Everyman's

DICTIONARY OF
PICTORIAL ART

VOLUME TWO

A Volume in
EVERYMAN'S REFERENCE LIBRARY

Volumes in Everyman's Reference Library

Other volumes in preparation

Everyman's Dictionary of

PICTORIAL
ART

Compiled by

WILLIAM GAUNT, M.A.(Oxon.)

VOLUME TWO

LONDON: J. M. DENT & SONS LTD
NEW YORK: E. P. DUTTON & CO. INC.

CONTENTS

VOLUME ONE

VOLUME TWO

J

Janssen, Cornelius, *see* JOHNSON, CORNELIUS.

Janssens van Nuyssen, Abraham (*b.* Antwerp, 1575; *d.* Jan. 1632), Flemish painter of religious and allegorical subjects, a pupil of Snellinck, who worked in the style of Rubens. He was in Rome, 1598–1601, and developed a dramatic light and shade derived from Caravaggio.

Japanese Pictorial Art had its origin in the sixth century when Buddhism was introduced into Japan and Korean and Chinese monks and craftsmen were encouraged to settle. Chinese influence was affirmed in the Nara period (A.D. 645–793), contemporaneous with the T'ang dynasty of China, the Buddhist paintings of this period showing a style which originated in India and had thence passed to China, the twelve frescoes in the main hall of the temple of

A. JANSSENS VAN NUYSSEN—Venus and Adonis—Kunsthistoriches Museum, Vienna.

JAPANESE SCREEN PAINTING (Yedo Period, Seventeenth Century)—Dancers—Kyoto Municipality.

Horyu-ji, near Nara (destroyed by fire, 1940), being the earliest known examples. Japan was comparatively isolated from China from the ninth to twelfth centuries and a national development of style followed. The wall-paintings and painted screens in the Chinese manner which had decorated imperial palaces and noble houses began to depict Japanese landscape scenes, and with the growth of Japanese literature illustrated manuscripts were produced. These were the source of Yamato-e or painting in a national style, the followers of this branch of painting delighting in quaint animals, insects, frogs, butterflies and hobgoblins depicted with great charm and vitality. A continuous picture-narrative in hand scrolls, dispensing with text, was developed in the Kamakura period (1185–1337). The contemplative sect of Zen Buddhism which came into prominence in the fourteenth century during the Muromachi period had an important influence on painting. The Zen monks brought from China examples of Sung landscape painting in ink washes. The reflective study of these works while drinking tea was the origin of the Tea Ceremony or Cha no yu, the aesthetic ritual which had a lasting effect on Japanese taste. The ceremonial isolation of the painting in a *tokonoma* or special wall recess dates from this time. Practitioners of ink painting were the monk Shūbun (early fifteenth century) and his pupil Sesshū (1420–1506). Kanō Motonobu (1475–1559), who combined the ink style with bright colour, is the founder of the Kano School which in its breadth of treatment, simplicity of conception and brilliant colour was long influential, and especially suited to the decoration of the Japanese house. Famous painters of the Momoyama period (1573–1638) were Kōetsu (1558–1637), Sōtatsu and Tōhaku (1539–1610), noted for beautifully decorated screens. Ogata Kōrin (q.v.) was a master of design inspired by Kōetsu. With the waning

JAPANESE SCROLL PAINTING (Kamakura Period, Twelfth Century)—Buddhist Deities of Mt Kasagi—Yamato Bunka-Kan Museum, Nara.

JAPANESE SCROLL PAINTING (Twelfth Century)—The Bodhisattva, Fugen Emmyo—Matsunoo dera, Kyoto.

Top right: KANŌ MOTONOBU (1476-1559) (attributed to)—Flowers and Birds (Hanging Scroll)—Daisen-in, Kyoto.

Bottom right: FUJIWARA TAKANOBU (1142-1205) (attributed to)—Portrait (Hanging Scroll, Colours on Silk)—Jingo-ji, Kyoto.

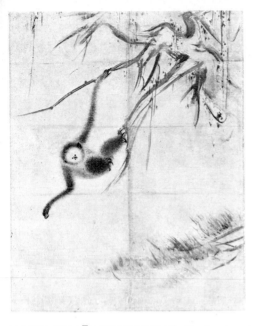

HASEGAWA TŌHAKU(1539-1610)—Monkey(one of a pair of Hanging Scrolls)—Ryūsen an, Kyoto.

JAPANESE LANDSCAPE (Muromachi period Early Fifteenth Century)—Nezu Museum, Tokyo

JAPANESE SCROLL PAINTING (Twelfth Century) —Portrait of the priest Gonzō—Fumon-in, Wakayama.

SŌAMI (attributed to) (d. 1525)—Landscape in the Chinese Manner (Section of a Hanging Scroll)— Daisen-in, Kyoto.

JAPANESE SCROLL PAINTING (Kamakura Period, Thirteenth Century)—Detail of a series supposed to satirize monks in animals' guise.—National Museum, Tokyo.

JAPANESE SCREEN PAINTING (Yedo Period, Seventeenth Century)—Europeans in Japan—Collection of Ataru Kobayashi, Tokyo.

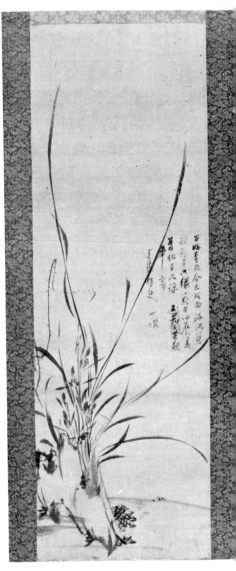

SHŪBUN (Fifteenth Century)—The Shokusan (Shu Shan Mountains of Kiangsu, China)—Seikado, Tokyo.

BOMPŌ (1344-1420)—Orchids and Rock (Hanging Scroll)—Rokuo-in, Kyoto.

KANO NAGANOBU (1775-1828)—Owl in the Moonlight—Victoria and Albert Museum.

JAPANESE HANDSCROLL (Kamakura Period, Fifteenth Century)—Portraits of Courtiers—
National Commission for the Protection of Cultural Properties, Japan.

KANO SCHOOL (Nineteenth Century)—Horses—Victoria and Albert Museum.

TAKEUCHI SEIHO (1864-1942)—Deer (Screen Colour on Silk)—Imperial Household, Tokyo.

HOKUSAI (1760-1849)—A Japanese Village—Victoria and Albert Museum.

KIOSAI (1821-89)—A Sage Fishing—Victoria and Albert Museum.

HISHIDA SHUNSO (1875-1911)—Black Cat, 1910 (Hanging Scroll, Colour on Silk)—Collection Moritatsu Hosokawa, Tokyo.

SOSEN (1749-1821)—Buck and Deer—Victoria and Albert Museum.

of the Kano School a new form of popular art appeared in the Yedo period (1615–1867). This was the Ukiyo-e school of woodcut artists which flourished chiefly in Yedo and Osaka. It is represented by Moronobu (d. 1694), Harunobu (1725–70), who worked in Tokyo and perfected the art colour printing from a number of wood blocks, Hiroshige (q.v.), famous for his views of rural life and landscape, Hokusai (q.v.), whose prints and drawings constitute him in western opinion one of the world's greatest masters, Sharaku (late eighteenth century), noted for his prints of actors, and Utamaro (q.v.), with his beautiful studies of women and birds and flowers. The Japanese colour print was a great and salutary influence on European art in the later nineteenth century. In the late nineteenth and early twentieth centuries Japan's enthusiasm for western culture caused native painting to be neglected, but an effort was made by some to revive it. Hishida Shunso (1875–1911) was a gifted artist in this field, others being Takeuchi Seiho (1864–1942) and Tomioka Tessai (1836–1924). The Academy of Fine Arts has taught the styles of the Kano School and of Ogata Kōrin. The contribution of Japanese painting and graphic art to the art of the world may be summed up as a splendid simplicity arising from the concentration on essentials.

Jawlensky, Alexei von (b. Kuslowo, Russia, 26 Mar. 1864; d. Wiesbaden, 15 Mar. 1941), Russian-born painter, associated with the development of German Expressionism. He first studied art at the Academy in St Petersburg and in 1896 went to Munich, where he met Kandinsky. He was influenced both by him and by the French Fauves, making bold use of brilliant colour in portraits and landscapes. In 1924, together with Kandinsky, Klee and Feininger, he was a member of the 'Blue Four', an offshoot of the Blue Rider group of Munich, exhibiting in Berlin and New York. His later works were abstract in tendency.

Jeanneret, Charles-Édouard, see CORBUSIER, LE.

Jode, Pieter de (b. Antwerp, 1570; d. 9 Aug. 1634), Flemish engraver, the pupil of Hendrik Goltzius and engraver of many plates after Flemish masters. His son, also Pieter (b. Antwerp. 22 Nov. 1606; d. England, after 1674), was his pupil and one of the engravers employed in reproducing the paintings of Rubens and van Dyck. Van Dyck painted the portrait of father and son together.

John, Augustus Edwin (b. Tenby, 4 Jan. 1878; d. Fordingbridge, 31 Oct. 1961), Welsh painter. He studied at the Slade School, taught art at the University College, Liverpool, 1901–3, and began to exhibit at the New English Art Club in 1903. His exceptional ability as a draughtsman and gifts as portrait and figure painter were early recognized, the 'Smiling Woman' of 1910 (Tate Gallery) being accounted a masterpiece. This was also a period of wandering in nomad fashion in Ireland and Wales, when he produced many poetic small oil-paintings of figures in landscape. He was an official artist to the Canadian Corps in the war of 1914–18, and R.A., 1928, resigning in 1938 because of the Academy's rejection of a sculpture by Epstein

A. JOHN—Study of the Nude (Pencil)—Fitzwilliam Museum, Cambridge.

but accepting re-election in 1940. He received the Order of Merit in 1942. His portraits are outstanding in their combined certainty of drawing and temperamental handling of paint and include those of many famous writers, Hardy, Shaw, Yeats, Joyce, Roy Campbell and Dylan Thomas among them. His sense of colour and a modified Post-Impressionism appear in his landscapes of the South of France and his flower-pieces. His cartoon for a mural decoration, 'Galway', 1916 (Tate), shows an inclination for large-scale work of this kind but never fully realized. He produced beautiful drawings of the figure at every stage of his career, and also some etchings. His autobiography, *Chiaroscuro*, 1952, was a distinguished excursion into prose.

Johnson, Cornelius (*b*. London, 14 Oct. 1593; *d*. Utrecht or Amsterdam, 1661–2), portrait painter, associated with both Holland and England, born in London of a family from Antwerp and originally of Cologne. Sometimes referred to as Janssen, he called himself Johnson or in later life Jonson van Ceulen (Cologne). He was probably the pupil of Marc Gheeraerts and worked for James I (of whom he painted several portraits) and Charles I (portrait at Chatsworth). His 'William Harvey' (Royal College of Physicians) is another notable work. He left England for Holland at the time of the Civil War (1643), living at Middelburg and elsewhere.

Johnson, Eastman (*b*. Lovell, Maine, 29 July 1824; d. 5 April 1906), American painter of portraits, landscape and subject pictures. He studied art at Düsseldorf and worked for some years as a young man at The Hague. Returning to America in 1855 he painted some scenes of Indian and frontier life in Wisconsin, made drawings of the Union Army during the Civil War and settled in New York, as a portrait painter mainly, though also painting *genre* scenes of American life.

A. JOHN—Cartoon for Decoration—'Galway'—Tate Gallery.

J. B. JONGKIND—Canal Barge—Photo: Arthur Tooth & Son.

J. JORDAENS—Portrait of a Man and Woman—National Gallery, London.

Jongkind, Johan Barthold (*b*. Latrop, nr Rotterdam, 1819; *d*. Côte St André (Isère), 1891), the greatest Dutch painter of the nineteenth century next to van Gogh. He left Holland early, going first to Düsseldorf, then to Paris, afterwards leading a wandering career spent mainly in France, though he returned to Holland from time to time. His favourite painting grounds were Paris and the region round Le Havre, where he met and greatly impressed both Boudin and Monet. His atmospheric landscapes and fresh and broken colour (in water-colours as well as oils) heralded the spirit and technique of Impressionism. The Barbizon painters and some critics, notably the de Goncourts, were quick to see his merits, but he lived in poverty, eventually becoming subject to persecution mania. He is often considered to belong to the French School.

Jordaens, Jacob (*b*. Antwerp, 19 May 1593; *d*. there 18 Oct. 1678), Flemish painter of religious and mythological subjects, *genre* scenes, still life and portraits, designer of tapestries and etcher. He was the pupil of Adam van Noort (q.v.), whose daughter he married, and his development is parallel with that of Rubens, in whose studio he worked. He painted with immense gusto and might be called a coarser Rubens. After the latter's death he was the leading figure of Flemish baroque painting. Though he never went to Italy, it is interesting to see how strongly he reflects in some works not only the Flemish spirit but the lighting and gesture of Caravaggio, as in the 'Meleager and Atalanta' (Antwerp). His vivacious earthy manner (in which Sir Joshua Reynolds found 'neither grace nor dignity') is well illustrated by 'The Royal Toast' (Brussels).

Juan de Flandes (active after 1496; *d*. 1519), painter associated with the Spanish School, though possibly, as his name 'John of Flanders' would indicate, Flemish in origin. He was appointed court painter to Queen Isabella in 1496 and after her death spent the last years of his life in Palencia. A characteristic work is the 'Raising of Lazarus' (Prado), one of a series of six panels originally in the church of St Lazarus at Palencia. Considered a typically Spanish feature is the disproportionate size of the figures in relation to the architecture.

Juan de Juanes, *see* MASIP, JUAN VICENTE DE, THE YOUNGER.

'Judgment of Sisamnes', paintings by Gerard David for the Hall of Justice in Bruges, executed in 1498. The subjects were taken from Herodotus, according to whom Sisamnes, one of King Cambyses's judges, convicted of selling a verdict, was ordered to be flayed alive. The first panel shows the arrest of the corrupt judge, the second the gruesome punishment being carried out. The paintings are in the Musée Communal, Bruges.

Jugendstil, *see* ART NOUVEAU.

K

Kaiser Friedrich or **National Museum, Berlin,** named after the Emperor Frederick III, one of the most important collections before the Second World War, though the building in East Berlin was then destroyed and the works of art dispersed, a number going to Wiesbaden until rebuilding at Berlin. The gallery included such famous works as Holbein's portrait of George Gisze, Rembrandt's 'Daniel's Vision', van Dyck's portrait of the Marchesa Geronima, Vermeer's 'Pearl Necklace', Hals's 'Hille Bobbe' and Signorelli's 'Pan' (a major loss in the war).

Kakemono. characteristic form of Japanese picture, a silk- or brocade-framed paper scroll with rollers at either end. It is hung in the *tokonoma*, an alcove for painting and flower arrangement, but the traditional practice is to change pictures frequently and the *kakemono* can be conveniently rolled up, stowed in a box specially designed for the purpose and replaced on the wall by another.

Kalf, Willem (*b.* Amsterdam, *c.* 1619; *d.* there, buried 3 Aug. 1693), Dutch *genre* and still-life painter, trained by Hendrik Pot (q.v.). He is regarded as the most distinguished of the Dutch still-life painters, depicting the luxurious appurtenances of the Dutch table—its Turkey rug covering, Chinese porcelain, ornamented goblets, fruits, etc.— with much feeling for material textures and sheen.

W. KALF—Still Life—
Kunsthalle, Hamburg.

[17]

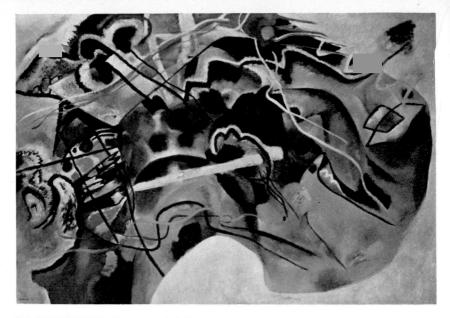

W. KANDINSKY—Picture with White Edge—Solomon R. Guggenheim Museum, New York.

Kandinsky, Wassily (*b*. Moscow, 5 Dec. 1866; *d*. Neuilly-sur-Seine, 13 Dec. 1944), Russian painter, associated with the modern German School and an international influence in art. He first studied law and turned to painting when thirty, moving to Munich, where with Franz Marc and others he founded the celebrated 'Der Blaue Reiter' group (q.v.) of Expressionists. He painted in entirely abstract fashion as early as 1910 and set out its theory in *Über das Geistige in der Kunst*, 1912, translated in an English version as *Concerning the Spiritual in Art*. From 1914 to 1921 he worked in Russia, his abstractions taking on a geometric character. When the Soviet enthusiasm for experimental art cooled he returned to Germany and was a teacher at the Bauhaus, 1922–3, leaving for Paris, 1933, when the Nazis came into power. He died a naturalized Frenchman. Believing that painting as distinct either from representing objects or decorating a surface could convey profound emotion or spiritual experience, he heralded the 'abstract-expressionist' movement of the 1950's.

Kauffmann, Angelica /*b*. Coire, Grisons, 30 Oct. 1741; *d*. Rome, 5 Nov. 1807), Swiss painter, the daughter of a painter who gave her lessons in both music and visual art. She lived in Italy for three years as a child, painting precociously, and on a second visit, 1763–6, painted the portrait of Winckelmann and was no doubt affected by the neo-classic tendencies he fostered. She came to London in 1786, was befriended by Reynolds and became popular as a portraitist and for classical and allegorical subjects of a fragile charm. Through the

[18]

C. S. KEENE—Figure Study —National Gallery of Scotland.

medium of Bartolozzi's engravings these had a wide distribution, and were extensively adapted in the Adam style of interior decoration in wall and ceiling panels, on painted furniture and in porcelain, though only two overdoors at Knowsley and roundels at Burlington House are assigned to her with certainty. She was an original member of the Royal Academy, 1768, and continued to exhibit there until 1797, though her later years were spent in Rome.

Keene, Charles Samuel (*b*. London, 10 Aug. 1823; *d*. there, 4 Jan. 1891), English graphic artist who worked in youth in the studio of a wood-engraver. Though he became famous as a *Punch* artist in the 1860's in succession to John Leech, his quality as an artist is best appreciated in a comparatively few pen drawings, water-colours and etchings. His serious studies of landscape and figure were highly admired by such fastidious critics as Degas and Whistler.

Kells, The Book of, greatest product of the Irish art of manuscript illumination, a manuscript of the Gospels written in Latin and dating from the eighth or early ninth century. It is preserved in the library of Trinity College, Dublin. The knots and interlacings characteristic of Celtic art are entwined with a variety of grotesque or legendary animals and painted with wonderful minuteness. Kells in county Meath was a centre of monastic culture. (Colour, *see* list.)

Kensett, John Frederick (*b*. Cheshire, Connecticut, 22 Mar. 1816; *d*. New York, 14 Dec. 1872), American landscape painter who carried on the romantic tendencies of the Hudson River School though developing a style of greater realism. He was noted for his paintings of mountain lakes.

Kent, Rockwell (*b*. Tarrytown Heights, New York, 21 June 1882), American painter and graphic artist. He turned to painting after

[19]

studying architecture and spent much time in travel, going to sea as a ship's carpenter and recording impressions of his voyages in painting and written description. Paintings of lonely and mountainous shores were followed by much decorative illustration in wood-engravings, those for *Moby Dick* being notable.

Key, Adriaen Thomas (*b.* Antwerp, *c.* 1544; *d.* ? 1568), Flemish painter of religious subjects and portraits. He was the nephew and probably the pupil of Willem Key (q.v.). He is noted more especially for his portraits.

Key, Willem (*b.* ? Breda, 1529; *d.* Antwerp, 1596), Flemish painter of religious subjects and portraits. He was the pupil of Lambert Lombard at Liège.

Key, prevailing tone of a picture, a high key being light, a low key dark.

Keyser, Thomas de (*b.* Amsterdam, 1596–7; *d.* there, buried 7 June 1667), Dutch painter, son of the sculptor and architect Hendrick de Keyser. He is noted mainly for portraiture, including group and equestrian portraits.

Kirchner, Ernst Ludwig (*b.* Aschaffenburg, 6 May 1880; *d.* Davos, by suicide, 15 June 1938), German painter, whose use of free, brilliant colour parallels that of the Fauve painters in France. He studied architecture first, then turned to painting, which he studied at Munich, and in 1905 was a leading spirit in the formation of the 'Die Brücke' group (q.v.) in Dresden. Settling in Switzerland in 1917, he painted landscapes and peasant life and finally turned to abstract painting.

Kisling, Moïse (*b.* Cracow, 1891; *d.* Paris, 1953), painter of Polish origin associated with the School of Paris (q.v.). He went to

E. L. KIRCHNER—Self-portrait with Model—Kunsthalle, Hamburg.

Paris, settling in Montparnasse, and served in the Foreign Legion during the First World War, becoming a French citizen. Influenced by the various tendencies that stemmed from the work of Cézanne, he showed distinction in figure subjects treated in a broad and simplified manner.

Kit-cat, size of canvas, about 36 by 28 inches, suited to a half-length portrait; so called from the series of portraits of this type and size of members of the Kit-Cat Club by Sir Godfrey Kneller (q.v.) (National Portrait Gallery).

Klee, Paul (*b.* München-Buchsee, nr Bern, 18 Dec. 1879; *d.* Muralto, nr Locarno, 29 June 1940), German-Swiss painter, draughtsman and etcher, an outstanding personality in twentieth-century art. He studied at Munich under Franz Stuck and absorbed a variety of impressions from painters old and modern (Blake, Goya, Hans von Marées and Cézanne among them) before setting out—in his own words—to work 'as one new-born'. With Kandinsky, Marc and Macke he took part in founding the 'Blaue Reiter' group, 1912 (q.v.), taught at the Bauhaus, 1920–6 (q.v.), and the Düsseldorf Academy, 1930. He moved to Bern in 1933 when the Nazis came into power. A very large output in oil, water-colour, pen and pencil drawings and etchings reflects his independent and original imagination, his wit and charm of colour and line. In his theoretic study, *Über die Moderne Kunst*, 1945, he likens the transformation of life by the artist to the process by which the soil is converted into the foliage of the tree, and his own art illustrates this transformation, in human terms, through the subconscious. Klee, however, unlike the Surrealists, attached great importance to both observation and technique, as well as to more or less 'automatic' processes of expression.

Klitias (early sixth century B.C.), Greek vase painter, one of the

[21]

P. KLEE—The Golden Fish—Kunsthalle, Hamburg.

individual artists who appeared with the great development of the pottery industry. His minute and elaborate work in the black-figured style is seen in the 'François Vase' (Florence, Etruscan Museum), with hundreds of elegant figures in successive rows.

Kneller, Sir Godfrey (*b.* Lübeck, 8 Aug. 1646; *d.* London, 19 Oct. 1723), portrait painter of German origin (original name, **Gottfried Kniller**), trained at Amsterdam under Rembrandt's pupil, Ferdinand Bol (q.v.). He went to Italy with a view to settling there but a successful visit to England in 1674 caused him to stay in London, where he built up a vast practice in portraiture, succeeding Lely as chief court painter. His portraits (which include those of Charles II, Louis XIV, James II, William III, Peter the Great, Queen Anne and George I) totalled nearly 6,000. He was made a baronet in 1715. Greatly talented and skilled in a direct technique, he was neverthe-less often hasty and superficial, numerous assistants working for him to a set convention. Walpole said: 'Where he offered one picture to fame he sacrificed twenty to lucre.' His set of portraits of the Augustan notabilities of the Kit-Cat Club, *c.* 1702–17 (National Portrait Gallery), is a famous series, others being the 'Beauties' (Hampton Court) and 'Admirals' (National Maritime Museum), and he is seen at his best in 'The Chinese Convert' (Kensington Palace). He had an influence both as teacher and technician, instituting a pioneer academy (in Great Queen Street, 1711) for instruction and having many followers in his method of painting.

SIR G. KNELLER—The Chinese Convert—Royal Collection.

Kokoschka, Oskar (*b.* Pöchlarn, on the Danube, 1 Mar. 1886), Austrian painter, one of the outstanding personalities of modern art in Germany. Born in what is now Czechoslovakia, he studied at the School of Arts and Crafts in Vienna, went to Berlin in 1907 and then travelled to Switzerland and Italy. A strong prejudice against formal and academic rules already appeared in his work, and after the First World War, in which he was wounded, he violently conveyed in pictures and writings a sense of human suffering and cruelty. This Expressionism (q.v.) led eventually to his being proscribed by the Nazis. Before that he had spent a period as teacher at Dresden, 1920–1924, and in Mediterranean travel. He moved to Vienna, 1931, to Prague, 1934, and to London, 1938, becoming a naturalized British subject. He has since lived in Switzerland. In portraits, landscape and still life he shows a restless and romantic vigour. 'The Tempest', 1914 (Basel, Kunstmuseum), is a notable symbolic work, and his views of the Thames are outstanding among modern landscapes.

Kollwitz, Kaethe (*b.* Königsberg, East Prussia, 8 July 1867; *d.* 22 April 1945), German graphic artist and sculptor, noted for the powerful drawings, woodcuts, etchings and lithographs in which she expressed proletarian and pacifist sympathies. Her father, Karl Schmidt, was an ardent radical, and her husband, Dr Karl Kollwitz, worked among the poor of Berlin, both influencing the trend of her thought and the subject-matter of her art. Among her principal works were the 'Peasants' War' series, 1902–8, and her poster 'Never Again War' after the First World War. Both the Kaiser Government and the Nazis regarded her with suspicion. Her house in Berlin was hit in the bombing of 1943 and much of her work was then destroyed, though a number of drawings have found their way into American collections.

[23]

O. KOKOSCHKA—Large Thames Landscape, 1959—Photo: Marlborough Fine Art.

Koninck, Philips (*b*. Amsterdam, 1619; *d*. 1688), Dutch painter, perhaps the pupil of Rembrandt. He is noted for his panoramic landscapes of the Dutch lowlands. His brother, Jacob (*c*. 1616–*c*. 1708), was also a landscape painter.

Kōrin, Ogata (1658–1716), one of the most famous Japanese artist-craftsmen, son of a rich silk merchant of Kyoto. He was related to the painters Kōetsu and Sotātsu and admired and was influenced by their work. Trained in the classic Kano style, he diverged from it in a bold and simplified style of his own. His vigour and breadth of design are shown in his lacquer screens. In smaller paintings he showed great mastery of calligraphic brushwork. His art was forgotten for some time after his death but was re-established in esteem by his follower Sakai Hōitsu (1771–1828), who published his paintings and designs in woodcut books.

Kröller-Müller Museum, Otterlo, Dutch collection of modern paintings, the main feature of which is the series of works by Vincent van Gogh.

Ku K'ai-chih (*c*. 344–406), Chinese painter, a native of Wu-si in Kiangsu province, the most famous of early Chinese artists. He was

[24]

BOOK OF KELLS—Opening of St Matthew's Gospel—Trinity College, Dublin.

P. KONINCK—Landscape; a View in Holland—National Gallery, London.

essentially a figure painter though he also painted animals and land-scapes. Inspired by Taoist thought, he first expressed the idea that painting is not merely the representation of externals but the revelation of an inner character or spirit. Works by him are the 'Admonitions of the Instructress in the Palace', a scroll consisting of a series of illustrations to a text by the poet Chang Hua (British Museum), and the earliest known Chinese landscapes, represented by a scroll, probably a Sung copy, in the Metropolitan Museum.

Kunsthalle, Hamburg, important gallery of German painting, including works by the fourteenth- and fifteenth-century masters Master Bertram and Master Francke and a notable collection of nineteenth- and twentieth-century works, by Runge, Friedrich, Nolde, Marc, Heckel, Schmidt-Rottluff and others. Its collection of French moderns was removed and sold abroad by the Nazi regime.

Kunsthistorisches Museum, Vienna, historical gallery of art, originally the Imperial Gallery formed by Ferdinand I, brother of Charles V. All the imperial collections were regrouped in the museum under its present title in 1891 and a further regrouping was completed in 1936, making the picture section comparable with the

OGATA KŌRIN—Wind God and Thunder God Screen (part)—National Commission for Protection of Cultural Properties, Japan.

OGATA KŌRIN—The Sage (Hanging Scroll, Ink on Paper)—Collection Mosaku Sorimachi, Tokyo.

Louvre, National Gallery or Prado. The gallery is rich in early Netherlandish and Dutch, Flemish and Venetian works. Of special note are the superb series of paintings by Pieter Brueghel the Elder, Giorgione's 'Three Philosophers', Titian's 'Ecce Homo' and other works, and Tintoretto's 'Susanna and the Elders'. The museum buildings were damaged in the Second World War but the pictures, preserved in the salt-mines of Upper Austria, were unharmed.

Kupka, František (*b.* Opocno, Czechoslovakia, 23 Sept. 1871; *d.* Puteau, France, 1957), Czech-born painter, associated with the School of Paris (q.v.). He studied in Prague and Vienna before going to Paris in 1895. His early work there consisted of neo-Impressionist pictures and book illustrations but under the modern stimuli of Paris his work underwent a complete change about 1910, and he was one of the first to produce entirely non-representational paintings. In these he was parallel with or perhaps even anticipated Delaunay (q.v.), Malevich and Mondrian (q.v.). His 'colour music' was of the kind for which Guillaume Apollinaire found the description 'Orphism'. The Czechoslovakian Government sponsored a retrospective exhibition of Kupka's work in 1946.

KU KA'I CHIH—Family Group—British Museum.

L

Laer, Pieter van (*b.* Haarlem, before 1595; *d.* 30 June 1642), Dutch painter who went to Italy to study in 1623 and stayed in Rome until about 1639, enjoying a considerable vogue there for his paintings of Roman street life, country fairs, rustic types and soldiers. He may be said to have created a *genre*—Le Bambocciate—or scene of low life which delighted some but offended the adherents of the classical tradition. He was nicknamed 'Il Bamboccio' in reference to his style of picture and not because of any grotesqueness or deformity in his person.

La Farge, John (*b.* New York, 31 Mar. 1835; *d.* 14 Nov. 1910), American painter, French by descent, designer and writer and lecturer on art, influenced by Pre-Raphaelite ideals of craftsmanship and design. He first studied with his grandfather, a miniaturist, and going to Europe in 1856 worked in Paris in the studio of Couture. A visit to England aroused his admiration for the Pre-Raphaelites, some of whom he met, and his own work in stained glass for churches and mansions in the United States has some parallel with that of Morris and Burne-Jones. In 1886 he travelled in Japan and the South Seas, making pictorial records of life in Samoa, in which he found a 'classic' dignity.

La Fresnaye, Roger de (*b.* Le Mans, 1885; *d.* Grasse, 1925), French painter, descendant of an ancient noble family in Normandy. First attracted to the art of Gauguin, he later became a follower of Cubism (q.v.) and before 1914 produced still lifes of distinction in the Cubist manner. After the war, in which he was seriously affected in health by a gas attack, he settled at

C. LAIB—The Crucifixion — Kunsthistorisches Museum, Vienna.

Grasse in the south of France, his art then tending towards a classic severity, and including many drawings.

La Hyre, Laurent de (*b.* Paris, 28 Feb. 1606; *d.* there, 28 Dec. 1656), French painter, influenced (though he did not visit Italy) by the style of Caravaggio probably through other painters, e.g. Vouet (q.v.), who had been to Rome. The example of Poussin during the latter's stay in France, 1640–2, directed him towards a delicate classicism not only in his decorative and religious paintings but in his landscapes, in which especially he achieved a personal manner.

Laib, Conrad (active Salzburg, mid fifteenth century), painter of the Austrian School whose work shows both Italian and German traits of style. An example of note is his crowded and ornamental 'Cruci fixion' (Vienna).

Lancret, Nicolas (*b.* Paris, 22 Jan. 1690; *d.* Paris, Sept. 1743), French painter, the son of a coachman and fellow pupil with Watteau of Claude Gillot. Like Watteau he painted the characters of Italian comedy and numerous *fêtes galantes*, though he lacked Watteau's poetry of colour and design. He introduced several personalities of the stage into his pictures, among them the celebrated dancer Mlle Camargo. Typical examples of his works are in the Louvre and the Wallace Collection.

N. LANCRET—The Snare—Louvre.

Landscape Painting, comparatively late product of art in the West, though the contemplation of mountain and water and their rendering in pictures were cultivated in China in the early centuries of our Christian era (*see* CHINESE PAINTING). In western art it first appears as a background and as such became a delightful element in the illuminated manuscripts and paintings of the Middle Ages. The 'Très Riches Heures du Duc de Berry', early fifteenth century, is notable for its pictorial calendar representing the changes of the seasons. Landscape gives interest of detail in the work of Jan van Eyck (q.v.) and with Pieter Brueghel (q.v.) becomes a dramatic accessory of the subject, as in the snow-covered landscape of his 'Census of Bethlehem'. The Flemish painter Patenier (q.v.) is usually credited with having first made landscape a primary feature of interest in pictures ostensibly containing some other element of subject. It developed with the interest of artists travelling to Italy in their new surroundings, Dürer, for example, leaving a notable record of his journey in water-colour. What is known as 'classical landscape' developed in seventeenth-century Rome, through the efforts of such northern artists as Paul Bril and Adam Elsheimer (qq.v.) and the Italian painters Annibale Carracci and Domenichino (qq.v.), and is superbly represented by Claude Lorraine (q.v.), who gave a new importance to light and space. The seventeenth century saw the cultivation of a familiar and domesticated landscape as in the compositions of Rubens and especially in the paintings of the Dutch School—van Goyen, Rembrandt, Ruisdael, Hobbema, Koninck, Cuyp and others. English landscape, much influenced by the Dutch, attained its great development next in the eighteenth and early nineteenth centuries. Wilson, Crome and the Norwich School, Gainsborough, Constable and Turner appear in succession and their work in oils is paralleled by that of water-colour landscapists—Paul Sandby, J. R. Cozens, Cotman, Turner, Girtin, Bonington and a host of minor men. After Constable and Turner the great development of landscape was in France and the study of light and atmosphere was pursued with further brilliant results. Corot and the Barbizon School (qq.v.) were followed by Courbet (q.v.) and then by the Impressionists (*see* IMPRESSIONISM), Monet, Pissarro and Sisley (qq.v.) being characteristic in their use of colour. Impressionism was the last great phase of landscape objectively treated, though not a terminus. Cézanne made landscape into a study of essential structure underlying all natural forms. Vincent van Gogh made it a vehicle for expressing personal emotion. A highly poetic form of landscape is that of the Far East (*see* CHINESE PAINTING; JAPANESE PICTORIAL ART).

Landseer, Sir Edwin (*b.* London, 7 Mar. 1802; *d.* there, 1 Oct. 1873), English animal painter, the pupil of his father, John Landseer, engraver, and B. R. Haydon (q.v.). He began to draw animals at an early age and developed great facility, becoming famous throughout Europe for the pictures which gave quasi-human expression and traits to domestic animals (e.g. 'Dignity and Impudence', 1839), and for the sentiment of such works as 'The Monarch of the Glen', 1851,

SIR E. LANDSEER—
Dignity and Impudence—
Tate Gallery.

which remain symbols of
Victorian taste. Scottish
landscapes and portrait
sketches (e.g. of his
friend Sir Walter Scott)
show him at his best.
R.A. in 1831, he was
knighted in 1850. The
neurosis and depression
by which he was tragic-
ally affected are in con-
trast to the humours
of his paintings and the
placidity of his famous
lions in Trafalgar Square,
unveiled in 1869.

Lanfranco, Giovanni
(b. Parma, 26 Jan.
1582; d. Rome, 30 Nov.
1647), Italian painter, the pupil of Agostino Carracci and later of
Annibale Carracci (q.v.). He was influenced in style by the ceiling
paintings of Correggio at Parma and decorated the domes and apses
of many churches in Rome and Naples, developing a baroque
illusionism as in the dome of St Andrea del Valle, 1625–8, in which,
according to the historian Passeri, he was 'the first to irradiate the
opening of a celestial glory with a splendour of light'.

Largillierre, Nicolas de (b. Paris, 10 Oct. 1656; d. there, 20 Mar.
1746), French portrait painter, taken in childhood to Antwerp, where
he received his first instruction in art. Later he went to London and
worked for Lely, putting in still-life and landscape details in Lely's
portraits. Going to Paris in 1682 he became a favourite painter with
the rich official and administrative class, his works showing little
depth of character but much accomplishment in handling.

Laroon, John Marcellus (b. London, 2 April 1679; d. Oxford, 1 June
1774), English painter, son of the Dutch-born painter Marcellus
Laroon the Elder, who was one of Kneller's assistants. In the course
of an adventurous career he travelled about Europe, was an actor and
singer at Drury Lane for two years, fought in the army under Marlborough and in 1712, a returned prisoner of war, worked in Kneller's
academy. He remained in the army, however, becoming a half-pay
captain in 1732. A friend of Hogarth, he imitated him in conversation
pieces and made spirited drawings of concerts and music parties not
unlike the drawings of Hogarth in style.

N. DE LARGILLIERRE—The Artist and his Family—Louvre.

'Last Judgment, The', by Michelangelo, the great fresco on the altar-wall of the Sistine Chapel, about 66 feet wide by 33 feet high, painted 1534–41, nearly thirty years after Michelangelo's ceiling in the Chapel. Christ appears as Judge surrounded by Apostles and saints and below is a vision of hell inspired by Dante. In the judge Minos Michelangelo portrayed Biagio of Cesena, master of ceremonies to the Pope, who had criticized the work because of the nudity of the figures. Some of the figures were covered with drapery by Daniele da Volterra under Paul IV, and others by Pozzo in the eighteenth century under Clement XII.

'Last Supper, The', subject of which Leonardo da Vinci gave the greatest of all interpretations in his world-famous fresco on a wall of the refectory of the Dominican friary of Santa Maria delle Grazie, Milan. It was painted between 1495 and 1498 when he was staying in the city in the service of the Sforza family. He had already worked out theoretically in his treatise on painting the dramatic and psychological interrelation of a group such as that of Christ and the Apostles in terms of action and gesture, and this he applied to his fresco with unique power. He also increased the effect by the painted interior perspective which, while it gave the illusion of extending the space of the refectory, also seemed to bring the Supper table actually into the room. Unfortunately Leonardo's love of experiment led him

G. DE LA TOUR—The Hurdy-gurdy Player—Musée de Nantes.

to use oil on plaster. The masterpiece, already decaying in his lifetime, has suffered progressive damage since, though expert restorers
in this century have done all that could be done to repair the ravages
of time, damp and much repainting.

Lastman, Pieter Pietersz (*b.* Amsterdam, 1583; *d.* there, buried 4
April 1633), Dutch painter and engraver, trained at Amsterdam.
Visiting Italy he was influenced by Elsheimer and Caravaggio. He is
less noted for his own history pictures than as the master of Jan
Lievens and Rembrandt, for whom his 'Romanist' experience had a
certain value.

La Tour, Georges de (*b.* Vic-sur-Sielle, 1593; *d.* Lunéville, 30 Jan.
1652), French painter, whose life was mainly spent at Lunéville in
Lorraine, where he had a flourishing studio. Nothing is known of his
training but his work suggests acquaintance with that of the Dutch
'candlelight' painters, e.g. Honthorst (q.v.), and it is probable that
he visited Italy. The style of Caravaggio and the Netherlandish
practice of illuminating a scene by artificial light are transformed in
his paintings into a grave and simplified beauty, 'The New-born
Child' (Musée de Rennes) being a famous example. Other masterpieces are 'The Hurdy-gurdy Player' (Nantes), an early work, and
the 'St Sebastian mourned by St Irene' (Berlin). La Tour was long a
forgotten master and it is only in the present century that he has
been acclaimed one of the greatest seventeenth-century French
painters.

La Tour, Maurice Quentin de (*b.* St Quentin, 1704; *d.* there, 1788),
French painter of pastel portraits, who studied in Paris with the
engraver Tardieu and the Flemish artist, J. J. Spoëde. The vogue for
pastel, initiated by the Venetian, Rosalba Carriera (q.v.), turned him
to this medium, to which he devoted himself exclusively, attaining
great celebrity. A member of the Académie, 1737, he became painter
to the king, 1750, though his portraits, brilliant in their characteriza-
tion, included those of people in every walk of life. His 'préparations',
preliminary studies of heads, are especially valued for their sense of
character. His later years, when his mind failed, were spent under the
care of his brother in his native place, where an important part of his
work is preserved.

'Laughing Cavalier, The', painting by Frans Hals, executed in 1624
and now one of the best-known pictures in the Wallace Collection,
representing a military officer of the d'Artagnan type, the details of
whose dress, rich in embroidery and lace, are depicted with fascinat-
ing skill. The 'laughter' of the cavalier is apparent only in his look of
humorous disdain.

Laurencin, Marie (*b.* Paris, 31 Oct. 1885; *d.* there, 9 June 1956),
French painter and graphic artist who first exhibited in 1907. She
became celebrated in the 1920's for charming stylized figure paintings,
the features suggested rather than drawn, carried out in pastel pinks
and blues. Her work included drawings, lithographs, mural decorations and dress design for Paul Poiret.

F. HALS—The Laughing Cavalier—Wallace Collection.

SIR T. LAWRENCE—
Portrait of Queen Char-
lotte — National Gallery,
London.

Lawrence, Sir Thomas
(*b*. Bristol, 1769; *d*.
London, 7 Jan. 1830),
English portrait painter.
An infant prodigy, he
was already successful
and celebrated for his
likenesses at Bath be-
fore he was twelve and
with little instruction he
quickly became accom-
plished in oil painting,
receiving the homage of
society as the heir of
the eighteenth-century
tradition. On Reynolds's
death in 1792 he was
made King's Painter
in Ordinary, was R.A.,
1794, knighted in 1815
and P.R.A., 1820. After
the Napoleonic wars
he was commissioned
by the Prince Regent
to paint the allied sovereigns and dignitaries, travelling in state for
this purpose to Aix-la-Chapelle, Vienna and Rome; the portraits are
now in the Waterloo Room, Windsor, and include some of his most
brilliant works, e.g. the ' Pope Pius VII '. He belongs to the Romantic
period in the restless glitter of his style, which interested both Géricault and Delacroix (qq.v.), though it descends in a number of paintings into a superficial showiness. A man of cultivated and discerning
taste, Lawrence has a secondary celebrity for his great collection of
old master drawings, especially rich in Michelangelos and Raphaels.
It realized £20,000 in the sale after his death, and though not acquired
entire by the nation as he had wished, part of it went to Oxford
University and is in the Ashmolean Museum.

Lawson, Ernest (*b*. San Francisco, 22 Mar. 1873; *d*. Miami, 18 Dec.
1939), American landscape painter who studied in Kansas City and
New York. He was one of the group of Eight and his later work
reflected the growing influence of modern currents of art since the
time of Cézanne.

Le Brun, Charles (*b*, Paris, 24 Feb. 1619; *d*. there, 12 Feb. 1690)

French decorative artist, chief representative of the grandiose art of the age of Louis XIV. The son of a sculptor, he showed precocious talent, studied under Vouet (q.v.) and at Rome, learning much from Poussin (q.v.), was a painter to the king at nineteen and a founder member of the Académie in 1648. He was patronized by Fouquet (q.v.), for whom he decorated the Château de Vaux, then by Colbert, who found in him the perfect instrument for creating a comprehensive system of art and manufacture, ultimately glorifying the absolutism of the Grand Monarque. He became the first painter to the king, 1662, director of the Manufacture Royale des Meubles, 1663, turned the Académie into a monopoly under his dictatorship, directed the decoration of Versailles, his chief work (notably the Staircase of the Ambassadors and the Galerie des Glaces), and made the Gobelins into a great centre of art industry employing painters, sculptors, weavers, dyers, goldsmiths and other craftsmen. His prodigious output included religious and history paintings, e.g. the 'History of Alexander' series (Louvre) designed for tapestry, portraiture such as the group of the banker Jabach and his family (Berlin), and countless designs for decorative projects. After the death of Colbert in 1683 he was replaced in authority by his enemy Mignard, though Louis XIV remained his loyal admirer.

Le Brun, Marie Elisabeth Louise (*née* **Vigée**) (*b.* Paris, 11 Jan. 1755; *d.* there, 30 Mar. 1842), French portrait painter, a pupil of Gabriel Biard. She was patronized by Marie Antoinette, whose portrait she painted, became a member of the Académie, 1783, and was fashionable in Paris before the Revolution, having painted four hundred portraits by 1789. She travelled widely in Europe, 1789–1805, her portraits including those of Lady Hamilton, Mme de Staël and Lord Byron. Portraits of herself and her daughter (Louvre) show her charm and skill. She published her *Souvenirs*, 1835.

'Legend of St Ursula', series of paintings for the confraternity of St Ursula at Venice, painted, 1490–6, by Vittore Carpaccio and now in the Accademia, Venice. They represent episodes from the fabled story of Ursula, daughter of a British king, demanded in marriage by a pagan monarch but warned in a dream to require its postponement during which time she should have 11,000 virgins as her companions in visits to holy places. Carpaccio gives to this legendary story (which was handed down with a number of variations) a clear-cut contemporary character, translating it into terms of Venetian types, costume and architecture. 'The Dream of St Ursula' is perhaps the most famous of the series.

Léger, Fernand (*b.* Argentan, 4 Feb. 1881, *d.* Paris, 17 Aug. 1955), French painter of the modern School of Paris. Originally trained as an architect, he turned to painting in 1903, studying at the École des Beaux Arts, the Académie Julian and in the Louvre. At first attracted by Impressionism, he came under the Cubist influence between 1909 and 1914 and during a period of war service took an interest in machine forms which became an important factor in his work from 1917 onwards. He made use of such things as railway signal boxes

and street signs in 'mechanised' composition, though in his later work he returned to human themes—always, however, with a strongly simplified decorative element. From 1940 to 1945 he was in U.S.A. but returned to Paris in 1945. In addition to paintings he produced a number of lithographs and book illustrations and designs for wall decoration, mosaic and stained glass.

Legros, Alphonse (*b.* Dijon, 8 May 1837; *d.* Watford, 8 Dec. 1911), French painter, etcher and sculptor. In early years he worked in Paris as a scene painter and exhibited at the Salon from 1857. Coming to England at Whistler's suggestion in 1863 he settled there and as Slade Professor at University College, London, 1875–92, gained esteem as a teacher. He is mainly of note for etchings in a sombre vein.

Leibl, Wilhelm (*b.* Cologne, 23 Oct. 1844; *d.* Würzburg, 4 Dec. 1900), German painter, whose work marks the nineteenth-century return to realism, inspired in his case by the doctrine of Courbet and the style of Holbein. He studied at Munich and in Paris and worked in Munich and elsewhere in Bavaria, depicting peasant folk with a precision of detail recalling that of the English Pre-Raphaelites. His 'Three Women in Church', 1881 (Hamburg, Kunsthalle), is a typical work.

Leighton, Frederic, Lord (*b.* Scarborough, 3 Dec. 1830; *d.* London, 25 Jan. 1896), English painter and sculptor. Comprehensively trained in Italy, Germany and France, he became the main representative of classicism in its late-Victorian form, i.e. in subject pictures inspired by ancient Greece and the Parthenon frieze. Many landscapes also resulted from his extensive travels, and his visits to the Middle East suggested the *décor* of the famous Arab Hall at his house in London (now a gallery and museum). His decorative art in fresco and mosaic can be studied in the Victoria and Albert Museum; his bronzes 'The Sluggard' and 'Athlete struggling with Python' are in the Tate Gallery. His varied talents, learning and personal charm contributed

W. LEIBL—Three Women in Church — Kunsthalle, Hamburg.

to make him a great success as President of the Royal Academy, and he was the first, and only, painter to be elevated to the peerage.

Lely, Sir Peter (originally **van der Faes**) (*b.* Soest, nr Utrecht, 14 Oct. 1618; *d.* London, 1680), painter of Dutch origin. He studied at Haarlem under Frans Pietersz de Grebber and came to England in 1641, soon afterwards changing his style to emulate the courtly elegance of van Dyck. He painted Charles I during his captivity at Hampton Court and during the Commonwealth period reverted to a plainer manner (as his portrait of Oliver Cromwell shows), but is mainly associated with the Restoration period, when in response to fashionable demand his output became very large and even the replicas required of him fully employed an army of assistants. The portraits of the female beauties of Charles II's court for which he is popularly celebrated are in fact so far turned out to a standardized pattern as to be often indistinguishable, but Lely shows a sense of individual character in his male portraits—as in those of the admirals and commanders in the victory against the Dutch at Solebay, 1665 (National Maritime Museum).

Le Nain, The Brothers, three seventeenth-century French painters, all born at Laon and active in Paris: Antoine, the eldest (*b. c.* 1588; *d.* Paris, 25 May 1648), Louis (*b. c.* 1593; *d.* Paris, 23 May 1648) and Mathieu, the youngest (*b. c.* 1607; *d.* Paris, 20 April 1677). Nothing is known of their training, though all became members of the Académie in 1648. They seem to have collaborated, in some works at least, though the signature on pictures 'Le Nain', without initial, does not distinguish them. The paintings, however, have been divided into three (not very determinate) groups: 'Antoine', small figures painted on

[39]

SIR P. LELY—Countess of Shrewsbury—National Portrait Gallery.

LOUIS and (?) MATHIEU LE NAIN—The Young Violinist—Petworth House Collection.

copper; 'Louis', larger in scale and subdued in colour; 'Mathieu', subjects reflecting a higher social level than the peasant scenes of the other two. From this classification Louis emerges as the main representative of the family genius and one of the great French artists of the early seventeenth century in the sympathetic realism and beauty of painting in his compositions drawn from peasant life, such as the 'Peasants' Meal' (Louvre).

Leonardo da Vinci (*b.* Vinci, nr Empoli, 1452; *d.* Château de Cloux, Amboise, 2 May 1519), Italian painter, sculptor, engineer, architect and scientist, one of the world's greatest artists and supremely the universal type of Renaissance genius. He was the son of Ser Piero da Vinci, a Florentine lawyer, and his mother, Catarina, was of humble birth and unmarried. The child was brought up in his father's household and showed unusual gifts from his earliest years, youthful pursuits being music, modelling and drawing. His father placed him in the studio of Andrea del Verrocchio (q.v.), where he was the fellow pupil of Botticelli, Perugino and Lorenzo di Credi (qq.v.). It is probable that he painted the kneeling angel in Verrocchio's 'Baptism' (Uffizi), in which according to legend the master recognized the pupil's superiority. In 1472 he was enrolled in the painters' guild at Florence and in 1477 Lorenzo the Magnificent took him under his protection. Before 1481 he began to devote himself to those projects and studies, in architecture, hydraulics, mechanics, engineering, astronomy, geology and anatomy, whose diverse nature still arouses wonder. To this period belong the 'Virgin and Child' (Munich), doubtfully regarded by some authorities but containing many Leonardesque details, the portrait of Ginevra de Benci (Liechtenstein Collection) and the unfinished 'Adoration of the Magi' (Uffizi). He left Florence for Milan about 1482, offering his services to Lodovico Sforza, primarily as a military and naval engineer, as a sculptor next and as a painter incidentally. Soon after his arrival he painted Lodovico's mistress, Cecilia Gallerani (the 'Lady with an Ermine', Cracow, Czartoryski Collection), and in 1483, in partnership with Ambrogio da Predis, the altar-piece to which Leonardo contributed the central panel, 'The Virgin of the Rocks'. The existence of two versions, one in the Louvre and one in the National Gallery, may be explained by the revision of the altar-piece in 1506 after a long period of haggling, when presumably a first version of the panel was sent to France and the other was finally accepted by the confraternity of the Immaculate Conception. Other great undertakings were the bronze equestrian monument to Francesco Sforza, of which only the model was completed, and the world-famous fresco of the 'Last Supper' (q.v.) in the refectory of Santa Maria delle Grazie. This masterpiece, in which he used an experimental oil medium, suffered also from the damp wall on which it was painted; modern restoration by Cavaliere Cavenaghi has restored, as far as it was possible, a painting which lives always as a great conception.

In 1500 Leonardo was in Venice, where he may have met Giorgione, who was greatly impressed by his treatment of light and shade. In

[41]

LEONARDO DA VINCI—The Virgin and St Anne (Cartoon)—Royal Academy.

LEONARDO DA VINCI
—The Virgin of the Rocks
—National Gallery, London. Compare with illustration on page 67.

1502 he was in the employ of Caesar Borgia, mapping out the country and planning canals, harbours and other works, and in 1503 was commissioned by the Signory of Florence to produce a battle scene on the walls of the Council Hall, Michelangelo being at the same time commissioned for a similar work. The cartoons of both aroused the greatest admiration, Leonardo's cartoon of the 'Battle of Anghiari' being finished in two years and exhibited with that of Michelangelo. Raphael, aged nineteen, saw them both at work. As so often, however, Leonardo left the work unfinished, an experimental technique again destroying what he had done. The portrait of Mona Lisa ('La Gioconda'), the wife of Francesco Zanobi del Giocondo, that mysterious smiling picture with all the subtle elusiveness of expression that Leonardo loved, was finished in 1504. Francis I later bought it for 4,000 gold florins and it was placed in the Louvre. The picture was stolen in 1911, but eventually recovered. In 1506 Leonardo returned to Milan, now under French domination, later spent some unsatisfactory years in Rome and then accepted Francis I's invitation to France, spending his last years in the small castle of Cloux near the royal residence of Amboise on the Loire. His last painting was the St John the Baptist, c. 1514–15, now in the Louvre.

The fame of Leonardo rests on an imagination which variously inspired all his undertakings. His voluminous notebooks and diagrammatic drawings, of which the Royal Library, Windsor Castle, contains the greatest collection, show a profound research into general scientific laws demonstrable by observation and experiment. In applied science he had all the equipment of a great inventor, anticipating

[43]

the aeroplane, the armoured vehicle, the submarine. On the subject of architecture and town planning he had a modern attitude towards acoustics, light and space, and conceived two-level highways. His notes for a treatise on painting and his remarks on the observation of accidental effects in nature are still stimulating to artists. Superb examples of his powers as a draughtsman, apart from his scientific and anatomical studies, are his drawings of horses and warriors for the 'Battle of Anghiari', his silverpoint bust of a warrior (British Museum) and his self-portrait in sanguine (Turin), while his cartoon for the 'Virgin and St Anne' (Royal Academy) is a monochrome masterpiece. Another aspect of his imagination is seen in the paintings, which have so much of mystery and subtlety that have never ceased to inspire the world's wonder. The work of his pupil Boltraffio shows how little of his magic was directly communicable, though Correggio and Giorgione demonstrate what could be learnt from his mastery of light and shade. A wax bust of 'Flora', discovered and attributed to him in 1909 and bought as his by the Kaiser Friedrich Museum, Berlin, remains of doubtful authenticity. In person Leonardo is described as singularly handsome, and his sanguine self-portrait (Turin) shows the grandeur of his head in old age.

Lépine, Stanislas Victor Edmond (*b.* Caen, 3 Oct. 1835; *d.* Paris, 28 Sept. 1892), French landscape painter, a pupil of Corot, who painted many delightful small pictures of Paris and of quiet canal and river views in its neighbourhood and in Normandy. He worked, like his friends, Boudin and Jongkind (qq.v.), on the lines that led to Impressionism.

Leslie, Charles Robert (*b.* Clerkenwell, 11 Oct. 1794; *d.* London, 5 May 1859), painter, born in London of American parents. After an early period in Pennsylvania and a brief interlude in 1833 as a drawing master at West Point, he lived and worked in England and became R.A., 1826, producing anecdotal and illustrative paintings. He is now mainly of note as the author of the sympathetic *Memoirs of John Constable, R.A.*, 1845.

Le Sueur, Eustache (*b.* Paris, baptized 19 Nov. 1616; *d.* there, 30 April 1655), French painter, much influenced in his early work by Vouet (q.v.), his master, and later by the classicism of Poussin. Too prone to imitate others, he became finally an insipid follower of Raphael. The Louvre has many of his works, chief among them his decorative paintings for the Hôtel Lambert and the series of twenty-two paintings for a Carthusian monastery representing the Life of St Bruno.

Lewis, John Frederick (*b.* London, 14 July 1805; *d.* Walton-on-Thames, 5 Aug. 1876), English painter, the son of an engraver. He became noted for Egyptian subjects, e.g. 'The Hareem', 1850 (Victoria and Albert Museum), which combined minuteness of detail with brilliance of colour and were admired by Ruskin as an anticipation or a special form of Pre-Raphaelitism.

[44]

E. LE SUEUR—Ganymede
—Louvre.

J. F. LEWIS—Lilium Aura-
tum—Birmingham Art
Gallery.

Lewis, Percy Wyndham (*b.* Nova Scotia, 1884; *d.* London, 7 Mar. 1957), English painter and author. He studied art at the Slade School and invented the variant of Cubist and Futurist ideas known as Vorticism, proclaimed in the two numbers of *Blast*, 1914–15, opposing the 'everyday visual real' and favouring machine-like forms. Both in numerous written works and in his paintings he was an intellectual independent, and one of his later literary products, *The Demon of Progress in the Arts*, 1954, was an attack on formalized extremism. 'The Surrender of Barcelona', 1936 (Tate), applies mechanistic treatment to an imagined scene of the past. In addition to works of a semi-abstract kind he painted a number of portraits, including those of Edith Sitwell, Ezra Pound and T. S. Eliot.

Leyden, Lucas van (*b.* Leyden, *c.* 1494; *d.* there, 1533), Dutch painter and engraver, the pupil of Cornelisz Engelbrechts. He settled at Antwerp, where he met Dürer in 1521, and the engravings and woodcuts by which he won early fame show Dürer's influence though possessing a decorative charm of their own which is characteristic in all his work. His unusual colour and pictorial imagination are well exemplified in the painting 'Lot and his Daughters' (Louvre).

Leyster, Judith, *see* MOLENAER.

Lhote, André (*b.* Bordeaux, 5 July 1885), French painter, art teacher and writer on art. He studied at Bordeaux, where he was apprenticed to a wood sculptor for a number of years, and came to Paris in 1908. There he 'discovered' Cézanne and attached himself to the Cubist movement, though later he rejected the attempt to 'sacrifice the appearance of the real world'. His own work was somewhat rigid, but he shone as teacher and critic and inaugurated a celebrated teaching school in 1922.

[46]

L. VAN LEYDEN—Lot and his Daughters—Louvre.

J. M. W. TURNER—Junction of the Severn and Wye—Plate from the 'Liber Studiorum' (Etching and Mezzotint).

'**Liber Studiorum**', series of etched and mezzotinted plates by Turner designed to illustrate various styles of landscape, published between 1807 and 1819. Of a projected 100 plates, 71 were completed. Turner took the idea of such a collection of monochrome studies from Claude's 'Liber Veritatis' (q.v.). He etched all the plates in outline but left it to professional engravers, e.g. Charles Turner, William Say and Thomas Lupton, to complete them in mezzotint.

'**Liber Veritatis**', collection of 200 drawings by Claude Lorraine compiled by him *c.* 1675–80 and made up in book form as a souvenir of paintings he had disposed of and perhaps in some cases projects for paintings. It does not seem to have been a complete register of authentic works to guard against forgery as Baldinucci and others have supposed, important pictures painted after the collection was initiated not being represented in it. Claude valued it highly and specially mentioned it in his will. From the Gellée family it passed through various hands and about 1770 was bought by the Duke of Devonshire, having since remained at Chatsworth. It was reproduced in mezzotint by Richard Earlom and published in two volumes in 1777, a third volume being later added of drawings from other sources. In the original book each drawing has the painter's signature, generally a monogram C and L, sometimes with a date and a note on the subject. They were executed in pen and bistre, 70 being on tinted paper with high lights touched in with white.

[48]

E. DELACROIX—Liberty leading the People—Louvre.

'**Liberty leading the People**', 'Le 28 juillet. La Liberté guidant le Peuple', painting by Delacroix, representing the French Revolution of 1830 and its three days' War of the Barricades in Paris, 27–9 July 1830, which led to the abdication of Charles X and the proclamation of Louis Philippe as king. The event is treated realistically except for the allegorical figure of Liberty. The picture, signed and dated 1830, is now in the Louvre.

Liebermann, Max (*b.* Berlin, 20 July 1847; *d.* there, 8 Feb. 1935), German painter of landscape, portraits and peasant *genre*. He studied in Berlin, Weimar and Paris, 1873–8, and paid regular visits to Holland, 1879–84, afterwards working in Berlin. Both France and Holland were influential in his development. A visit to Barbizon, 1873, made him a student of nature in the spirit of Daubigny and Corot and, impressed by the work of both Millet and Josef Israels (qq.v.), he painted many peasant subjects, some in the Dutch fishing villages where Israels found his themes. Though he is considered the leading German Impressionist it was only in later life that he took to *plein-air* painting, and as chairman of the Berlin Secession from 1899 was a leader in modern ideas. He was President of the Berlin Academy, 1919–33.

[49]

Liechtenstein Gallery, Vienna, collection of Renaissance and baroque art notable for its paintings by Rubens and van Dyck.

Lievens, Jan (b. Leyden, 24 Oct. 1607; d. Amsterdam, buried 8 June 1674), Dutch painter, fellow pupil of Rembrandt under Pieter Lastman (q.v.). He worked with Rembrandt for a time, their early paintings sometimes being confused. He visited England, stayed for some time in Antwerp, where he was influenced by Rubens and van Dyck, and on his return to Holland carried out a number of officially commissioned decorative works, e.g. at the Town Hall, Amsterdam.

Limner, archaic term, derived from 'illuminator' (of manuscripts). It described the Elizabethan miniature painters, e.g. Hilliard, and was later applied to the simple and usually anonymous craftsmen who painted portraits in colonial America.

Lindisfarne Gospels, or St Cuthbert's Evangelistarium, most celebrated production of the Anglo-Hibernian monastery of Lindisfarne founded by St Aidan and the Irish monks of Iona or Icolmkill in 634. It was conceived as a memorial volume to St Cuthbert, who died in 687, and under Ethelwold, Bishop of Lindisfarne, the manuscript was enriched early in the eighth century by an elaborate painting of an evangelist to each of the four Gospels and illuminated capital letters at the commencement of each book. Its wonderfully decorative interlaced ornament is similar in style to that of the Book of Kells (q.v.), by which alone it is surpassed. It is now in the British Museum.

Line Engraving, intaglio process in which lines are incised on a metal plate with a tool called the graver or burin. The plate is covered with printing ink, the surface then being wiped clean, leaving the ink only in the incised lines, and a print taken by laying a sheet of

M. A. RAIMONDI—St Paul Preaching at Athens (Line Engraving after Raphael)—Victoria and Albert Museum.

1. SCHONGAUER—Christ before the High Priest (Line Engraving)—Victoria and Albert Museum.

A. MANTEGNA—The Virgin of the Grotto (Line Engraving)—Victoria and Albert Museum.

A. DÜRER—Melancolia (Line Engraving)—Victoria and Albert Museum.

W. HOGARTH—Gin Lane (Line Engraving)—Victoria and Albert Museum.

moistened paper over the plate and passing through a press. Originally a form of decoration used by goldsmiths and armourers (*see also* NIELLO), it was not used for printing on paper until the fifteenth century. The earliest dated example known is the 'Flagellation' by a German artist (1446), one of a number of anonymous engravers in Germany and the Netherlands. In Italy the earliest engraver was Maso Finiguerra (1426–64). Famous in the history of line engraving are Antonio Pollaiuolo, Andrea Mantegna, Albrecht Dürer, Marcantonio Raimondi and Lucas van Leyden (qq.v.). Portrait engraving flourished in the seventeenth century, Robert Nanteuil (1623–78) being outstanding in France and William Faithorne (1616–91) in England. Eminent in English engraving, eighteenth to nineteenth century, are Hogarth (q.v.) and Blake (q.v.). As a reproductive craft, the process fell into disuse during the nineteenth century (*see also* ENGRAVING).

Linnell, John (*b*. London, 16 June 1792; *d*. Redstone, 20 Jan. 1882), English painter who studied under John Varley (q.v.) and at the Royal Academy Schools. He was successful in portraiture though now remembered for his landscapes and more especially for befriending Blake and encouraging the production of his final masterpieces. Linnell, however, became one of the Victorian family despots, exercising an unfortunate influence on his son-in-law, Samuel Palmer (q.v.).

Lippi, Filippino (*b*. Prato, *c*. 1457; *d*. Florence, 18 April 1504), Italian painter of the Florentine School, the son of Fra Filippo Lippi. He studied under Fra Diamante, his father's pupil, and Botticelli, being the latter's most distinguished pupil. He painted many altarpieces and frescoes in a graceful and delicate style, both as regards the human types represented and in the treatment of fluttering draperies and other accessories. His earlier works include the 'Vision of St

FILIPPINO LIPPI—Music —Staatliche Museum, Berlin.

FRA FILIPPO LIPPI—Madonna adoring the Child—Uffizi, Florence.

Bernard', 1480, an altar-piece in the chapel of the Badia, Florence, the famous 'Madonna and Child with Sts Victor, John the Baptist, Bernard and Zenobius', 1485 (Uffizi), and the 'Virgin and Child with Sts Jerome and Dominic', 1485 (National Gallery). In 1484 he completed the frescoes left unfinished by Masaccio in Santa Maria del Carmine. He was in Rome for some years from 1488 and painted frescoes of scenes from the life of St Thomas Aquinas for a chapel in Santa Maria sopra Minerva. Frescoes for the Strozzi Chapel in Santa Maria Novella, Florence, 1500–2, were his last important undertaking. A notable altar-piece of the later Florentine period is 'The Adoration of the Magi', 1496 (Uffizi).

Lippi, Fra Filippo (*b.* Florence, *c.* 1406; *d.* Spoleto, 9 Oct. 1469), Italian painter of the Florentine School. A Carmelite monk in early life, he is first mentioned as a painter in 1431 and in his early work formed his style on that of Masaccio (q.v.). He was much patronized by the Medici family but lost two church offices after being convicted of forgery. Though pardoned and made chaplain of the convent of Santa Margherita in Prato, he again distinguished himself by eloping with a nun, Lucrezia Buti, by whom he had two children, one of them the painter, Filippino Lippi. A dispensation arranged by the Medici sanctioned their marriage. His main work was the frescoes in the choir of Prato Cathedral, 1452–64, depicting events in the lives of St John the Baptist and St Stephen, the best being the 'Death of St Stephen', in the background of which he introduced a portrait of himself, and that of Salome dancing. His last years were spent at Spoleto, where with his pupil, Fra Diamante, he worked on frescoes of the life of the Virgin for the cathedral. He also painted many panel pictures and created that wistful type of beauty in his Madonnas (owing something to Fra Angelico) which was to be an ideal pursued by many Florentine masters of the fifteen century. (*See* p. 55.)

Lithography, form of graphic reproduction based on the antipathy of grease and water, invented in the late eighteenth century by the Austrian printer Aloysius Senefelder. The artist draws on the surface of a stone grained or polished or a zinc plate similarly prepared,

R. P. BONINGTON—Rue de la Grosse Horloge, Rouen, 1814 (Lithograph). Victoria and Albert Museum.

PERSIAN MANUSCRIPT PAINTING (Poems of Nizami)—Old Woman complaining
to Sultan Sanjar—British Museum.

S. LOCHNER—The Presentation in the Temple—Darmstadt Regional Museum.

usually with a greasy crayon which gives the effect of a chalk drawing, though for line or a flat tone he may also use pen and brush with a greasy lithographic ink. Treating the surface with dilute nitric acid desensitizes the area that has not been drawn upon, and when the stone or plate has been moistened with water an ink roller passed over it causes ink to adhere only to the greasy image, the water repelling it in the other parts. It is possible to take a large number of impressions without loss of quality. Colour prints can be obtained by using a number of stones or plates, the image-area of each representing a particular tint determined by the artist. Many artists have made brilliant use of the process since the early nineteenth century, including Delacroix, Goya, Isabey, Bonington, Daumier, Gavarni, Whistler and Toulouse-Lautrec, the last-named devising colour effects of the most striking and original kind. Bonnard and Vuillard are other artists who have produced beautiful work in colour lithography, a form of the process now much favoured. (Colour, *see* list.)

Local Colour, colour belonging to a particular object unmodified by effects of light or colour reflected from other objects. In painting it is secondary in importance to these modifications or to the use of colour for emotional rather than descriptive value.

Lochner, Stefan (*b.* Meersburg, Lake of Constance; *d.* Cologne, Sept.–Dec. 1451), German painter, the leading master of the Cologne School, whose work is noted for its freshness of colour and charm of style and expression, appearing to owe something in style to the Gothic miniature. His most famous work is the altar-piece, *c.* 1426, in Cologne Cathedral, the central panel of which depicts the Adoration of the Kings (seen in 1520 by Dürer ' with wonder and astonishment '). Other works by him are the ' Madonna and Child in the Rose Garden ' (Wallraf-Richartz Museum, Cologne) and the ' Presentation in the Temple' (Darmstadt) (*see* page 57).

Lombard, Lambert (*b.* Liège, 1505; *d.* there 1566), Flemish painter. He was also architect, poet and engraver and is noted for his influence as a ' Romanist' on his many pupils after a visit to Italy, 1537–8.

London Group, society of British artists formed in 1913 with the aim of breaking away from academic tradition and allowing British painting to take a course of its own parallel with that of modern art in Paris. Walter Sickert was one of its promoters and its first president was Harold Gilman (1876–1919). *See also* CAMDEN TOWN GROUP. Its members have included Paul Nash, Sir Matthew Smith, Duncan Grant and other leading painters of the modern British school. The society still exists and holds regular exhibitions, now representing varied directions of effort.

Longhi (Falca), Pietro (*b.* Venice, 1702; *d.* there, 8 May 1785), Italian painter of the Venetian School, son of Alessandro Falca, a goldsmith. He studied under Crespi (q.v.) at Bologna, and returning to Venice developed a form of *genre* painting, treating in a light fashion and with freshness of view the social life of the city. Regarded by a group of masked figures, the rhinoceros brought to Venice for the

P. LONGHI—The Water-cress Seller—Collection of the Marquess of Bath.

P. LORENZETTI—The Deposition—Lower Church of St Francis, Assisi.

A. LORENZETTI—The Presentation of Jesus in the Temple—Uffizi, Florence.

carnival of 1751 is the subject of a well-known example of his gay, minor and documentary art (National Gallery). His son, Alessandro Longhi (1733–1815), was a portrait painter and engraver (reproducing some of his father's *genre* scenes). He published in 1762 a biographical account of the more important contemporary Venetian painters, with his own portrait engravings.

Lorenzetti, Italian painter brothers of the early Sienese School. The elder seems to have been **Pietro** (active 1306 1347), who was possibly the Petruccio Lorenzo known to have been active at Siena in 1306. Authenticated works by him include an altarpiece in the Pieve at Arezzo, 1320, frescoes at Assisi and the 'Birth of the Virgin' in the cathedral museum at Siena. His art is related to that of both Duccio and Giotto. His brother **Ambrogio,** or Ambrogio di Lorenzo (active 1319–47), was his pupil and influenced in style by Giotto and Giovanni Pisano. He did some work in Florence as well as in Siena. 'The Presentation of Jesus in the Temple', 1342 (Uffizi), and 'The Allegory of Good and Bad Government', frescoes in the Palazzo Pubblico, 1337–9, are his principal works. It is possible that both died in the plague that ravaged Siena in 1348.

Lorenzo Monaco, Don (b. c. 1370; d. 1422+), Italian painter of the Florentine School. Lorenzo 'the monk', as he is known, was Piero di Giovanni, who came it would seem from Siena to Florence and in 1391 took his vows and the name of Lorenzo at the Camaldolese monastery of Santa Maria degli Angeli, Florence. His work consisted of manuscript illuminations, altar-pieces and frescoes, his style in painting

[61]

deriving partly from Siena and partly from the Giottesque tradition represented by Agnolo Gaddi (q.v.). Two of his best-known works are the 'Coronation of the Virgin', 1413, and the 'Adoration of the Magi', 1420–2 (both in the Uffizi), a variant of the 'Coronation' being in the National Gallery. He introduced a Gothic element into Florentine art, to be seen in his elongated figures and decorative colour, and his 'Annunciation' (Florence, Accademia) is already close in feeling to the work of his successor, Fra Angelico (q.v.).

Lorrain, Lorraine, Claude, *see* CLAUDE.

Lotto, Lorenzo (*b.* Venice, *c.* 1480; *d.* Loreto, 1556), Italian painter of the Venetian School, noted for both his religious paintings and his portraits. He led a nomadic life and was active not only at Venice but at Treviso, Bergamo and various cities of the Marches as well as at Rome, where he stayed for some years from 1509 onwards. Various influences have been detected in his work, that of Giovanni Bellini to begin with, then of Raphael (at Rome), Correggio, and even Dürer and Holbein, though his mature work relates him to Titian, Giorgione

L. LOTTO—A Lady as Lucretia—National Gallery, London.

and Palma Vecchio. He evolved, however, a quite distinct style, rich and imaginative, and in portraiture approached greatness, as in the 'Prothonotary Apostolic, Giuliano' (National Gallery). 'A Lady as Lucretia' (also National Gallery) well represents a type of his work which inspired the young Caravaggio. His most celebrated altarpieces are in the churches of the Carmine and SS. Giovanni e Paolo, Venice, the cathedral at Asola and at Monte San Giusto near Ancona, where the church contains a 'Crucifixion' with twenty-three life-size figures. The last two years of his life were spent in monastic retreat in the Santa Casa monastery at Loreto.

Louvre, The, largest national gallery in the world, containing in addition to antiquities and sculpture a superb representation of all the European schools, though numerically strongest in French painting. Among its great treasures are Cimabue's 'Madonna Enthroned', Leonardo's 'Mona Lisa' and 'Virgin of the Rocks', Raphael's 'La Belle Jardinière' and 'Baltasar Castiglione', Giorgione's 'Concert Champêtre', Rembrandt's 'Pilgrims at Emmaus', Veronese's 'Marriage at Cana' and Poussin's 'The Arcadian Shepherds'. The history of French art unrolls in works that represent its every phase from the Master of Avignon to Cézanne.

Luini, Bernardino (b. Luino on Lake Maggiore, c. ? 1470+; d. 1532), Italian painter of the Milanese School, probably the pupil of

B. LUINI—Marriage of the Virgin—Saronno.

Ambrogio Borgogne (q.v.). Some early fragments of fresco, such as the 'Head of a Girl' (Wallace Collection), cut from a large decoration at the Villa Pelucca, a country house near Milan, are fresh and original, but Luini's natural talent was swamped by his efforts to imitate Leonardo da Vinci in the smile, light and shade, and pose of numerous Madonna pictures. His best-known later frescoes are those of Santa Maria dei Miracoli, Saronno, *c.* 1525. There are many copies and studio works after him.

Lurçat, Jean (*b.* Bruyères, Vosges, 1 July 1892), French painter and decorative designer. Cézanne and Picasso were influences on his early work. In the 1920's he travelled extensively and his acquaintance with Spain and the Sahara led him to produce a number of paintings evoking the poetry of barren landscape. He has been better known since by his magnificent tapestry designs and has been largely responsible for the modern French revival of tapestry as an art.

Luteri, Dosso and **Battista,** *see* Dossi.

Luttrell Psalter, The, illuminated manuscript executed *c.* 1340 for Sir Geoffrey Luttrell, of Irnham, Lincolnshire, who appears in one of the miniatures with his wife, Agnes Sutton, and his daughter-in-law, Beatrice Scrope. It represents the art of the East Anglian School in its decadence but its marginal illustrations are of great value in depicting the English life and labour of the time. It was acquired by the British Museum in 1929.

Luxembourg, Paris, palace erected by Marie de' Medici, which in 1879 became the meeting-place of the Senate. Attached to it is a gallery the role of which in the past was to represent modern European art. Reorganization after the Second World War transferred its best works to other galleries leaving only a conservative residue.

LUTTRELL PSALTER (detail)—Ploughing—British Museum.

M

Ma Yuan (early 13th century), Chinese painter, member of an artist family, who worked at the court under the Sung Dynasty. His landscapes were famous and frequently copied, expressing the romantic spirit of contemplation for which Sung painting was especially distinguished.

Mabuse, *see* GOSSART.

McEvoy, Ambrose (*b.* 1878; *d.* London, 1 April 1927), Irish painter, a contemporary of John and Orpen at the Slade School. He painted interiors with figures and portraits, being especially noted for portraits of women to whom his own refinement of style added distinction.

Macke, August (*b.* Meschede, Rhineland, 3 Jan. 1887; killed in action, 1914), German painter, one of the 'Blaue Reiter' group (q.v.) at Munich with Kandinsky and Marc, joining them in 1909. He studied art at Düsseldorf; enlarged his experience by travel (Italy, Holland, Belgium, London, Paris, 1905–8); and visited Tunis with Klee, April 1914. In design and colour his pictures of park and street scenes and his landscapes gave brilliant promise, regrettably cut short at an early stage of the First World War.

Maclise, Daniel (*b.* Cork, 25 Jan. 1806; *d.* London, 25 April 1870), Irish painter of historical subjects. He studied at the Royal Academy Schools and was elected R.A., 1840. He is remembered mainly by his series of portrait drawings of eminent

A. McEVOY—The Earring—Tate Gallery.

* C

A. MACKE—Farewell—Wallraf-Richartz Museum, Cologne.

literary men and women, 1830–8, and the two frescoes in the House of Lords, 'The Interview between Wellington and Blücher' and 'The Death of Nelson', on which he lavished immense but imperfect and little-appreciated effort.

'Madame Récamier', famous portrait by Jacques Louis David, begun in June 1800 but left unfinished, possibly because the sitter had asked Gérard also to paint her. Juliette Récamier, wife of a rich banker, noted for her beauty, wit and the distinguished circle of her *salon*, was then twenty-three. The interior detail depicted is of interest as reflecting the severely classical taste by which David gave an impetus to 'Empire' furniture design. The *chaise-longue* belonged to his studio and was one of the designs carried out for him by the cabinet-maker, Georges Jacob.

'Madonna of the Rocks', subject of two paintings, both of which have been attributed to Leonardo, one in the Louvre, the other in the National Gallery. They have a history which is not altogether clear. On 25 April 1483 Leonardo, in partnership with Ambrogio de Predis and the latter's half-brother Evangelista, contracted to paint a work for the confraternity of the Immaculate Conception at Milan in the chapel adjoining their church of San Francesco. The centre-piece was to be painted by 'the Florentine', i.e. Leonardo, the side panels by de Predis. Between 1490 and 1494 the artists claimed more

LEONARDO DA VINCI—Madonna of the Rocks—Louvre.

N. MAES—The Idle Servant—National Gallery, London.

pay. Argument dragged on for years and the picture was reclaimed. In 1506 the confraternity agreed to pay an extra sum but the work finally delivered seems to have been a different version from that originally painted. The first version is generally considered to be the painting now in the Louvre. A question on which there have been different opinions is whether the National Gallery picture, which was definitely that finally accepted and hung in the confraternity's chapel, was by Leonardo or his assistant. Comparison with the wings of the altar-piece by de Predis also in the National Gallery shows so different a level of workmanship as to lead to the conclusion that the London 'Madonna' is indeed a mature and superb masterpiece by Leonardo himself. Compare illustration on page 43.

Maes, Nicolas (*b.* Dordrecht, Nov. 1632; *d.* Amsterdam, buried 24 Dec. 1693), Dutch *genre* and portrait painter, a pupil of Rembrandt at Amsterdam. His early work includes such masterpieces as 'The Idle Servant' (National Gallery) and the 'Old Woman at the Spinning Wheel' (Rijksmuseum), but after a period spent in Antwerp he turned to fashionable portraiture with a marked change of style, in which, however, the Rembrandtesque technique could still be discerned.

Maestà (It. 'majesty'), abbreviated title for paintings of the Madonna and Child, enthroned in majesty and attended by angels or saints.

Magnasco, Alessandro (*b.* Genoa, 1681; *d.* there, 12 Mar. 1747), Italian painter, son of the painter Stefano Magnasco. He studied in Milan and worked there and also at Florence and Genoa. In a tempestuous, febrile and romantic style he carried on the tradition of Salvator Rosa (q.v.) and was much admired in his own time for his pictures of social life in which there was a fantastic and perhaps satiric element. Market scenes, gipsy encampments, Jewish synagogues and monks at prayer in wild landscape settings were among his subjects, and his method of painting with dashing touches seems to have had its effect on the style of Guardi (q.v.). After a long period of neglect interest in him has revived in modern times.

Magritte, René (*b.* Lessines, 1898), Belgian Surrealist painter, a principal exponent of the art of metaphor in painting. Inspired by the work of Chirico (q.v.) he began about 1925 to produce a new kind of pictorial imagery and was associated with an active group of Surrealist painters and poets in Brussels, illustrating a number of books of an imaginative order and contributing to 'advanced' reviews. Paintings by him are in the Museum of Modern Art, New York, the Art Institute of Chicago, the galleries of Antwerp and Brussels and many private collections in various parts of the world.

Mahlstick (Maulstick), wooden stick tipped with a pad of cloth or leather used by painters as a support for the wrist when painting fine detail.

Mainardi, Sebastiano (active 1493; *d.* 1513), Italian painter of the Florentine School, a pupil and assistant of Ghirlandaio (q.v.), whose

[69]

A. MAGNASCO—The Bohemian Wedding—Louvre.

sister he married. He is said to have collaborated with Ghirlandaio in a fresco of the 'Assumption of the Virgin' (Santa Croce, Florence), and a series of frescoes at San Gimignano has been attributed to him, but many works have been ascribed to him of which it is only possible to say that they were from the studio, or by a follower, of Ghirlandaio.

Malbone, Edward Greene (*b*. Newport, Rhode Island, Aug. 1777; *d*. Savannah, Georgia, 7 May 1807), American miniature painter, trained at an early age by Samuel King in Boston and beginning his independent career in Providence at seventeen. He accompanied Allston to London for study, returning to America in 1801. He worked in Boston, New York and Philadelphia and his delicate art is now held in high regard.

Malevich, Kasimir (*b*. Kief, 1878; *d*. Moscow, 1935), Russian painter and theorist who invented the form of completely non-figurative art called 'Suprematism'. He studied at Kief and going to Moscow, *c*. 1900, was impressed by the modern French paintings then being collected there by wealthy merchants. He passed through Fauve, Cubist and Futurist phases but in 1915 turned dramatically to simple geometric forms. His 'White on White', 1918 (New York Museum of Modern Art), is a celebrated product of his theories, which he vigorously propagated in the early years after the Bolshevik Revolution. The return to conservatism in art in the U.S.S.R., *c*. 1930,

[70]

marked the end of his influence, but he was a gifted artist and has a pioneer importance in the history of abstraction.

Malouel (Maelwael), Jean (*b.* (?) Gelderland: *d.* 1415), painter of the Franco-Flemish School who worked in Paris for Isabeau de Bavirèe and then at Dijon, where he was appointed court painter to the Dukes of Burgundy, Philip the Bold and John the Fearless. He had some (uncertainly known) part in the decoration of the Chartreuse of Champmol built under the auspices of Philip the Bold. It has been suggested that he began the 'Crucifixion and Martyrdom of St Denis' (now in the Louvre) which is mainly the work of Henri Bellechose, his successor as Burgundian court painter; and also a circular 'Pietà' (Louvre), both being paintings for Champmol, though definite evidence is lacking of his contribution. He seems to have been more primitive in style than Bellechose.

Mander, Karel van (*b.* Meulebeke, 1584; *d.* Amsterdam, 1606), Dutch painter and writer. He studied art at Ghent and after a wide variety of experience settled at Haarlem, where he had a successful academy of painting. He is best known, however, for his biographical work on artists, published 1604, a valuable source of information on Dutch and Flemish art.

Manessier, Alfred (*b.* St Ouen, 5 Dec. 1911), French painter who studied in the architecture section of the École des Beaux-Arts. After undergoing the influence of Cubism and Fauvism he turned to non-figurative painting, producing works of exceptional richness in colour. He has designed stained-glass windows in which the abstract quality of his painting is impressively applied.

Manet, Edouard (*b.* Paris, 25 Jan. 1832; *d.* there, 30 April 1883), French painter and outstanding figure in nineteenth-century art. The son of a magistrate, he was allowed (after a trial voyage as naval cadet, 1848–9) to enter the studio of Thomas Couture (q.v.), with whom he studied for six years, gaining, in spite of frequent clashes with his academic master, a sound technical training. He copied Titian and Velazquez in the Louvre, and though he did not visit Spain until 1865 his early work shows the influence of seventeenth-century Spanish masters, this being underlined by his paintings of Spanish dancers in Paris, e.g. 'Lola de Valence', 1861–2 (Louvre). The first picture he sent to the Salon, the 'Buveur d'Absinthe', 1859, was refused, inaugurating a long series of sensational rejections. He brilliantly succeeded in his aim of handling an old master subject in contemporary fashion in the two celebrated pictures of the 1860's, 'Le Déjeuner sur l'Herbe', 1863 (translating Giorgione's 'Concert Champêtre' into modern terms), and 'Olympia', 1865 (Titian's Venus brought up to date), but both pictures were misunderstood, their unconventional nudities causing a scandal. Exhibited in the Salon des Refusés, 1863, the 'Déjeuner' became the symbol of revolt against academic and Philistine prejudice, and Manet, though no rebel by nature, became the centre of the group of younger artists whose meetings and discussions at the Café Guerbois were the

[71]

seeding-ground of Impressionism. For political rather than aesthetic reasons his 'Execution of Maximilian', 1867 (of which there are four versions, at Boston, Mannheim and Copenhagen, with fragments of the second version in the National Gallery), was barred from his one-man show of that year. After the Franco-Prussian War, in which he served as an officer in the National Guard, he took to *plein-air* painting under the influence of Monet and Berthe Morisot, his pupil and sister-in-law (qq.v.), working at Argenteuil with Monet and Renoir in 1874; though he abstained from exhibiting at the Impressionist exhibitions. His colour freshened, though he was impressionistic rather in giving the vividness of the first sketch than in systematic division of colour. The cabaret and its frequenters figure largely in his later work (as in that of Degas), the 'Bon Bock', a success of 1873, being followed by 'La Servante de Bocks', 1878–9, and the famous masterpiece (executed after the first onset of fatal illness), 'Un Bar aux Folies-Bergère', 1881–2 (London, Courtauld Institute Gallery). Conservative by nature and in ambition, Manet was unconventional only in genius.

Manfredi, Bartolommeo (*b.* Ustiano, nr Mantua, 1580; *d.* Rome, 1620), Italian painter who worked in Rome at the beginning of the seventeenth century, and is mainly known as an imitator of Caravaggio in secular subjects, transmitting the style of that master to foreign artists in Rome, such as Gerard Honthorst (q.v.).

Mannerism, in a general sense some idiosyncrasy, extravagance or affectation of style or manner in art, though it has more specific reference to Italian painting in the sixteenth century and represents a distinct phase between the art of the High Renaissance and the rise of baroque. It was largely based on an admiration for Michelangelo and a consequent exaggeration of the emphasis of his composition and the expressive distortion of his figures. Mannerist characteristics are an excessive muscularity or elongation of the figure; violent

or strained gesture; crowded composition, often showing many discrepancies of proportion and scale; and a corresponding violence of colour. These tendencies developed in Florence, Rome and Bologna, and the unrest they show may be partly related to the disturbing effect of the Reformation and also to that disruptive episode the sack of Rome in 1527, which upset the routine of many painters. Principal Mannerists were Parmigianino, Daniele da Volterra, Jacopo da Pontormo, Salviati, the brothers Federigo and Taddeo Zuccaro, and Perino del Vaga (qq.v.). A particular and graceful form of Mannerism was that introduced into France by the Italian artists whom Francis I employed, Giovanni Battista Rossi (Il Rosso), Primaticcio and Niccolò dell' Abbate (qq.v.). *See also* FONTAINEBLEAU, SCHOOL OF. Pellegrino (1527–92) introduced Mannerism into Spain. Late representatives of the style in Italy were Bronzino (q.v.), the pupil of Vasari, and the Cavaliere d'Arpino (q.v.) with whom it is considered to have reached its nadir. In England William Blake and Fuseli show how something of a Mannerist result might be independently reached at a much later date through an admiration for Michelangelo.

Mantegna, Andrea (*b.* Isola di Carturo, between Vicenza and Padua, 1431; *d.* Mantua, 13 Sept. 1506), Italian painter and engraver, who was brought up and trained by Francesco Squarcione (q.v.) at Padua, his master entering him in the guild of painters before he was eleven. Like Squarcione, and indeed all the north Italian artists who saw Donatello's work at Padua, he was later impressed by the great sculptor's achievement as well as by the paintings of the Florentines, Uccello and Filippo Lippi; and one might say the spirit of Florence is joined with that of Venice in his art, for he was also influenced in style by Jacopo Bellini, whose daughter Lodovisia he married in 1453. Early paintings which won him fame were his frescoes in the

Eremitani church at Padua, 1449–54, mainly destroyed in the Second World War though two sections moved to Venice remain. The nature of his art about this period can be intimately studied in the panel 'The Agony in the Garden' (National Gallery), splendidly designed as a formal composition. The background was probably taken in essentials from a drawing by Jacopo Bellini, but the sculptural quality, the effects of perspective and foreshortening, and the austerity of form were Mantegna's own. In 1459 he went to Verona and painted an altar-piece for the church of St Zeno, then moved to Mantua in 1460 at the invitation of Lodovico Gonzaga, remaining in the service of the Gonzagas for the rest of his life. Among the frescoes he undertook for them was the bridal chamber of the Castello di Corte at Mantua, the painted cupola of the ceiling representing figures foreshortened round a balcony with open sky beyond, the first feat of an illusionism later practised by Correggio and the baroque painters. Cartoons for the decoration of a theatre in this palace (not carried out) constitute the famous 'Triumph of Caesar', in nine sections each nine feet square, painted in tempera, 1482–92, bought with other treasures of the Gonzagas by Charles I and now at Hampton Court. While this work was in process he visited Rome to paint frescoes in the chapel of the Belvedere (since destroyed). The cartoons show a growing addiction to classical antiquity and an attempt to rival Roman narrative relief sculpture in painting, which in spite of its grandeur tended to divert him too far from the study of reality. Principal later pictures were the 'Lamentation' (Milan, Brera), with its dramatic foreshortening of the body of the dead Christ, the 'Madonna della Vittoria' (Louvre), celebrating a Mantuan victory over the French, and two paintings intended for the boudoir of

A. MANTEGNA—The Agony in the Garden—National Gallery, London.

Isabella d'Este at Mantua, the 'Parnassus' and 'Virtue triumphant over Vice' (Louvre), in which Mantegna shows a graceful fancy strikingly different from his usual austerity. They show how little he was a man of set formulas. As an engraver he was highly original in the style and straight-line shading of his religious and mythological copperplates.

Manuel Deutsch, Nicolaus (*b*. Bern, 1484; *d*. 1530), Swiss painter, poet and reformer. He studied painting at Colmar and in Venice under Titian. His works included a 'Dance of Death' (of which only copies exist) for a monastery at Bern and the 'Beheading of John the Baptist' (Basel) in an ornate and fanciful style with much curious detail. He was active in later years in diplomacy and public affairs and as an advocate of the Reformation.

Maratta, Carlo (*b*. Camerano, 15 May 1625; *d*. Rome, 15 Dec. 1713), Italian painter in the later baroque style, the pupil of Andrea Sacchi (q.v.). He worked in Rome and was entrusted by Clement XI with the care and restoration of the frescoes of Raphael (whom he admired and copied) in the Vatican. He led a reaction towards the classic serenity of Raphael as distinct from the theatricalism of baroque. He was a prolific painter of Madonnas and other religious subjects as well as portraits.

[75]

F. MARC—Landscape with Horse—Folkwang Museum, Essen.

Marc, Franz (*b*. Munich, 8 Feb. 1880; killed in action nr Verdun, 4 Mar. 1916), German painter, associated with the 'Blaue Reiter' group (q.v.). He studied at Munich and after travel to Italy and Paris was influenced by Post-Impressionist art, applying its lessons of colour and design to animal painting and in particular a series of horses. Acquaintance with Kandinsky and Macke in 1910 led to his adopting their free use of brilliant colour and in 1912 a meeting with Delaunay in Paris added a Cubist influence, as in his 'Roes in the Wood', 1913–14 (Karlsruhe). His animals were subjective and symbolic creations rather than studies of nature and in this sense he was an Expressionist. The trend of his development, cut short by war, was towards abstraction.

Marcantonio (Marcantonio Raimondi) (*b*. Bologna, *c*. 1480; *d*. there, ? 1534), Italian engraver. He worked at Bologna as goldsmith and engraver under Francia until 1510 and was also influenced by Dürer, whose engravings he copied. He lived in Rome from 1510 until its sacking in 1527 by imperial forces and mercenaries, engraving many works by Raphael and his pupils. He was the first and perhaps the most eminent of reproductive engravers, but he may be called an original artist inasmuch as he elaborated and interpreted Raphael's drawings, Raphael encouraging his independent skill. He died in obscurity.

Marcoussis, Louis (*b.* Warsaw, 1883; *d.* Vichy-Cusset, 1941), Polish-born painter who worked in Paris and was drawn into the sphere of Cubist influence. He produced semi-abstract paintings in the flat decorative style of synthetic Cubism.

Marées, Hans von (*b.* Elberfeld, 24 Dec. 1837; *d.* Rome, 5 June 1887), German painter who studied in Berlin and Munich and spent a number of years in Rome. He is noted for introducing a new simplicity and force of expression into figure painting as in his 'The Oarsmen', 1873 (Berlin), though his works found little appreciation or understanding in his own time.

Margarito (Margaritone) of Arezzo (active *c.* 1262), Italian painter, sculptor and architect, signed works by whom are at Arezzo, Siena and in the National Galleries, London and Washington. The retable or altar frontal in the National Gallery, London, 'The Virgin and Child Enthroned with Scenes of the Nativity and Lives of the Saints', shows in its panels of detail the survival of the Byzantine tradition, though the central figure has Romanesque simplicity. It was bought in 1857 to show 'the barbarous state into which art had sunk even in Italy previously to its revival'; a view repeated by Anatole France in *L'Ile des Pingouins*. Revision of these judgments would nevertheless place it in a more naïve and provincial category than the art of either Cimabue or Duccio.

Marin, John (*b.* Rutherford, New Jersey, 23 Dec. 1870; *d.* Cape Split, Maine, 1 Oct. 1953), American painter especially noted for his water-colours in which the feeling of landscape or seascape is conveyed

MARGARITO OF AREZZO—The Virgin and Child Enthroned with Scenes of the Nativity and Lives of the Saints—National Gallery, London.

J. MARIN—London Omnibus (Water-colour)—Stieglitz Collection, Metropolitan Museum, New York.

by forceful, cubistically broken shapes and patterns of colour. He began his career as an architect, studied painting in Philadelphia and New York and travelled much in Europe, 1905–11, subsequently settling in New Jersey. Many of his original inventions in water-colour were inspired by the coast of Maine and the streets of Manhattan.

Maris, name of three brothers prominent in the nineteenth-century revival of Dutch landscape, **Matthijs** (*b.* The Hague, 1835; *d.* 1917), **Jakob** (*b.* The Hague, 25 Aug. 1837; *d.* Carlsbad, 8 Aug. 1899) and **Willem** (*b.* The Hague, 1843; *d.* 1910). Jakob is noted as a painter of water, clouds and misty skies, Willem painted peaceful sunlit meadows. Influenced by the Barbizon School (q.v.), they in turn had some influence on British artists, especially the Glasgow School.

Marmion, Simon (*b.* Amiens, active 1449; *d.* 1489), painter and miniaturist of the Franco-Flemish school, who worked at Amiens, Valenciennes and Tournai and illuminated manuscripts for Philip the Good, Duke of Burgundy. He painted panels (now lost or dispersed) illustrating the Life of St Bertin for the abbey of St Omer of which there are parts at Berlin and in the National Gallery, these showing a notable delicacy of style.

[78]

M. MARIS—Souvenir of Amsterdam—Rijksmuseum, Amsterdam.

J. MARIS—Landscape with Windmills—National Gallery, London.

S. MARMION—Altar-piece of St Bertin—Staatlichen Museum, Berlin.

Marquet, Pierre Albert (*b.* Bordeaux, 27 Mar. 1875, *d.* Paris, 14 June 1947), French landscape painter, one of the first Fauves. He went to Paris in 1890 and studied at the École des Beaux-Arts, later meeting Matisse, with whom he often painted on the banks of the Seine. In his many paintings of towns, harbours and rivers he showed a particular gift of simplification which seized unerringly upon the essentials in the scene before him.

'Marriage-à-la-Mode', series of six paintings by Hogarth, completed in 1744 and engraved by G. Scotin, B. Baron and F. S. Ravenet in 1745. It shows (1) the signing of a marriage contract between the daughter of a wealthy commoner and the son of a peer; (2) the boredom of the ill-matched pair soon after the marriage; (3) and (4) the follies of the countess; (5) the discovery of the countess with her lover by the earl and his death in the sword fight following; (6) the remorse and death of the countess. The series is now in the Tate Gallery.

'Marriage at Cana'. The first miracle of Jesus when He turned water into wine at a marriage feast at Cana in Galilee (John ii) has been variously depicted by the old masters, but the most famous version is that of Veronese, painted, 1652–3, for the refectory of the Benedictines of San Giorgio Maggiore at Venice and now in the Louvre. Containing more than 130 figures in a palatial setting, this huge painting, mundane in its opulent detail and general conception, caused Veronese to be taken to task by the Inquisition for treating a religious subject lightly. The artist introduced the portraits of many contemporaries, Charles V, Francis I, Sultan Soliman II, the poet Aretino and Vittoria Colonna among them. Venetian painters— Titian, Bassano, Tintoretto and Veronese himself (q.v.)— were portrayed as musicians and many anonymous figures represented aspects of luxurious Venetian life.

Marsh, Reginald (*b.* Paris, 14 Mar. 1898; *d.* Bennington, Vermont, 3 July 1954), American painter of city life. After working as an illustrator and cartoonist in New York, he studied painting there and produced pictures of the Bowery, the Elevated Railway, Coney

Island and other aspects of the metropolitan scene. densely crowded with figures. These are unresolved as works of art but convey something of the teeming excitement of life in the mass.

Marshall, Benjamin (*c.* 1767–1835), English painter of animals and sporting subjects, a follower of George Stubbs (q.v.). He painted a number of portraits of racehorses and their owners, which were exhibited at the Royal Academy, the portrait of Emilius, winner of the Derby in 1823, being a good example.

Martin, Homer Dodge (*b.* Albany, New York, 28 Oct. 1836; *d.* St Paul, 12 Feb. 1897), American landscape painter, largely self-taught. He worked in France for some years and was influenced by the Barbizon School as well as by Whistler (qq.v.). He is one of those who mark the decline of the Hudson River tradition and the search for fresh stimulus in Europe.

Martin, John (*b.* nr Hexham, 19 July 1789; *d.* Douglas, Isle of Man, 17 Feb. 1854), English painter of imaginative subjects. He began his career as heraldic coach painter in Newcastle but, settling in London, made his mark by scenes of fantasy, of doomed cities and supernal wrath, stupendous in the theatrical effect attained by placing small figures in vast settings with tunnel-like effects of perspective. The

R. B. MARTINEAU—The Last Day in the Old Home—Tate Gallery.

Bible and Milton suggested many of his themes. He might be called the Cecil de Mille of the Romantic period.

Martineau, Robert Braithwaite (*b.* London, 19 Jan. 1826; *d.* there, 13 Feb. 1869), English painter of subject pictures, a pupil of Holman Hunt. He is famous for his 'The Last Day in the Old Home', 1862 (Tate Gallery), in which a theme like that of a Victorian novel is elaborated with Pre-Raphaelite detail.

Martini, Simone (Simone Memmi) (*b. c.* 1283; *d.* 1344), Italian painter of the Sienese School, a pupil of Duccio (q.v.). French Gothic art and the Gothic element in the sculpture of the Pisani contributed to give his art a new direction, dominant in Siena for the two centuries following. It appears in the 'Virgin and Child' of 1315 in the council chamber of the Palazzo Pubblico, and the decorative beauty of his line and colour is fully seen in the 'Annunciation' of 1333 (Uffizi), a work in which, it has been said, Northern Gothic and the Sienese tradition meet in perfect union. A link with France and court life was first established by his visit to Naples in 1317, where he painted for Robert of Anjou his altar-piece in the church of San Lorenzo, showing St Louis crowning Robert, King of Naples. In 1339 he went on public business to Avignon and remained in that centre of an exiled Papacy and a chivalric culture for the rest of his life. There he was the friend of Petrarch and painted a portrait (now lost) of Petrarch's Laura. In Avignon he exerted an influence of great effect on French art and the development of an international Gothic style, as well as on Italy. His work includes in fresco his early 'Maestà' for the Palazzo Pubblico, Siena, 1315, 1321, the equestrian portrait of

S. MARTINI—Christ returning to His Parents after disputing with the Doctors—Walker Art Gallery, Liverpool.

[83]

S. MARTINI—Guidoriccio dei Fogliani on Horseback—Palazzo Pubblico, Siena.

Guidoriccio dei Fogliani with panoramic background, and frescoes in the Lower Church of St Francis, Assisi, in which the scene of the knighting of St Martin expresses all the courtly gaiety of his *milieu*. An interesting signed and dated work of the Avignon period is the 'Christ returning to His Parents after disputing with the Doctors', 1342 (Liverpool, Walker Art Gallery), and a noble product of his studio is the polyptych (three panels of Sts Ambrose, Michael and Augustine) in the Fitzwilliam Museum, Cambridge.

Masaccio (*b.* San Giovanni Valdarwo, 21 Dec. 1401; *d.* Rome 1427–9), Italian painter of the Florentine School, properly called Tommaso di Giovanni and nicknamed Masaccio ('shiftless'), Vasari explains, because of his carelessness in practical affairs. His master may have been Mariotto di Cristofano, who came from the same town. He worked in Florence from 1422, was in Pisa in 1426 and died in Rome. In succession to Giotto he brings us a stage nearer the Renaissance, and is sometimes called the father of modern painting from his ability to represent the mass and volume of objects in the round and their relation in space. To this must be added a narrative and dramatic power obtained by a strict choice of essentials in which he continues Giotto's work. He is celebrated for his frescoes in the Brancacci Chapel in the Carmine and at Santa Maria Novella, Florence. Not all the Brancacci frescoes have survived and opinions have varied as to whether all were by Masaccio or only the most powerful, others (apart from later additions by Filippino Lippi, q.v.) being attributed to Masolino (q.v.), who seems to have shared the original commission. Without doubt, however, the 'Expulsion of Adam and Eve from Paradise', the 'Tribute Money', 'St Peter healing the Sick with his Shadow', 'St Peter baptizing', 'St Peter enthroned' and 'St Peter distributing the Goods of the Community' are by him. The frescoes were long the inspiration of Florentine artists, Michelangelo among them. The central panel of an altar-piece for the church of the Carmine at Pisa, 1426, now in the National Gallery, has the majesty characterizing the work of this short-lived genius.

Masip, Juan Vicente de (*c.* 1475–*c.* 1550), Spanish painter who worked at Valencia. It is probable that he visited Italy and his religious paintings show the influence of Raphael and the Roman

[84]

MASACCIO—The Tribute Money—Santa Maria del Carmine, Florence.

School, though individual in colour and detail. 'The Visitation' and 'Martyrdom of St Agnes' (Prado) are two notable works. His son, **Juan Vicente de Masip the Younger** (?1523–79), also known as Juan de Juanes, whose reputation long overshadowed that of his father, developed a dramatic but artificial mannerism from the Raphaelesque style, as in his 'Last Supper' (Prado). He was capable of vigorous portraiture, as in his 'Don Luis de Castellà de Vilanova.' (Prado).

Maso di Banco (active late fourteenth century), Florentine painter, one of the principal followers of Giotto, mainly known by his frescoes of the Life of St Sylvester in the Bardi Chapel of Santa Croce at Florence. He has been identified with Giottino (q.v.), but they are now regarded as two distinct artists.

Masolino (b. ? Panicale, c. 1383; d. c. 1447), Italian painter of the Florentine School, a goldsmith in youth who is stated to have worked under Ghiberti on the baptistery doors at Florence, 1403–7, but who later turned to painting. He executed some of the frescoes in the Brancacci Chapel of the church of the Carmine, Florence, 1424–7, the remainder being by Masaccio (q.v.). In other works Masolino—unlike Masaccio—still shows attachment to the decorative Gothic conventions of style, but in the Brancacci Chapel he seems to have made an effort to match the younger painter's boldness and realism. Other paintings include a Madonna, dated 1423 (Bremen), frescoes at

[85]

MASOLINO—Virgin and Child with Angels—Church of San Stefano, Empoli.

Castiglione d'Olona, and an altar-piece, parts of which are in the galleries of Naples, Philadelphia and London.

Mass in painting refers not to bulk but to the principal areas in which form is distributed and arranged as distinct from detail.

'Mass of Bolsena, The', fresco by Raphael in the Stanza d'Eliodoro of the Vatican, painted between 1512 and 1514, one of his greatest works. Commemorating the pontificate of Julius II, it shows an unbelieving priest convinced of the doctrine of transubstantiation by the miraculous bleeding of the host, and has reference to the Pope's suppression of schism.

'Massacre of Scio, The', 'Scènes des Massacres de Scio' (Chios), painting by Delacroix exhibited in the Salon of 1824, representing an episode of 1822 in the Greek War of Independence, Greek families 'awaiting death or slavery' at the hands of the Turks, a mounted Turkish officer being dominant in the composition. Delacroix is said to have repainted some part of the picture after seeing Constable's 'Hay-wain' (q.v.), also exhibited in the Salon in 1824. The 'Massacre' is one of the major products of French Romanticism.

Masson, André (*b*. Balagny, 4 Jan. 1896), French painter who settled in Paris in the 1920's and was influenced by Picasso and the painters and poets then developing the ideas of Surrealism. His work

RAPHAEL—The Mass of Bolsena (detail)—Vatican, Rome.

E. DELACROIX—The Massacre of Scio—Louvre.

A. MASSON—Insect Ballet—Photo: Leicester Galleries.

has passed through several stages—from strange images in which plants, insects and human figures had a part, e.g. the 'Metamorphoses' of 1939, to a kind of calligraphic abstraction — but its general trend was towards finding a visual equivalent for a mental or emotional state. Working in the United States during the 1940's he influenced such painters as Jackson Pollock (q.v.), and he has his part in the growth of what is known as 'Abstract Expressionism.'

Massys (also **Quentin Matsys, Metsys**), **Quinten** (*b*. Louvain, 1465–1466; *d*. Antwerp, 1530), Flemish painter of religious subjects, portraits and studies of secular life, the son of a metalworker and clockmaker at Louvain and trained there and perhaps in the studio of Dirck Bouts (q.v.). His art represents two phases of transition, from the later period of early Netherlandish art, represented by Memlinc and Gerard David (qq.v.), to that of Italian influence, and from declining Bruges to the newly flourishing city of Antwerp, where he became a member of the Painters' Guild in 1491. He is noted for the refinement and delicacy of his female types, in which he seems to show acquaintance with the work of Leonardo, and for landscape backgrounds related in character to those of his contemporary at Antwerp, Patenier (q.v.). He branched out also in the vein of 'The Moneychanger and his Wife' (Louvre), which he made a popular subject among painters such as van Reymerswael (q.v.). His sons Cornelis (*c*. 1508–80+) and Jan (*c*. 1509–75) were also painters and pupils of Quinten.

Master, term applied in a general sense to any artist of outstanding ability but with a more specific historical meaning, implying admittance to a Painters' Guild, as in the Dutch and Flemish centres of art, a 'masterpiece' not being necessarily of exceptional merit but simply one which proved competence. Alternatively, 'master' describes historically artists with a studio-workshop employing pupils, such as the European painters of the thirteenth to seventeenth centuries, more

Q. MASSYS—The Money-changer and his Wife—Louvre.

especially, though the term 'Old Master' in this sense, as regards both excellence and date, is nowadays very flexibly used. The term 'little masters' applies, strictly, not to minor artists necessarily but to those working on a small scale. 'Master' plus the title of a painting roughly establishes the personalities of a number of anonymous artists, known only, or mainly, by works thus cited.

Master of Avignon, anonymous fifteenth-century French painter of the School of Avignon, author of the superb 'Pietà' (Louvre), *c.* 1450, a unique work for its time in its emotional feeling and simplicity and breadth of treatment. The artist was at one time identified with Charonton (q.v.) but later analysis of style has rejected this supposition.

Master of Flémalle (so called from a group of pictures in Frankfurt (wrongly) supposed to have come from the Belgian town of Flémalle), Flemish painter of the early fifteenth century, identified in 1909 by Georges Hulin with Robert Campin (q.v.), and as the author of a group of works previously ascribed to a 'Master of Mérode' (after an 'Annunciation' formerly belonging to the Mérode family and now in the Metropolitan Museum, New York). The same anonymous artist was also called 'Master of the Mousetrap', from a detail in the Mérode work. Paintings attributed to the same hand are the Weil Altar (Prado) and the 'Virgin and Child before a Fire-screen' (National Gallery). Experts do not unanimously accept the identification with Campin, but the important point involved is that of a personality and style in early Netherlandish art evidently distinct from that of van Eyck but with some influential relation to that of Rogier van der Weyden (qq.v.), who, there is reason to believe, was Campin's pupil.

Master of 1499, anonymous Flemish painter active at the end of the fifteenth century who worked at Bruges. There are four works attributed to him in the Musée des Beaux-Arts at Antwerp, the reverse of a panel of the Madonna bearing the date 1499.

D   [89]

Master of Moulins (active *c.* 1480–*c.* 1500), painter of the French School, also known as the 'Master of the Bourbons', from the triptych in Moulins Cathedral (with Pierre II, duc de Bourbon, as donor and his wife and daughter in the wings). The influence of Hugo van der Goes (q.v.) appears in the 'Nativity' (Autun) and the 'St Victor with a Donor' (Glasgow), but the beauty of his work is of France rather than of the Netherlands. Identification with Jean de Perréal is dubiously regarded by experts, but under any title he is an outstanding master.

Master of St Giles, painter of Netherlandish training, active at Paris, *c.* 1500, named from two pictures in the National Gallery, 'St Giles and the Hind' and 'The Mass of St Giles', in style belonging to the School of Bruges.

Master of Spes Nostra. Anonymous Netherlandish painter active in the latter part of the fifteenth century, a notable work by whom is the allegorical 'The Vanity of Human Life' (Rijksmuseum).

Master of the Death of the Virgin, Netherlandish painter, active 1507–37, author of a large group of works, and deriving his title from two altar-pieces of 'The Death of the Virgin' at Cologne and Munich. He is usually identified with Joos van Cleve (q.v.)

MASTER OF MOULINS—St Victor and a Donor—Glasgow Art Gallery.

MASTER OF SPES NOSTRA—The Vanity of Human Life—Rijksmuseum, Amsterdam.

Master of the Female Half-lengths, Netherlandish painter active in the early sixteenth century, probably of the Antwerp School, though related in style to the Bruges masters, Benson and Isenbrant,(qq.v.). He is the author of a large group of works with figures distinctive in their oval features and almond-shaped eyes.

Master of the Housebook, German painter and engraver active in the Rhineland in the latter part of the fifteenth century, so called from the drawings in the *Hausbuch* of Schloss Wolfegg. The engravings, of which there is an especially large and representative collection at Amsterdam, show scenes of everyday life. A well-known painting is 'The Lovers of Gotha' (Gotha, Castle Museum).

Master of the Legend of St Lucy, Netherlandish painter of the late fifteenth century, named from the altar-piece in the Church of St Jacques, Bruges. He worked at Bruges in the style of Memlinc (q.v.).

Master of the Legend of St Ursula, Netherlandish painter active in Bruges at the end of the fifteenth century whose work shows the influence of Memlinc (q.v.). Named from the diptych in the Convent of Les Sœurs Noires, Bruges.

Master of the Life of Mary, anonymous German painter and stained

[92]

MASTER OF ST GILES—The Mass of St Giles—National Gallery, London.

MASTER OF THE VIRGO INTER VIRGINES—The Virgin and Child with Female Saints
—Rijksmuseum, Amsterdam.

glass designer of the School of Cologne, active in the second half of the fifteenth century. He is named from the panels of the Life of the Virgin (Munich) from the church of St Ursula, Cologne. Their style suggest a Netherlandish training.

Master of the Magdalen Legend, Netherlandish painter of religious subjects and portraits, active in Brussels in the early sixteenth century, possibly identical with Bernard van Stockt.

Master of Trebon (active at Prague, second half of fourteenth century), Czech painter named from the paintings forming part of an altar-piece in the Augustinian church at Trebon, now in the National Gallery at Prague. They combine the Gothic tradition of art in Bohemia with influences coming from Italy and France. 'The Resurrection' is a masterpiece which shows its author to have been an innovator in the use of light and shade and a designer of great originality and power.

Master of the Virgo inter Virgines, Dutch painter of the second half of the fifteenth century, named from the distinguished painting of 'The Virgin with Female Saints' (Rijksmuseum).

Matisse, Henri (*b.* Cateau Cambrésis, 31 Dec. 1869; *d.* Nice, 3 Nov. 1954), French painter, one of the most eminent representatives of the School of Paris (q.v.). He studied law in Paris as a young man, was a lawyer's clerk for a while in his native district but soon went back to Paris to take up painting. He went first to the studio of Bouguereau, then studied under Gustave Moreau (q.v.) at the École des Beaux-Arts, receiving a sound academic training. He was attracted towards Impressionism about 1897 and a period of experiment followed.

H. MATISSE—Woman with Headdress (Pencil Drawing) — E. le Bas Collection.

[95]

H. MATISSE—The White Plumes—Minneapolis Institute of Arts.

For a while his work was similar in technique to the Intimist paintings of Bonnard (q.v.), as in 'La Desserte' of 1898. Colour in its various Post-Impressionist aspects, in the work of Cézanne, van Gogh and above all Gauguin, then engaged his attention, and from 1904 to 1906 he was associated with a group of like enthusiasms, Marquet, Vlaminck, Derain, Dufy, Rouault, Braque, Friesz and van Dongen. In the famous Salon d'Automne of 1905 the bold flat colour of Matisse and his associates earned them the title of Fauves—'wild beasts'. Matisse opened a school in 1907, though the students who expected encouragement in wild excesses of paint were told to copy casts and work from nature, and on these admirable but conservative lines the school lasted only a few months. Distortion for the sake of expressing movement and a stridency of colour appear in his famous 'The Dance', commissioned by the wealthy Russian tea merchant Tschoukine, with its brick-red nude figures against a background of raw blue and green, but Matisse was by nature inclined to measure, tranquillity and refinement in art. The luxurious subtleties of Persian art attracted him about 1910 and in developing a related sense of colour and in a decorative simplification of line and mass he diverged from the movement which succeeded Fauvism in the limelight, Cubism (q.v.), for which he had little sympathy. For some years he travelled about the world, but in 1917 settled at Nice, devoting himself to paintings of Mediterranean interiors, still life and 'Odalisks', characterized by great economy of means, brilliant colour and the free use of textile patterns as a subsidiary decorative element. He made some early essays in sculpture in 1899 and in later years resumed the practice of free and unconventional modelling. He also produced etchings, lithographs and wood-engravings and illustrated Mallarmé's poems, Joyce's *Ulysses* and other works. He designed and built the chapel for the Dominicans of Vence, consecrated in 1951, a late work of importance in applying an entirely modern decorative sense to a religious interior. Matisse's work figures in most of the principal collections of modern art, the largest number of his paintings being in the Moscow Museum of Western Art (enriched by the collections of the Moscow merchants) and the Barnes Foundation, Pennsylvania.

Matsys, Quentin, see MASSYS, QUINTEN.

Matteo di Giovanni (*b* ? Sansepolcro, *c*. 1435; *d*. 1495), Italian painter of the Sienese School, a pupil of Vecchietta. His work had the traditional delicacy and charm of Siena, a notable example being the 'Assumption of the Virgin' (National Gallery). He painted parts of a triptych for the cathedral of Sansepolcro (now in the museum at Sansepolcro), of which the centre panel, by Piero della Francesca (q.v.), is 'The Baptism of Christ' in the National Gallery.

Mauve, Anton (*b*. Zaandam, 18 Sept. 1838; *d*. Arnhem, 5 Feb. 1888), Dutch landscape painter, a friend of Israels and Maris (qq.v.) and an admirer of the Barbizon School (q.v.). He worked at The Hague, where Vincent van Gogh, his nephew, was his (transitory) pupil.

MATTEO DI GIOVANNI—The Assumption of the Virgin (Altar-piece)
—National Gallery, London.

A. MAUVE—Morning Ride on the Beach—Rijksmuseum, Amsterdam.

Mazo, Juan Bautista del (*b*. Beteta, Cuenca, *c*. 1512–16; *d*. Madrid, 10 Feb. 1667), Spanish painter, a pupil of Velazquez, whose daughter he married in 1634. He may have collaborated with Velazquez in some works; he made copies and adaptations of his paintings and succeeded him as court painter in 1661. He painted landscapes and hunting scenes in addition to court portraits, the 'View of Saragossa,' 1647 (Prado), being an example, but remains a somewhat insubstantial figure. The painting in the National Gallery, once fancifully called 'A Duel in the Pardo' and attributed to him, is now considered too feeble for his hand; the 'Don Adrián Pulido Pareja' in the National Gallery, long thought to be by Velazquez, is now ascribed, as a feeble imitation of Velazquez, to Mazo.

Medium, liquid vehicle—oil, gum arabic, etc. with which pigments are mixed for use, first to bind the pigment and subsequently as a diluent in execution. The term is commonly extended to denote any technical means employed by artists—oil-painting, tempera, water-colour and the various forms of graphic art.

Meissonier, Jean Louis Ernest (*b*. Lyons, 21 Feb. 1815; *d*. Paris, 31 Jan. 1891), French painter of historical *genre*, who worked on a small scale in emulation of the Dutch and Flemish seventeenth-century masters, borrowing many of their subjects. Extremely popular in his own day, his pictures have shared the general disrepute into which the romanticization of the past has fallen. A typical work is 'The Brawl', presented by Napoleon III to Queen Victoria, and the Wallace Collection has a number showing his minute though much misused skill.

[99]

MAZO—The Painter's Family—Kunsthistoriches Museum, Vienna.

Meléndez, Luis Eugenio (*b.* Naples, 1716; *d.* 1780). Spanish painter who studied in Naples and Rome and going to Spain became court painter to Charles III. He painted portraits and religious subjects but is best known for the excellent still lifes which caused him to be styled the 'Spanish Chardin'. His paintings of fruit and flowers, intended for the decoration of the royal palaces, returned to the sobriety and simplicity of the seventeenth century, and are in the tradition of Zurbarán (q.v.).

Melozzo da Forli, Francesco (*b.* Forli, 1438; *d.* there, 8 Nov. 1494), Italian painter of the Umbrian School, a disciple of Piero della Francesca (q.v.). He worked in Rome and at Urbino, where he probably collaborated with the Flemish painter Joos van Ghent on the portraits of famous men and personifications of the liberal arts for the Duke of Urbino's library. A fresco in the church of Santi Apostoli, Rome, is an example of his work which includes characteristic figures of angelic musicians. He is said to have been the inventor of the type of foreshortening which caused figures on a painted ceiling or interior dome to appear floating overhead in space.

H. MEMLINC—The Mystic Marriage of St Catherine—Hospital of St John, Bruges.

Memlinc (Memling), Hans (b. Seligenstadt, nr Mainz, or ? Möm-
lingen, c. 1430; d. Bruges, 11 Aug. 1494), Flemish painter, probably of
German origin, possibly a pupil of Rogier van der Weyden (q.v.). He
settled at Bruges, c. 1466, where he had a prosperous career, producing religious paintings of great beauty and portraits of dignified
reticence, anticipating those of Holbein in quality. His landscape
backgrounds have singular charm. Though taking elements of style
from van Eyck, Dirck Bouts and van der Weyden (qq.v.), and showing little development in his work (save in his later years the intro-
duction of some Italian decorative motives), his delicate sense of
beauty makes him an outstanding master. Notable works are the
'Mystic Marriage of St Catherine' and the panels of the 'Shrine of St
Ursula' (Hospital of St John, Bruges); the Donne Triptych (Chatsworth), which includes a self-portrait; 'Bathsheba' (Stuttgart), a

[101]

A. R. MENGS—Portrait of Frau Thiele—Dresden Art Gallery.

life-sized nude; and such fine portraits as that of Guillaume Moreel and his wife (Brussels).

Memmi, Lippo, di Filippuccio (*d.* 1356), Italian painter of the Sienese School, son and pupil of the painter Memmo di Filippuccio, and brother-in-law of Simone Martini (q.v.), with whom he often worked. He was mainly active between 1332 and 1351. The fresco over the door of the convent of the Servites at Siena and a Madonna (Berlin) are two of his principal works.

Memmi, Simone, *see* MARTINI.

Mengs, Anton Raphael (*b.* Aussig, 12 May 1728; *d.* Rome, 29 June 1779), German painter, son of Ismael Mengs, court painter at Dresden. He was taken to Rome as a boy and had an early success with pastel portraits, later rivalling Batoni (q.v.) in portraiture. He married an Italian and lived and worked mainly in Italy though executing some commissions in Madrid. His friendship with Winckelmann and the ideas he expressed in writing gave him a certain importance in the neo-classic development, but his 'Parnassus' (Villa Albani) has been generally considered a poor piece of eclecticism and his emptiness of style was severely criticized by Goethe.

'Meniñas, Las', 'The Maids of Honour', famous painting in the Prado executed by Velazquez in 1656. It shows the artist at work on a portrait of the little Infanta Margarita Maria, who is being kept amused by the attentions of her maids of honour and the presence of her mastiff and dwarfs. The presence of the king and queen, who have arrived to look on, is indicated by their reflections in the mirror on the far wall and by the fact that one of the ladies in waiting is evidently curtsying to them.

Menzel, Adolf von (*b.* Breslau, 8 Dec. 1815; *d.* Berlin, 9 Feb, 1905), German painter and graphic artist, famous for his portrayal of the life and age of Frederick the Great. He first worked as lithographer

[102]

D. VELAZQUEZ—Las Meniñas—Prado.

and illustrator, illustrated works by Goethe with pen drawings, then revived the art of wood-engraving and made his name by his illustrations to Kugler's *History of Frederick the Great* and Frederick's own works, 1843–9, taking great pains to ensure historical accuracy in architecture, decoration, costume and portraiture. Self-taught as a painter, he produced, apart from pictures of ceremonial and historic occasions in his own time, a number of oil studies of a realistic kind, not exhibited in his lifetime but since highly esteemed in Germany.

Mesdag, Hendrik Wilhelm (*b.* Groningen, 25 Feb. 1831; *d.* The Hague, 7 July 1915), Dutch marine painter, who gave up banking and began to study art at the age of thirty-five. He worked at The Hague and to some extent returned to seventeenth-century tradition.

Metaphysical Painting, term used by the Italian painters Giorgio de Chirico and Carlo Carrà, describing their efforts to convey an intensity or strangeness of mood and idea by still-life objects in incongruous settings or unusual relationships. This *pittura metafisica*, dating from about 1917, foreshadows a later trend of Surrealism (q.v.).

Metropolitan Museum of Art, New York, one of the world's greatest art collections, comprehensive in range and including both ancient and modern works of art. It has been enriched by the legacies of private collectors such as Benjamin Altman and Henry Frick, thus acquiring some of the finest examples of the work of Rembrandt, Hals and other European masters.

Metsu (Metzu), Gabriel (*b.* Leyden, 1629; *d.* Amsterdam, buried 24 Oct. 1667), Dutch painter, a pupil of Gerard Dou (q.v.). He settled at Amsterdam as a painter of *genre* pictures, being among the foremost of those who depicted interiors and scenes from well-to-do Dutch family life, sometimes attempting to emulate Vermeer and sometimes recalling the polish of Ter Borch. A masterpiece, personal in style, is the famous ' The Sick Child ' (Rijksmuseum).

[103]

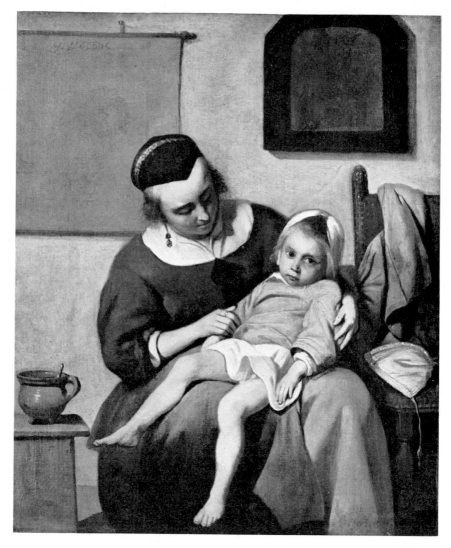

G. METSU—The Sick Child—Rijksmuseum, Amsterdam.

A. F. VAN DER MEULEN—
The Capture of the Town of
Salins—Musée National,
Versailles.

Metsys, Quentin, *see*
MASSYS, QUINTEN.

Metzinger, Jean (*b.*
Nantes, 1883; *d.* France,
1956), French painter
who went to Paris at the
age of twenty and was
there first influenced by
the art of Seurat (q.v.)
but later by Cubism
(q.v.), to his own idea
of which he remained
faithful throughout his
life. Scientifically and
theoretically minded, he regarded Cubism as a systematic and
standardized technique for representing objects. He collaborated
with Albert Gleizes (q.v.) in the book *Du Cubisme*, 1912.

Meulen, Adam Frans (François) van der (*b.* Brussels, Jan. 1632; *d.*
Paris, 15 Oct. 1690), Flemish painter, a pupil of Snyders (q.v.), who
worked mainly in France, adopting French nationality. He was
appointed battle-painter to Louis XIV, travelling with the French
armies, and took part with Le Brun (q.v.) in the decoration of Marly
and Versailles, co-operating with him in the design of the Gobelins
tapestries. He popularized in France the Flemish style of panoramic
landscape.

Mexican Painting. Painting in Pre-Columbian America took the
form of mural decoration and the ornamentation of pottery but is
most compactly and vividly represented by the painted manuscript
books (or 'codices') of the Mexican cultures. They consist of a form of
picture writing, the key to which has been given by the interpretations drawn up after the Conquest by Spanish-educated Mexicans.
The subject-matter was historical, legendary and concerned with
religious rites. The artists worked on strips of deerskin or paper made
from tree bark, prepared with a white ground, using a black outline
and flat brilliant colour, their pictorial symbols being strongly geometrical in character. The strips were folded into book semblance,
constituting the 'library' of temple or palace. Important codices are
at Rome in the Vatican, in Vienna, Paris, the British Museum, the
Bodleian Library, Oxford, and Mexico City. The Codex Mendoza in
the Bodleian, prepared for the first Viceroy of New Spain as a
description of the country to be sent to Charles V, is of prime importance in being the work of native artists, the meaning of whose

pictographs is conveyed by an explanation in Spanish. Many religious manuscripts were destroyed by the Spanish conquerors, though for some time after the Conquest the old picture writing remained a means of communication and its characteristic combinations of colour are still favoured by the Mexican peasant. In the art of the colonial period during the sixteenth and seventeenth centuries there was an admixture of Spanish and Mexican art forms, though painting in subject was now divided between Christian religious themes and portraiture conceived in the European style. The Royal Academy of San Carlos, the oldest school of art in the American continent, was established at the end of the eighteenth century. The century following produced little that was outstanding in pictorial art but the feeling of independence, political and cultural, has produced what may be called a renaissance in recent times. While they have absorbed some artistic influences from Europe and North America, painters in modern Mexico have devoted themselves to patriotic themes and have shown great aptitude for fresco. Outstanding representatives of this national spirit are Diego Rivera, José Clemente Orozco and David Alfaro Siqueiros (qq.v.), among other artists of note being Miguel Covarrubias (b. 1904), Juan O'Gorman (b. 1905), Rufino Tamayo (b. 1899) and Alfredo Zalce (b. 1908).

Mezzotint, tone process of engraving invented in the seventeenth century by an amateur artist, Ludwig von Siegen. The surface of a copper plate is uniformly indented by means of a tool with a slightly curved edge, serrated with fine teeth, called a rocker, which is drawn

D. LUCAS—Salisbury Cathedral (Mezzotint) (after J. Constable).

over the surface of the plate at several angles. It raises also a 'burr' of metal which as in drypoint (q.v.) holds the ink in printing and adds richness of effect. An impression from the plate at this stage would be a dense black. The mezzotinter then scrapes away the burr and levels the surface in those parts that are meant to be lighter, the artist working from dark to light in making his picture. Mezzotint was introduced into England by Prince Rupert, c. 1657, and by the end of the seventeenth century it was generally known as *la manière anglaise*. It was introduced into America by Peter Pelham (c. 1684–1751). It was largely used for the reproduction of paintings, especially portraits, in the eighteenth century. Notable landscape mezzotints of the nineteenth century are those of Turner's *Liber Studiorum* and the plates after Constable by David Lucas. Exponents of the method are John Smith (1625–1742), James MacArdell (1729–65), Valentine Green (1739–1813) and David Lucas (1802–81). Some mezzotints were produced in colour, J. C. Le Blon (1667–1741) being the first to experiment in this direction.

Michel, Georges (*b.* Paris, 12 Jan. 1763; *d.* there 7 June 1843), French landscape painter, a solitary forerunner of the Barbizon School (q.v.). A pupil of Taunay, a minor painter of the late eighteenth century, he assimilated something of the outlook of the Dutch landscape masters through restoring and cleaning their pictures. Content with his immediate surroundings, and never exhibiting, he painted in obscurity and without appreciation views of the then village of Montmartre, its windmills and the country round. His directness and vigour, as in 'Aux Environs de Montmartre' (Louvre), has brought him high posthumous regard.

Michelangelo (Michael Angelo) Buonarroti (*b.* Caprese, 6 May 1475; *d.* 18 Feb. 1564), Italian sculptor, architect, painter and poet, one of the greatest and most universally gifted of artists. His father was an impoverished Florentine gentleman who was given a temporary administrative post at Caprese by the Medici from 1474 to 1475. His second son, Michelangelo, was born there, though the family returned soon after to Florence. At thirteen he was allowed to become apprentice to the successful painter Domenico Ghirlandaio (q.v.). He also studied Giotto and the frescoes of Masaccio in the Brancacci Chapel. (It was there, tradition relates, that his nose was broken in a fracas with a fellow pupil, Torrigiano.) Chosen as one of the young artists whom Lorenzo allowed to work in the school and collection of classical sculpture in the Medici gardens under the custodian, Bertoldo, he was encouraged to develop his natural gift and liking for sculpture. In rivalry with the antique, he produced the 'Head of a Faun' that delighted his patron and the relief, 'Battle of Centaurs and Lapiths' (Florence, Casa Buonarotti). The Medicean atmosphere of Platonic philosophy and classical study typical of the Renaissance made a lasting impression on him, though after the death of Lorenzo in 1492 and in the now uneasy political atmosphere of Florence he was seized by that presentiment of disaster which caused him to flee to Bologna. He returned to Florence after a year to find it changed

MICHELANGELO—Youth with Arm extended (Pen and Brown Ink)—British Museum.

by the stern theocracy of Savonarola. Aged twenty-one, he went to Rome in 1496, where a Cupid in which he had counterfeited the antique attracted notice, and during five years' stay he produced two famous works of sculpture, strangely contrasting in style and spirit, his 'Bacchus' (Florence, Museum) and 'Pietà' (St Peter's, Rome), the latter showing his true grandeur. He returned to Florence in 1501 at the family request and was next occupied by the famous and colossal 'David', carved from a block of Carrara marble that had been discarded as spoilt. Michelangelo had not abandoned painting altogether. The 'Entombment' and 'Madonna and Child with St John and Angels' (National Gallery) have been regarded as works of about his twentieth year; the Holy Family (Uffizi) of 1503 was a masterpiece executed for his and Raphael's patron Angelo Doni; and in 1504 he was commissioned to paint a large fresco in the council hall of the new Florentine Republic as a companion piece to the 'Battle of Anghiari' by Leonardo da Vinci. Michelangelo chose an incident from the Battle of Cascina during the Pisan War when Florentine soldiers had been surprised by the enemy while bathing. Both great artists left their work unfinished, though Michelangelo, while he seems to have disliked Leonardo personally, may well have learned from the latter's cartoon a new energy of movement and intensity of expression. He was, however, summoned to Rome by Julius II to work on the famous tomb on which he was to toil at intervals during forty years. A fresh project of the impetuous Pope was among the circumstances first diverting him from the task; the decoration of the vaulting of the Sistine Chapel. The architect,

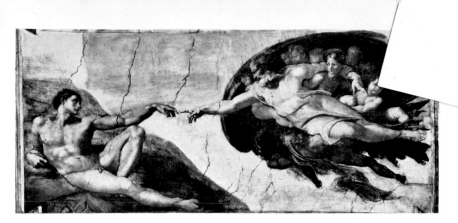

MICHELANGELO—The Creation of Adam—Vatican, Sistine Chapel.

Bramante, suggested that the commission should be given to Michelangelo, out of jealousy, it was presumed, in the belief that he would fail in the undertaking or produce a minor work. Though reluctant, Michelangelo accepted the challenge and in an astonishingly short space of time, working without assistants and under most difficult conditions, painted the famous ceiling that is one of the wonders of art. A tremendous biblical symphony, it interprets the Creation of the World and of Man, the Fall and the Flood in nine great compositions flanked by the figures of prophets and sibyls, and with supporting 'slaves' or 'atlases'. The conception is conveyed with the utmost force and lucidity by the human figure and gesture alone, as in the magnificent 'Creation of Adam'. Michelangelo was then thirty-seven. He went back to sculpture to become again involved in the 'tragedy of the tomb'. It was not until 1545 that it was finished, on a far less ambitious scale than had been planned, only the tremendous figure of Moses being the artist's own work. Vicissitudes also attended the commission given him by Clement VII, 1520, to design the Medici supulchral chapel in San Lorenzo, Florence. This, with its famous figures of Day and Night, Morning and Evening, was finished in 1535. In 1534 he was required by Clement VII to devote himself to painting the altar wall of the Sistine Chapel, which had previously been decorated by Perugino, a commission urgently affirmed by Clement's successor, Paul III. He took the Last Judgment as his subject and in six years produced his overwhelming masterpiece. It was in a different key from either the wall frescoes of other painters in the chapel or Michelangelo's own earlier work on the ceiling. It is sombrely majestic and one recalls the gloomy events then recent in memory—the siege of Florence, the sack of Rome—as well as the deep impression Dante had always made on the artist. It tells of torture and martyrdom, stern retribution and tragic fate. This tragic masterpiece lacks the beauty of the ceiling, yet in its command of movement in space it indicated the course Italian art was to follow for a century to come. The architectural designs of his later

[109]

MICHELANGELO—The Last Judgment—Vatican, Sistine Chapel.

M. MIEREVELD—Portrait of a Lady—National Gallery, London.

years in Rome (which included the magnificent dome of St Peter's) had a great influence on the emergence of the baroque style. Two frescoes in the Capella Paolina representing the Martyrdom of St Peter and the Conversion of St Paul, 1549, which completed his work in painting, were inevitably an anticlimax after the 'Last Judgment'. To the wonderful list of Michelangelo's achievements must be added his superb drawings, the earlier examples being executed with a pen, the later with black and red chalk; as well as the sonnets, celebrated being those addressed to Vittoria Colonna, the widow of the Marquis of Pescara, whose friendship was the artist's great solace, her death in 1547 leaving him disconsolate. Though he died in Rome, he was reburied in Santa Croce, Florence, with every honour.

Miereveld, Michiel Janzoon van (b. Delft, 1 May 1567; d. there, 27 June 1641), Dutch painter who spent his life at Delft. He studied under Willemsz and became court painter to the House of Orange, producing a large number of carefully finished portraits, among them 'Lord Vere of Tilbury' and 'Elizabeth, Queen of Bohemia' (National Portrait Gallery).

Mieris the Elder, Frans van (b. Leyden, 16 April 1635; d. there, 12 Mar. 1681), Dutch portrait and *genre* painter. He was the pupil of Gerard Dou (q.v.) and specialized in courtly conversation pieces such as 'The Cavalier and Lacemaker' (Vienna). His son Willem (b. Leyden, 3 June 1662; d. there, 26 Jan. 1747) was also a *genre* painter and his father's pupil of distinction. Frans the Elder is so called to distinguish him from Willem's son Frans (1689–1763), a *genre* painter too but better known as antiquary and historian.

Mignard, Pierre (b. Troyes, Nov. 1612; d. Paris, 30 May 1695), French painter of decorative works and portraits, a pupil of Jean Boucher and later of Vouet (q.v.). He spent twenty-one years in Italy, forming himself on the schools of Bologna and Rome, and returned to Paris in 1657, where he was successful in decorative schemes (of which the only remaining example is the cupola of the

W. VAN MIERIS—Fish and Poultry Shop—National Gallery, London.

Val-de-Grâce) and in portraiture. He was the rival of Le Brun (q.v.), though inferior to him in ability, and succeeded him as ruler of the Académie in 1690. His portraits have a mannered elegance, e.g. his 'Mme de Montespan' (Troyes). He cultivated the society of the writers of the age and his portrait of Molière is at Chantilly. His brother, Nicolas Mignard (1606–68), was also a painter, though of less note, who worked at the court of Louis XIV.

Milan, centre of the Lombard School which emerged in the fifteenth century with Vincenzo Foppa (q.v.), a follower of the Ferrarese, Squarcione (q.v.). A noted pupil of his was Ambrogio Borgogne (q.v.). The growth of Milanese painting was also encouraged by the great architect Bramante during his stay at Milan when he executed some paintings, his sense of architectural design appearing in the work of his Milanese pupil Bramantino (q.v.); but most of all Milanese work was dominated by Leonardo da Vinci (q.v.). Among his followers and imitators were Zenale, Leonardo's collaborator Ambrogio de Predis, Boltraffio (q.v.), Solario (q.v.), Bernardino Luini (q.v.) and Sodoma (q.v.). For the most part they reflected the master's work without originality.

Millais, Sir John Everett (b. Southampton, 8 June 1829; d. London, 13 Aug. 1896), English painter. He was precocious in talent and a student at the Royal Academy Schools at the age of eleven. Youthful acquaintance with Holman Hunt and Rossetti led to his joining them in the formation of the Pre-Raphaelite Brotherhood, 1848, and

SIR J. MILLAIS—Ophelia—National Gallery, London.

producing some of the best works inspired by its doctrine of 'truth to nature' during the 1850's, among them 'Christ in the House of His Parents', 1850 (Tate Gallery), and the painting of Miss Siddal as Ophelia, 1852 (National Gallery). His marriage to Euphemia Gray in 1855 after the annulment of her marriage with Ruskin estranged him from that early mentor and the *milieu* of Pre-Raphaelite idealism. His original style and quality disappeared from the popular subject pictures and portraits of an academically successful career, of which the 'Bubbles' of 1885 was one of the sensations. He was made a baronet, 1885, and elected P.R.A., 1896. His illustrations to the Moxon Tennyson of 1857 and for Trollope's *Orley Farm*, 1863, interestingly show the change from Pre-Raphaelite to mid-Victorian.

Millet, Jean François (*b.* Gruchy, nr Cherbourg, 4 Oct. 1814; *d.* Barbizon, 20 Jan. 1875), French painter and graphic artist who came of a poor peasant family. He first studied art at Cherbourg and obtained a municipal grant to study in Paris. He entered the studio of Delaroche (q v.), fellow pupils being Diaz and Rousseau (qq.v.), his later friends at Barbizon, and first exhibited at the Salon in 1840. After a long struggle to earn a living by paintings of shepherdesses and nude bathers in the eighteenth century *style galant*, he found his true vein in 'The Winnower' of 1848. He settled at the village of Barbizon in 1849, with his second wife and growing family, and there, still in poverty, devoted himself exclusively to the paintings of peasant life for which he is famous, such as 'The Gleaners', 1857, and

J. F. MILLET—The Sawyers—Victoria and Albert Museum.

'The Angelus', 1858–9 (Louvre). In the sombre melancholy of his pictures he may be called a realist, though the ethical or emotional element sometimes seems too prominent, and Baudelaire's criticism that he was determined at all costs to add something to the inherent poetry of his subjects remains pointed. Millet was also a faulty technician in oils, his paint often being lifeless and muddled in texture, but in pastels, drawings and etchings his great powers were fully displayed. He is distinct from his colleagues of the Barbizon School (q.v.) in the equal importance he attached to figure and land-scape, and to convey an essential harmony between them is one of his achievements.

Miniature Painting, commonly a description of portraits painted on a very small scale. The term miniature (from Lat. *miniare*, to colour with red ochre) was originally applied not to a small portrait but to the art of illustrating manuscripts. *See* ILLUMINATED MANUSCRIPTS. These illustrations being on a small scale it is possible that a con-fusion arose with Lat. *minuere*, to diminish. The sixteenth-century portrait miniaturists, however, were called 'limners' (illuminators), and like the painters of manuscripts worked on vellum or smooth card in body colour, something of the brilliance of the medieval miniature remaining in their use of colour. In the eighteenth century it became usual to paint on ivory in transparent water-colour. Holbein painted beautiful por-trait miniatures while in England (1531–43), and English artists have been conspicuous in the past as miniature painters, among the most notable being Nicholas Hilliard (q.v.), his pupil Isaac Oliver and the latter's son Peter Oliver, Samuel Cooper (q.v.), who was called a 'van Dyck in little', and Richard

ISAAC OLIVER—Sir Philip Sidney (Miniature)— Royal Collection, Windsor Castle.

Cosway (q.v.), whose miniatures for snuff-box lids were famous. The earliest French miniaturists were Jean and François Clouet (q.v.), and a number of specialists practised the art in France in the seventeenth and eighteenth centuries, while such well-known painters as Largillierre, Boucher and Prud'hon (qq.v.) produced some minatures. Petitot (1607–91) is noted for miniatures executed in enamel for Louis XIV. A special type of eighteenth-century French miniature was the *menu plaisir* picturing entertainments of the day, a noted exponent being Louis-Nicolas van Blarenberghe (1716–94). The leading artists of the late eighteenth century were Jean Baptiste Jacques Augustin (1759–1832) and Jean Baptiste Isabey (1757–1855), a favourite of the Napoleonic court. Friedrich Fuger (1751–1818), a German artist who worked for the Austrian court, is sometimes known as 'the Cosway of Vienna'. The art declined in the nineteenth century and though still practised has had no important revival.

Miró, Joan (*b.* Barcelona, 20 April 1893), Spanish painter who studied art in Barcelona but moved to Paris in 1919, being attracted by the Cubist art of his countryman, Picasso (q.v.). He is associated with the Surrealist developments of the School of Paris and evolved a fanciful 'sign language' with hints of a humour like that of Paul Klee (q.v.) and characterized by gay and brilliant colour. 'Dutch Interior' (New

J. MIRO—Carnival of Harlequin—Albright Art Gallery, Buffalo.

York, Museum of Modern Art) and 'Carnival of Harlequin' (Buffalo) are typical of his fantastic and decorative style of composition.

Modelling, in painting or drawing, refers to the effort to convey the three-dimensional character of a solid object by means of light and shade or modulations of colour.

Modersohn-Becker, Paula (*b.* Dresden, 8 Feb. 1876; *d.* Worpswede, 30 Nov. 1907), German painter and graphic artist, having a distinguished though somewhat isolated place in the Expressionist phase of modern German art. Frequent visits to Paris, 1903–7, led her to study the works of Gauguin and van Gogh and develop a style in which a strong feeling for humanity is combined with expressive colour and simplified form.

Modigliani, Amedeo (*b.* Leghorn, 12 July 1884; *d.* Paris, 25 Jan. 1920), painter and sculptor of an Italian-Jewish family who first studied art in Florence and Venice but settled in Paris in 1906. It is usual to associate him with the School of Paris, though he had in fact no place in its *avant-garde* movements except that he shared the Cubist interest in primitive and African sculpture. The study of Negro masks suggested the bold elongation and simplification of his sculptured heads, though these remained entirely European in character, while his paintings—portraits and nudes—despite similar exaggerations, were fundamentally Italian in colour and a sense of linear beauty that showed his sympathy with the School of Siena and with Botticelli. His drawings, of which he made a great number (often selling them for a few francs or a drink in a cafe), had equal distinction. After years

A. MODIGLIANI—
Peasant Boy—Tate Gallery.

[117]

J. M. MOLENAER—Musical Pastime—National Gallery, London.

J. DE MOMPER AND J. BRUEGHEL—Landscape with Coaches and Figures—Collection of Mrs Geoffrey Hart.

of Bohemian poverty he had some little success towards 1918, but privations, drugs, alcohol and tuberculosis combined to cut short his life while still young.

Molenaer, name of two Dutch painters, husband and wife, **Jan-Mienze Molenaer** (*b.* Haarlem, after 1605; *d.* there, 19 Sept. 1668), *genre* painter, and **Judith Leyster** (*b.* Haarlem, *c.* 1600; *d.* Heemstede, Feb. 1660), who married Molenaer in 1636. Both followed Hals closely in the style and spirit of his more Bohemian subjects, though in his later work Jan Molenaer was influenced by Rembrandt.

Momper, Joos (Jodocus) de, the Younger (*b.* Antwerp, 1564; *d.* there early in 1635), Flemish landscape and marine painter, the son of Bartholomeus de Momper, whose pupil he was, and son-in-law of Joos de Momper (1500–59). His landscapes are intermediate in style between those of Pieter Brueghel and Elsheimer (qq.v.), and a number of his contemporaries at Antwerp, Hendrik van Balen, Frans Francken (q.v.), Sebastian Vranckz (q.v.) and others, put in figures for him.

'Mona Lisa', world-famous painting of Leonardo da Vinci, was executed, 1503–6, while the artist was at Florence. The sitter was the daughter of Antonio Maria de Noldo Gherardini of Naples and was born in Florence in 1479. She married, 1495, Francesco di Bartolommeo di Zanobi del Giocondo (1460–1528), who according to Vasari gave Leonardo the commission to paint his wife. It is related that Leonardo 'retained musicians who played and sang and jested in order to dispel that melancholy that painters tend to give their portraits', though the renowned 'smile' seems rather a subtlety of shadow about the lips than a decided expression. The painting was

**LEONARDO DA VINCI
—Mona Lisa—Louvre.**

[119]

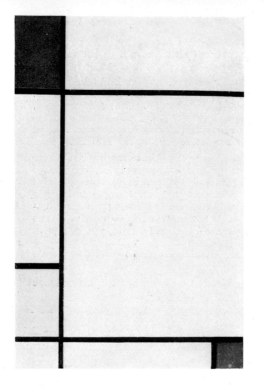

probably bought from Leonardo by Francis I. Stolen from the Louvre in 1911, it was later recovered and now hangs there.

Mondrian (originally **Mondriaan**), **Piet** (*b.* Amersfoort, Holland, 17 Mar. 1872; *d.* New York, 1 Feb. 1944), Dutch abstract painter. After studying art in Amsterdam he went to Paris in 1911, where he stayed until 1914, absorbing the influence of Cubism as practised by Picasso and Braque in their 'analytic' phase. Returning to Holland he joined with Theo van Doesburg and others in the formation of the de Stijl group (q.v.) and the production of a journal (in 1917) of the same title. In paintings composed of rectangular shapes he sought to apply a system of 'determined relations' related to the trend of modern architecture and its severe simplification. He later developed his entirely non-figurative and rigidly mathematical art under the title of 'Neo-Plasticism'. He went to New York in 1940 and had a period of success there before his death.

Monet, Claude Oscar (*b.* Paris, 14 Nov. 1840; *d.* Giverny, 6 Dec. 1926), French painter and leader of the Impressionists. He spent his youth at Le Havre, where he was diverted from boyish caricature to open-air landscape painting by the encouragement of Boudin (q.v.). Boudin and Jongkind (q.v.), with whom Monet became friendly in 1860, had taught him much about atmosphere before he went in 1862 to Gleyre's studio in Paris, where he met Renoir, Sisley (qq.v.) and Bazille. He painted with them in the forest of Fontainebleau and until 1870 was engaged in perfecting a new approach to which the realism of Courbet and the direct method of Manet both contributed, as may be seen in the beautiful 'Femmes au Jardin', 1867 (Louvre), and the Manetesque 'Plage à Trouville', 1870 (Tate). A wartime interlude followed, spent in Holland and London, where he admired

C. MONET—In the Garden—Louvre.

E

C. MONET—Argenteuil—Louvre.

the works of Turner. From 1872 to 1878 he worked at Argenteuil,
where he had a floating studio, his mature method of rendering light
in colour being now fully developed. His ' Impression' in the exhibition of 1874, in which he and his friends appeared as a fairly homo-
geneous group, brought the term Impressionism into currency for the
first time. He painted at Vétheuil, 1878–83, and afterwards settled at
Giverny, where in the garden of his house he painted his last remarkable studies of water-lilies. Although Monet was consistent in aim his
work is surprisingly varied. The study of different effects of light on
the same subject led to the production of paintings in series, and each
of these has its individuality, e.g. the snow scenes at Vétheuil, the
Haystacks, Poplars, Cathedrals (Rouen), Venice, the Thames, the
Nymphéas. He shows also great variety in composition, in which the
influence of the Japanese print is subtly present, and uses colour as
much poetically as for the rendering of atmosphere. Almost abstract
visions of colour, the studies of water-lilies, long regarded dubiously
as the most formless of his works, have been hailed in recent years as
outstanding examples of pure painting.

Monnoyer, Baptiste (*b.* Lille, 19 July 1634; *d.* London, 16 Feb.
1699), French decorative painter, trained in the Antwerp of Rubens
and Snyders, who, under Le Brun (q.v.), had a prominent part in the
decoration of Vaux, Versailles and Marly and in designing Gobelins

tapestries. He specialized in garlands of flowers depicted in ornamental vases and still life with birds, monkeys, etc., set in an architectural framework, either as individual pictures or integral parts of
a decorative scheme. A Protestant, he quitted France, to Louis
XIV's regret, after the Revocation of the Edict of Nantes, but found
patronage in England, where he collaborated with Kneller (q.v.).
There are two *dessus de porte* by him at Hampton Court.

Monotype, print taken from a plate painted with oil colours or
printing ink either positively or with the lights wiped away from a
dark ground. Only one good impression can be taken, hence the name
monotype, though the paint or ink remaining on the plate may serve
as a guide for the renewal of the painting and a further impression.
The only reason for the monotype is the special texture resulting
from the transfer. G. B. Castiglione (1616–70) and William Blake give
examples of its use and it was especially favoured by Degas.

Monro, Thomas (*b.* 1759; *d.* Bushey, 14 May 1833), English
physician and amateur painter, of historical, note for the encouragement he gave to young artists and especially to Thomas Girtin
and J. M. W. Turner. At his house in the Adelphi he amassed a
large collection of water-colours and drawings, including unfinished
works by J. R. Cozens, of whom he took care after that artist went
insane. Girtin and Turner were among those whom he employed to
complete or make copies of works by Cozens and others, his patronage
thus becoming the equivalent of an art school training and having
great influence on their development.

**Montagna, Barto-
lommeo** (Bartolommeo
Cincani) (*b.* Orzinuovi,
c. 1450; *d.* Vicenza,
1523), Italian painter,
influential in north
Italy, and largely in-
strumental in making
Vicenza a centre of art.
He worked mainly in
that city though he
seems to have been
trained in Venice and
various Venetian influ-
ences have been de-
tected in his work, e.g.
of Alvise Vivarini,

B . M O N T A G N A —
Madonna and Child—
National Gallery, London.

[123]

A. MOORE — Blossoms — Tate Gallery.

Gentile Bellini, Carpaccio and Mantegna. His paintings of religious subjects are noted for their majestic simplicity of design and sobriety of colour.

Monticelli, Adolphe Joseph Thomas (*b.* Marseilles, 14 Oct. 1824; *d.* there, 29 June 1886), French painter of Italian descent, noted for his rich, jewel-like colour. He learned to paint at Marseilles, and going to Paris in the 1840's became a devotee of Watteau and the Venetians, whose work he studied in the Louvre. Helped by Diaz (q.v.) he quickly became successful, artists as well as patrons admiring his work, In 1870, however, he retired to Marseilles, renouncing ambition and leading a solitary and eccentric life. His art is strangely compounded of Romantic memories in subject (*fêtes galantes*) and imagined scenes of medieval court life in Provence) and a heavily encrusted mosaic of glowing paint which has its own value and has earned him the title of the 'first Fauve'.

Moore, Albert Joseph (*b.* York, 1841, *d.* London, 1893), English painter, the son of an artist, noted for decorative figure composition, much influenced by the Parthenon frieze. He studied at York and in the Royal

H. MOORE—Pink and Green Sleepers (Chalk Drawing)—Tate Gallery.

Academy Schools and developed the characteristic style of which 'Blossoms' (Tate Gallery) is an example about 1865.

Moore, Henry (*b.* Castleford, Yorks, 30 July 1898), English sculptor and draughtsman. He served in the 1914–18 war and afterwards studied at the Leeds School of Art and the Royal College of Art. He has achieved international eminence as a sculptor, his works including his 'Madonna and Child' for St Matthew's Church, Northampton, 1943–4, Three Standing Figures, 1947-8 (Battersea Park), and several monumental versions of reclining figures making original use of both solids and voids. As a graphic artist he is famous for his wartime tube shelter drawings, produced in his capacity as Official War Artist, 1940–2. Distinct from his drawings for sculpture, these are pictorially conceived works of great power, an example being the 'Pink and Green Sleepers', 1941 (Tate Gallery).

Mor van Dashorst, Anthonis (also known as **Sir Anthony More** and **Antonio Moro**) (*b.* Utrecht, *c.* 1519; *d.* Antwerp, April 1576), Dutch painter, the founder of an international type of portraiture. He studied under Jan Scorel (q.v.) and in Italy, 1550–1, and was influenced by Titian. He came to England in 1553 and was court painter to Mary Tudor until her death in 1558, when he entered the service of Philip II at Madrid. In 1568 he returned to the Netherlands and settled at Antwerp. The varied forms of his name reflect his international success. His sense of character is well seen in his portraits of Sir Thomas and Lady Gresham (Rijksmuseum).

Morales, Luis de (*b.* Estremadura, *c.* 1509; *d.* Badajoz, *c.* 1586), Spanish painter of religious subjects, enthusiastically called 'el

[125]

Divino'. Little is known of his life, though it is thought possible he worked at Valencia and Seville as well as Badajoz. In style he seems to have acquired some Italian mannerisms through the Italianate Flemish painters of the time such as Quinten Massys (q.v.), though some affinity has been found with El Greco (q.v.). A typical work, often repeated with slight variations, is the charming 'Virgin and Child' (Prado).

Morandi, Giorgio (*b*. Bologna, 1890), Italian painter, one of the most distinguished living Italian artists. Early influences on his work were the still life of Cézanne and the 'metaphysical' painting of Chirico and Carrà, 1918–20, but he evolved a personal style in the treatment of a narrow range of subjects—especially simple still-life objects in a variety of subtly designed and abstract arrangements.

More, Sir Anthony, *see* MOR VAN DASHORST.

Moreau, Gustave (*b*. Paris, 6 April 1826; *d*. 18 April 1898), French painter of imaginative subjects taken from classical or religious story. He was academic in style, but a passionate and 'decadent' quality in his 'Salome' led Huysmans to admire and describe it in his novel *À Rebours*, and his work has points of resemblance to that of Odilon Redon (q.v.). Towards the end of his life he became an influential teacher, Matisse, Marquet and Rouault being among his pupils. He left 8,000 paintings and drawings to the nation, his house being converted into a museum.

Moretto, Il (Alessandro Bonvicino) (*b*. Rovato, Brescia, 1498; *d*. Brescia, 1554), Italian painter, generally known by his nickname, 'Il Moretto' ('the blackamoor'), belonging to the Venetian School of Brescia. He was the pupil of Fioravante Ferramola at Brescia and in general character and warmth of colour his art is related to that of Giovanni Bellini and Titian, though he is reputed also to have had a great enthusiasm for Raphael. He painted church frescoes, a number of altar-pieces and portraits, being especially distinguished, like his pupil Moroni (q.v.), in the latter branch of art. A fine example of his portraiture is the 'Count Martinengo Cesaresco' in the National Gallery.

Morisot, Berthe Marie Pauline (*b*. Bourges, 14 Jan. 1841; *d*. Paris, 2 Mar. 1895), French painter and perhaps the most distinguished of women painters. Brought up in a cultivated household, she early showed a wish to paint and benefited by the guidance of Corot (q.v.), 1860, working with him in the open air. She met Manet (q.v.) in 1868 (marrying his brother Eugène in 1874), and it was partly through her advocacy that Manet took to *plein-air* painting. Her championship of this ranged her with the Impressionists and she exhibited in most of the Impressionist exhibitions. Renoir, Degas and Mallarmé were among her friends and admirers of her art. Her studies of women and children in the open are highly sensitive in feeling and she painted some exquisite water-colours.

Morland, George (*b*. London, 26 June 1763; *d*. there, 29 Oct. 1804),

G. MORLAND—Inside of a Stable—National Gallery, London.

English painter of rustic scenes, the pupil of his father, Henry Robert Morland (1716–97), also a painter of *genre*. He exhibited drawings at the Academy when ten years old, studied art at the Royal Academy Schools and learned also by copying Flemish and Dutch masters, though his alehouses, cottages and farmyards are essentially English. He was a natural painter in a fluent easy style, his pictures popular in engravings by William and James Ward (whose sister he married), but many seem to have been dashed off to pay a debt or secure a dole from the dealers who profited by the careless, Bohemian mode of living which caused him to be imprisoned for debt, 1799–1802, and again in 1804. Many of his rural scenes were painted at Kensal Green and some coastal views resulted from visiting the Isle of Wight. 'Inside of a Stable', exhibited at the Academy in 1791 (National Gallery), shows him at his best.

Moro, Antonio, *see* Mor van Dashorst.

Moroni, Giambattista (*b.* Bondo, Bergamo), 1510; *d.* 2 May 1578), Italian painter, a pupil of Moretto (q.v.). He produced both religious paintings and portraits but is more highly esteemed for the latter, which won the praise of Titian. His quiet and straightforwardly realistic style, without formality of pose or deep analysis of individual character, enabled him to portray a type as perfectly as in his 'Tailor' and 'Lawyer' in the National Gallery, works in their way unsurpassable.

G. MORONI—The Tailor
—National Gallery, London.

Morris, William (b. Walthamstow, 24 Mar. 1834; d. London, 3 Oct. 1896), English poet and designer, with Burne-Jones, whom he met as an undergraduate at Exeter College, Oxford, leader in a second phase of Pre-Raphaelitism. Beginning as a painter under the influence of Rossetti (after being articled for a short while to the architect George Street), he contributed to the Oxford Union decorations in 1857, but only one canvas ('La Belle Iseult' Tate Gallery) remains of purely pictorial work, beauty in handicraft becoming his ideal and part of the general opposition to the Victorian way of life and art which his poetry and prose, inspired by medieval or earlier models, also represent. Designs for stained glass, wallpaper, chintzes, tapestry and carpets, furniture, illuminated MSS., book types and decoration are aspects of his work as designer, the firm he founded with others in 1861 and the Kelmscott Press, 1890, having great influence on the attitude towards design and the growth of interest in 'arts and crafts'.

Morse, Samuel Finley Breese (b. Charlestown, Massachusetts, 27 April 1791; d. New York, 2 April 1872), American painter and inventor, a pupil of Washington Allston (q.v.), whom he accompanied to England in 1811. His avowed ambition 'to revive the splendours of the fifteenth century' cannot be discerned in his work, though his 'Congress Hall' (Washington, Corcoran Gallery) has documentary interest and he was first President of the National Academy of Design, 1826–45. He is remembered rather as the inventor of the telegraph and the Morse Code than as an artist.

Mosaic, form of decoration provided by fitting together pieces of coloured stone, marble or glass. It was anciently used in Mesopotamia and Egypt for ornament on a small scale; jewellery and movable objects (such as the 'Standard' of Ur, now in the British Museum) giving examples. It is of more importance in art as an equivalent of painting in relation with architecture, cubes (*tesserae*) of marble and other materials being fastened in a cement bed and giving a

ROMAN MOSAIC (Pompeii) — Dioscorides of Samos—Scene from a Comedy—Museo Nazionale, Naples.

ROMAN MOSAIC (Pompeii)—Beware of the Dog—Museo Nazionale, Naples.

ROMAN MOSAIC—Various Marine Creatures —Victoria and Albert Museum.

MOSAIC (Sixth Century)—The Virgin and Child with Saints—Parenzo, Istria.

permanent decoration for wall or floor. The mosaic pavement, which seems to have originated with the ancient Greeks, reached its highest development among the Romans. Roman mosaic varies from the formal pattern to elaborately pictorial effect. Famous examples are the doves of Pliny at Hadrian's villa, Tivoli, represented with great delicacy of colouring, and the mosaic copy from Pompeii of the battle between Alexander and Darius after the painter Philoxenos. In the Byzantine period mosaic in the form of coloured and gilded glass was used for mural decoration on a large scale and of impressive splendour. The richness of gold-leaf and the vibration set up by calculated irregularities of surface and the juxtaposition of different colours are combined with a monumental simplicity of form. Mosaic remained the dominant form of mural 'painting' until the rise of fresco in Italy. The mosaics of Santa Maria Maggiore, Rome, fourth–fifth centuries A.D., are the first great examples of religious composition. Ravenna in the sixth century gives us the famous masterpieces of the church of San Vitale representing the Emperor Justinian, the Empress Theodora and their attendants. Other great examples are the mosaics of Santa Sophia, Constantinople, sixth century, the church of Daphni (between Athens and Eleusis), eleventh century, and the cathedral of Torcello, 12th century. Byzantine artist-craftsmen worked in many centres, not only in Greece and Italy but at Palermo and Monreale in Sicily, Cologne, Cordova, Jerusalem and

[131]

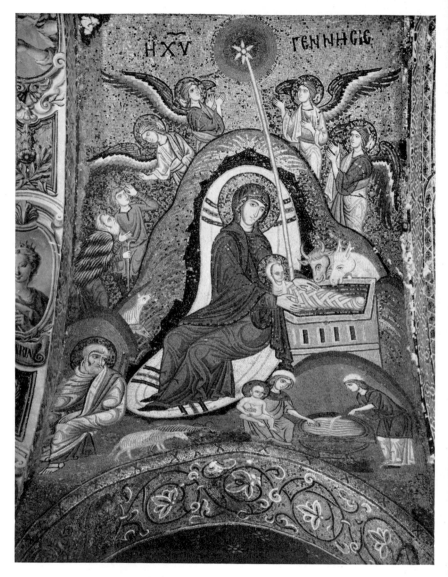

MOSAIC (Twelfth Century)—The Nativity—Palermo, Church of the Martorana.

Damascus. In modern times the art seems to have been well preserved only at Venice, where both Byzantine tradition and later developments are represented by St Mark's. Attempts to revive pictorial mosaic in the nineteenth century, as in Sir W. B. Richmond's work in St Paul's Cathedral, were not very successful, but it has had some revival in this century as a wall covering, with practical advantages as well as pleasant appearance and lending itself to styles of modern design. Among modern figurative mosaics, those of the Swedish artist Einar Forseth for the City Hall, Stockholm, and of Boris Anrep for the floor of the entrance hall of the National Gallery, London, are of note.

Moser, Lucan (*b*. ? Weil, nr Stuttgart, active *c*. 1430–50), German painter who worked at Ulm. He is known by the altar-piece of St Mary Magdalene, 1431, in the church at Tiefenbrunn, a work of advanced accomplishment for its time and place, its realistic detail suggesting some acquaintance with painting in France and the southern Netherlands.

Mostaert, Jan (*b*. Haarlem, *c*. 1475; *d*. there, *c*. 1556), Dutch painter of religious subjects and portraits, a follower of Geertgen tot Sint Jans (q.v.). He was court painter to Margaret of Austria and is noted for portraits of richly dressed sitters with elaborate backgrounds. He was one of the first to introduce a Renaissance element into Netherlandish painting.

Motherwell, Robert (*b*. Aberdeen, Washington, 24 Jan. 1915), American abstract painter and writer on art. He was educated at Stanford and Columbia universities and first exhibited in the International Surrealist Exhibition in New York in 1942. With Baziotes, Rothko and others he is one of the flourishing *avant-garde* of contemporary American art. He has edited the *Documents of Modern Art* series and is a teacher at the Hunter College, New York.

Motif, subject in a painting considered not as an end in itself but as developing some general intention in composition and design.

Mount, William Sidney (*b*. Setauket, Long Island, 26 Nov. 1807; *d*. there, 19 Nov. 1868), American *genre* painter. He studied in the schools of the National Academy of Design and for a time travelled about the country making studies of American rural life and its humours, some of which were reproduced in Currier and Ives prints (q.v.). He eventually settled in Long Island, which provided him with many subjects. In sentiment and humour his work may be compared with that of Wilkie.

Müller, William James (*b*. Bristol, 1812; *d*. there, 8 Sept. 1845), landscape painter, son of the curator of the Bristol Museum, a German. He adapted Cotman's methods in water-colour and travelled extensively in England, Europe and the Middle East, painting many eastern scenes. He gave lessons to David Cox (q.v.) in oil painting.

Multscher, Hans (*b*. Reichenhofen, *c*. 1400; *d*. 1467), German painter and sculptor, who worked at Ulm producing carved altar-pieces with painted wings. The wings of the Wurzach altar-piece, 1437 (Berlin), painted by him are a principal remaining work, the

J. MOSTAERT—Adoration of the Magi—Rijksmuseum, Amsterdam.

H. MULTSCHER—The Nativity (Wurzach Altar, 1437)—Staatliche Museum, Berlin.

'Nativity' showing dramatic use of a realism deriving from Netherlandish art in the strongly individualized figures.

Munch, Edvard (*b*. Löyton, Norway, 12 Dec. 1863; *d*. Ekely, 23
Jan. 1944), Norwegian painter and graphic artist, influential in the
development of Expressionism (q.v.). He studied in Oslo and Paris,
his work showing a certain debt to Gauguin and to 'Art Nouveau'
(q.v.). It had most effect in Germany, where in 1892 in a Berlin
exhibition it caused great controversy and found response in the
spiritual unease of many German artists. He left a large number of
paintings and drawings to the city of Oslo.

[135]

G. MÜNTER—Man at Table.

Münter, Gabriele (*b.* Berlin, 19 February 1877), German painter associated with the 'Blaue Reiter' (q.v.) group, She went to Munich to study when twenty-three, becoming closely attached to her teacher, Wassily Kandinsky. Influenced by his early work and by that of the French Fauves she developed a strong and simplified style in landscape and still life, free from the harsher extremes of German Expressionism. In later years, painting little, she lived in seclusion at Murnau.

Mural Painting, decoration of the wall either by painting on the surface or on a canvas which is subsequently affixed in position, the latter being a method frequently used in modern times. In painting directly on the wall various media have been used, principal among them being fresco (q.v.), though tempera, encaustic and oil have their examples also. Mosaic and stained glass (qq.v.) may be considered under the same general heading. Mural painting is found in all periods of art but mainly, as distinct from the domestic easel picture, in the palace, church or interior of public use or significance. Two main forms can be distinguished : that which emphasizes the flatness of the wall surface and is conceived in large areas of flat colour, as in ancient Egypt, Crete or in the work of Puvis de Chavannes (q.v.) ; and that which gives the illusion of imaginary perspective, breaking down the flatness of the wall, as in Pompeian wall-painting, baroque painting or the rococo style as represented by Tiepolo. In

[136]

either case, however, a largeness of treatment with relation to the architecture has always been found necessary.

Murillo, Bartolomé Esteban (*b.* Seville, baptized 1 Jan. 1618; *d.* there, 3 April 1682), popular Spanish painter of religious and *genre* pictures. He studied art under Juan Castillo at Seville and, having saved a little money by hawking pictures at fairs and painting church pictures for export to South America, seems to have gone to Madrid, where he benefited by the study of the works of Titian, Rubens and van Dyck in the royal palaces, and received some encouragement from Velazquez. He married a woman of wealth in Seville in 1645 and gained a fortune by his own efforts, receiving a vast number of commissions. The Academy of Seville was founded by him in 1660, and he remained in the city during the years of success, declining the honour of becoming court painter to Charles II in 1670. In early days he painted many pictures of peasant and street urchin types, but his later works were mainly religious and executed in his soft and melting *estilo vaporoso*, as in the 'Immaculate Conception' (Prado), a favoured theme of which there are many versions. The 'Melon Eaters' (Munich) and 'Two Peasant Boys' (Dulwich) are notable examples of his naturalism, traceable to Ribera and Velazquez but not free from the sentimentality which makes his religious works unpalatable to modern taste. Placed among the greatest masters until the nineteenth century, he has since been looked on with disfavour as the originator of much that was mawkish and empty in art. The dramatized *genre* of his 'Prodigal Son' series shows his later work at its best. He employed a number of assistants and many works still ascribed entirely to his hand may have been their work.

Musée d'Art Moderne, Paris, museum of modern art to which pictures were transferred from the Luxembourg, opened in 1945. It takes up the account of modern art where the Louvre and the Musée de l'Impressionisme leave off, with works by the Fauves, Cubists, Surrealists and the non-figurative and other painters of the present day.

Musée de l'Impressionisme, gallery of nineteenth-century French Impressionist paintings at the Jeu de Paume, an offshoot of the Louvre.

Museum of Modern Art, New York, founded in 1929, collection representing every new development in twentieth-century painting, sculpture and design in the widest sense. The result of enlightened and far-sighted planning, it fulfils an important function through its exhibitions, publications (models of their kind) and various educational activities.

Museum of Modern Western Art, Moscow, collection based on the magnificent private collections of the Moscow tea merchants Tschoukine and Morosov, including notable examples of Post-Impressionist, Fauvist and Cubist art from Cézanne and van Gogh to Picasso and Matisse. It is now divided between the Hermitage, Leningrad (q.v.), and the more recently formed Pushkin Museum.

MURILLO—Boys eating Melons and Grapes—Pinakothek, Munich.

Museums, *see* ART MUSEUMS AND GALLERIES.

Mytens, Daniel (*b.* The Hague, *c.* 1590; *d.* 1642), Dutch portrait painter, one of the foreign artists attracted to Stuart England. A member of the Guild of St Luke at The Hague, he went to England before 1618, worked for James I and became court painter on Charles I's accession, his duties including the copying of old masters. He returned to Holland about 1635. Dry and formal in portraiture, his work has been considered at its best in his portraits of Charles I, at Turin and in the National Portrait Gallery, London.

DANIEL MYTENS—King Charles I (1631)—
National Portrait Gallery.

N

Nabis, The, group of French painters formed towards the end of the nineteenth century in an effort to clarify modern purpose in painting. Paul Sérusier, follower of Gauguin, brought them together and invented the name for them from the Hebrew Nabiim ('the divinely inspired'). He was joined by Maurice Denis (q.v.), who became the theoretician of the movement, Paul Ranson, K. X. Roussel (q.v.), Pierre Bonnard (q.v.), Edouard Vuillard (q.v.) and Félix Vallotton. The subtitle of Denis's book *Théories*, 'From Symbolism and Gauguin towards a new Classic Order', sums up their aim. Reacting against Impressionism, they sought to give ideas aesthetic form (*see also* SYMBOLISM). The adherence of Bonnard and Vuillard seems fortuitous and it became necessary to invent a special term for their absence of theory (*see* INTIMISM). The movement is of note as part of the ferment of ideas that preceded Fauvism and Cubism.

Nanteuil, Robert (*b*. Rheims, 1623; *d*. Paris, 9 Dec. 1678), French graphic artist and engraver, trained as an engraver and influenced in his art by Philippe de Champaigne (q.v.). He was noted for portrait drawings and pastels, became 'Dessinateur et Graveur' to Louis XIV and ranks as the greatest of French portrait engravers, working from life and modelling features with much delicacy of linear shading. His portraits include those of Mazarin, Turenne and Anne of Austria.

Naples, centre of an Italo-Spanish School in the seventeenth century inspired partly by the work of Caravaggio and partly by that of the Carracci and the School of Bologna. Under the sternly religious and despotic government of Spain, it was noted for darkly shadowed pictures of martyrdom and torture of which the Spanish painter Ribera (q.v.) was the chief exponent. One of his principal pupils was Luca Giordano (q.v.). Salvator Rosa (q.v.) was formed as an artist at Naples and his landscapes of the surrounding country and coast were a unique product.

Nash, Paul (*b*. London, 11 May 1889; *d*. 11 July 1946), English painter and designer. He studied at the Slade School and as an official artist in the war of 1914–18 produced in a Cubist manner some of the most striking paintings of the Western Front (Imperial War Museum). 'Structural purpose' was an aim which led him into many forms of design, for textiles, ceramics, the stage and the book, but the Surrealist trend of the 1930's and exhibition of 1936 brought out an imaginative and poetic feeling already apparent in his oils and water-colours. Again an official artist in the Second World War, he showed this imaginative vision in paintings of the Battle of Britain. His brother, John Nash, R.A. (*b*. 1893), as a landscape painter has a related sense of design.

Nasmyth, Scottish family distinguished in both art and science.

P. NASH—The Menin Road, 1918—Imperial War Museum.

Alexander Nasmyth (1758–1840) was a portrait and landscape painter who worked at Edinburgh. His son, Patrick (1787–1831), was the most considerable artist of the family. He settled in London, c. 1797, and his landscapes of southern England earned him the title of the 'English Hobbema'.

National Gallery, London, most important collection of pictures in Britain. Its nucleus was the collection of the wealthy merchant John Julius Angerstein, bought for the nation in 1824 at the suggestion of George IV. The present building in Trafalgar Square was opened in 1838. The gallery has been constantly enriched by private bequests and by purchase, the National Art Collections Fund being an important private benefactor. It is extremely well balanced as a survey of European art from the fourteenth to the nineteenth centuries; its collection of large Italian altar-pieces is of special note, and its representation of the Venetian, Dutch, Flemish and British schools particularly rich. No other gallery, perhaps, has so many individual masterpieces of the highest quality.

National Gallery, Washington, D.C., gallery of painting and sculpture based on the collection and funds provided by Andrew W. Mellon in 1935 and housed in a building completed in 1940. It is supplemented by the earlier collections in the Smithsonian Institution, Washington, known as the National Collection of Fine Arts. The National Gallery has been enriched by a number of important bequests, including the Kress, Widener and Chester Dale collections, and represents mainly the Italian, Flemish, Dutch, British and American schools.

National Portrait Gallery, London, first collection of its kind and without rival, founded in 1856 and established in its present building in 1898. It contains the portraits of sovereigns, statesmen, divines,

[141]

writers, artists, military and naval leaders and others, as represented by contemporaneous artists. The 'Chandos' portrait of Shakespeare and the 'Kit-Cat' portraits of famous Augustans by Kneller are among its treasures.

Nattier, Jean Marc (*b.* Paris, 17 Mar. 1685; *d.* there, 7 Nov. 1766), French painter, a follower of Le Brun (q.v.), and a pupil of his father, Marc Nattier, whom he assisted in reproducing Rubens's 'Marie de' Medici' series for the engravers. He painted both history pictures and portraits but is especially noted for the latter and for his portrayals of Louis XV's daughters, represented in the rococo fashion in various allegorical roles. He worked also for Peter the Great.

Naturalism, in painting a close adherence to nature, which may accompany the interpretation of some ideal or imaginary subject. Thus Ruskin speaks of 'Gothic naturalism advancing from Byzantine severity'. In this sense it is to be distinguished from Realism (q.v.), which implies that the artist is concerned with what is contemporaneous.

Nazarener, group of German painters in the early nineteenth century who sought to revive a religious spirit in art by a return to the methods and outlook of the late medieval and early Renaissance period. Wackenroder and Schlegel, enthusiasts for the Middle Ages, gave a literary impetus to the movement initiated by Overbeck (q.v.) of Lübeck. With other young artists he established in 1810 a kind of monastic workshop in the disused monastery of San Isidoro in Rome, and by 1828 the group included Pforr of Frankfurt, Vogel of Zürich, Cornelius (q.v.) of Düsseldorf, Schadow and Veit of Berlin, Schnorr von Carolsfeld of Leipzig, Führich and Steinle of Vienna. They were sarcastically nicknamed by the early Christian title of 'Nazarenes' and their art was derisively described by Goethe and others as 'Religious-Patriotic', 'Art-Catholic', 'Romantic' and 'Pre-Raphaelite', none of these descriptions being quite beside the point. The

A. VAN DER NEER—Moonlight Scene—Rijksmuseum, Amsterdam.

NICCOLÒ DI LIBERATORE—Triptych, Christ on the Cross and other scenes—National Gallery, London.

revival of fresco was part of their plan and the frescoes for the Bartholdi Palace (now at Berlin) by Cornelius, Overbeck, Veit and Schadow were a result. A stiff and anaemic style characterizes the movement, which was an aesthetic failure though one of the formative influences on Pre-Raphaelitism (q.v.) in England.

Neer, Aert van der (*b.* Amsterdam, 1603; *d.* there, 9 Nov. 1677), Dutch landscape painter. His work is related to that of Hendrik Avercamp and Esaias van de Velde (qq.v.) and he was particularly successful in rendering effects of moonlight and in painting winter landscapes with skaters on ice.

Neithardt, Matthias, *see* GRÜNEWALD.

Neroccio di Bartolommeo Landi (*b.* Siena, 1447; *d.* 1500), Italian sculptor and painter of the Sienese School who worked in the tradition of Simone Martini. He was the brother-in-law of the painter Francesco di Giorgio, with whom he conducted a workshop.

Netscher, Caspar (*b.* Heidelberg, 1639; *d.* The Hague, 15 Jan. 1684), Dutch painter and engraver who studied under Ter Borch (q.v.). He tried to settle at Bordeaux in 1659 but the persecution of Protestants then in progress caused him to return to The Hague. He is noted for his delicate portraits of women.

Neue Sachlichkeit, Die, the 'new objectivity', a phase of the

German Expressionist movement in the 1920's, in which emotional expression was not self-centred but extended to social criticism and had some political implications. It is exemplified by the bitter pictorial comment of George Grosz and Otto Dix (qq.v.).

Nevinson, Christopher Richard Wynne (*b*. London, 13 Aug. 1889; *d*. there, 7 Oct. 1946), English painter and graphic artist. He studied at the Slade School and in Paris and was a Futurist rebel of 1914, afterwards making striking use of a Futurist style in paintings of the Western Front which companion those of Paul Nash (q.v.). In later works he abandoned experiment.

New English Art Club, society of artists founded in London in 1886 reflecting the aims and methods of French Impressionism. Wilson Steer and Walter Sickert (qq.v.) were among its original members. It is now one of the more conservative exhibiting societies.

Niccolò di Liberatore (Niccolò da Foligno) (*b*. Foligno, active *c*. 1456; *d*. 1502), Italian painter of the Umbrian School, mistakenly called Alunno by Vasari. His early work is related to that of Benozzo di Lese, though afterwards he appears to have been influenced by such Venetians as Antonio Vivarini and Carlo Crivelli. A number of signed and dated works exist. Though provincial in style, he was able to give the tenseness of emotion to his religious compositions which

SIR W. NICHOLSON—Mushrooms—Tate Gallery.

B. NICHOLSON—St Ives Harbour—Arts Council.

distinguishes such an example as the 'Christ on the Cross', 1487, of the triptych in the National Gallery.

Nicholson, Ben (*b.* Denham, 10 April 1894), English abstract painter, the son of Sir William Nicholson (q.v.). Not formally trained in art, he began with realistic still life but later became noted for abstract paintings and compositions in low relief, geometrically conceived and showing great refinement of line and spacing together with studied restraint of colour. These have won him international recognition.

Nicholson, Sir William Newzam Prior (*b.* Newark, 5 Feb. 1872; *d.* Blewbury, Berks, 16 May 1949), English painter and graphic artist. He studied art in Paris and won early fame as collaborator with his brother-in-law, James Pryde (q.v.), in the posters, 1894–6, of the 'Beggarstaff Brothers' which simplified cut-paper design with striking effect. Another early graphic achievement was his series of woodcuts in colour, comprising portraits, e.g. his 'Queen Victoria' and London types. Subsequently he painted in oils, portraits, landscapes and still life (being especially noted for the latter), with a fine technical quality.

[145]

Niello (It. form of Lat. *nigellum*, diminutive of *niger*, black), method of ornamenting a polished metal surface by filling in incised lines with a black metallic amalgam, consisting of silver, copper and lead heated with flowers of sulphur. The earliest specimens date from Roman times. It was favoured by goldsmiths of the fifteenth century, who sometimes took prints from the niello, this practice contributing to the invention of engraving on metal as a process of graphic reproduction.

'Night Watch, The', famous portrait group by Rembrandt depicting the officers of one of the companies of the burgher guard. 'The Company of Captain Frans Banning Cocq and Lieutenant Willem van Ruytenburch', painted in 1642 and now in the Rijksmuseum, Amsterdam. It is not a night scene but Rembrandt's characteristic deep shadows have caused it to be thus popularly described. It contains thirty-four life-size figures, not arranged in the usual way of such groups, which gave equal value to each portrait, but with a life-like informality which seems to have given some offence or at all events to have caused the artist's vogue as a portraitist to wane. The picture has been cut down on either side and in the foreground (which was the beginning of a bridge). A list of names was painted over the gate after Rembrandt's death. A small copy of the complete original, however, was made in 1660, before these alterations and disfigurements, by Gerrit Lundens, and is in the National Gallery.

Nocturne, 'night piece', term of musical use since the eighteenth century, appropriated to painting by Whistler in his famous night views of the Thames. His intention was not merely to describe a night scene but to indicate an equivalent of music in painting, in terms of design and a calculated harmony of colour, e.g. 'blue and silver', 'black and gold'.

Nolan, Sidney (*b.* Melbourne, 22 April 1917), Australian painter of Irish descent, noted for landscapes and figure paintings which vividly interpret the Australian continent and its history, many of his works dealing with incidents and legends of early colonial days. Between 1945 and 1955 he produced a series based on the life of the bushranger Ned Kelly which attracted widespread attention. His imaginative style, surrealist in background, is also strikingly illustrated by a 'Leda and the Swan' series, 1960. He is represented in the principal Australian galleries, the Tate Gallery and the Museum of Modern Art, New York.

Nolde, Emil (*b.* Nolde, Schleswig, 7 Aug. 1867; *d.* Schleswig, 7 Sep. 1956), German painter of the Expressionist school. He studied at Karlsruhe and Dachau and derived stimulus from a visit to Paris, *c.* 1906, being influenced by Gauguin and becoming interested in primitive art (journeying in 1914 to the Far East and South Seas). He joined the 'Die Brücke' group (q.v.) in 1906 and was associated with the other advanced movement of the 'Blaue Reiter' (q.v.) in 1913. He painted biblical subjects marked by a barbaric intensity of colour, still life and studies of the landscape of his native region on the German-Danish border, his work including brilliant water-colours.

S. NOLAN—Agricultural Hotel—Tom Collins Memorial, Perth University.

Non-figurative Art, that which neither attempts to represent natural objects nor takes them as the starting point of more or less abstract design but seeks for values in form and colour independent of associations, the latter being regarded as an 'impure' admixture and the desired ideal the 'purity' of art. Wassily Kandinsky (q.v.) was the first to produce entirely non-figurative painting, *c.* 1910. The idea was vigorously pursued for a while by artists in Russia, notably by Malevich (q.v.), under the name of Suprematism, and by various adherents of purely geometric design, the de Stijl group (q.v.) in Holland being of note. As a movement towards complete freedom of expression it was encouraged by the Surrealism of the 1930's and since then has gained devotees in every part of the world, either in its informal aspect ('Abstract Expressionism') or in clear-cut forms of geometric or quasi-mechanical aspect. The development has been amazingly swift since the Second World War in the United States, where Jackson Pollock (q.v.), Mark Rothko, Mark Tobey, Arshile Gorky and a number of other artists have claimed international attention. European artists who have played an influential part in the evolution of non-figurative styles are Piet Mondrian (q.v.), Nicolas de Staël (q.v.), Hans Hartung (q.v.), Alfred Manessier (q.v.), Gustave Singier, Pierre Soulages (q.v.), Michel Tapié, Jean Dubuffet, Georges Mathieu, E. W. Nay, Fritz Winter. Of note in Britain are Ben Nicholson (an early practitioner of the geometric abstract) (q.v.),

[147]

Peter Lanyon, William Gear, Alan Davie, Victor Pasmore. In spite of being assailed by much criticism, non-figurative art is now of world-wide currency, with a special attraction for the younger artists of many countries. *See also* ABSTRACT ART; ACTION PAINTING; TACHISME.

Noort, Adam van (*b.* Antwerp, 1557; *d.* 1641), Flemish painter, son of the painter Lambert van Noort (1520–71). He was an admirer of Venetian colour and is mainly of note as a master with many pupils, among whom were Rubens and Jordaens (qq.v.).

Northcote, James (*b.* Plymouth, 22 Oct. 1746; *d.* London, 31 July 1831), English painter, the pupil of Sir Joshua Reynolds, of whom he wrote a biographical memoir, 1813. He is of less note for his portraits or his compositions for Boydell's Shakespeare Gallery, 1786, than as the conversationalist on art and artists who lives for us in Hazlitt's *Conversations of James Northcote, Esq., R.A.* He was made R.A. in 1787.

Norwich School, painters belonging to the Norwich Society of Artists founded in 1803 by John Crome (' Old Crome') (q.v.) and his friend Robert Ladbrooke. The society flourished until about 1830, though it continued longer. It consisted of professional painters, drawing masters and amateurs, mainly inspired by Crome's attachment to nature in its local aspect but also by John Sell Cotman (q.v.), who joined the society in 1807. They constituted a local school of landscape unique in the history of British art, and offering a certain comparison with the French Barbizon School (q.v.). The many minor but interesting artists of the school included Crome's son, John Berney Crome, George Vincent, James Stark, Joseph and Alfred Stannard, John Thirtle, Thomas Lound, Henry Ninham and Samuel David Colkett. The East Anglian heath and woodland, the River Yare and the Norfolk coast provided many of their subjects.

O

'**Oath of the Horatii**', painting by Jacques Louis David of the three heroic Roman brothers pledged to win victory against the people of Alba by a fight to the death with three of the Alban family of Curiatii (seventh century B.C.). It established a new kind of classicism, hard and sculptural, in contrast with the melting softness of eighteenth century French art; also opposing stern republican virtue to the frivolous myths of artists like Boucher. It may be regarded as a revolutionary picture with a political as well as an aesthetic message, though it was a royal commission painted four years before the French Revolution broke out, being completed in Rome in August 1785. It was hailed with enthusiasm in the Paris Salon of that year.

Ochtervelt, Jacob (*b.* Rotterdam, 1635; *d.* Amsterdam, 1710), Dutch portrait and *genre* painter, according to Houbraken a pupil of Nicolaes Berchem. He worked in the vein of Terborch and Metsu in

J. L. DAVID—Oath of the Horatii—Louvre.

J. OCHTERVELT—Merry Company—Manchester City Art Gallery.

interiors with figures, though his work shows a transition from the typical seventeenth-century art of Holland towards its eighteenth-century decline.

Oil Painting, painting with pigments bound with oil and diluted as required with linseed oil or turpentine, the medium with the widest range of effect, from extreme delicacy to the greatest force and richness, and the most adaptable, lending itself equally well to the requirements of the small cabinet picture and the large decorative work. It is an error to suppose that it was invented by Jan van Eyck, but it first developed in a distinct form in the Netherlands and Germanic lands during the fourteenth century and with van Eyck attained a brilliance that has led to the belief that he possessed some secret process. His method, and the Netherlandish method in general, was to paint transparently on a white gesso ground, the picture being smoothly finished piece by piece with a luminous enamel-like result. The method was taken up in Italy, Antonello da Messina (q.v.) being a pioneer. In Venice Giovanni Bellini (q.v.) rivalled the brilliance of Flemish technique. A combination of a tempera underpainting with a final glaze of oil colour was a Renaissance technique used by Michelangelo. In the sixteenth and seventeenth centuries there was a further development of technique parallel with the desire to obtain greater depth and force of three-dimensional effect. The transparent method, still in essence that of the tempera painter, was replaced by a more elaborate process. The picture was first painted in monochrome, and on this basis the light parts were painted with thick opaque colour, the shadows being painted thinly. Successive glazes of transparent colour gave richness. *See* GLAZE; IMPASTO. The new phase of oil painting flourished in Venice and Titian represents its perfection. Rembrandt, Rubens and Velazquez give individual variants of what may be called the classic method. A decisive change came with the nineteenth century, when painters such as the Impressionists abandoned the old master process of building up a picture in stages in favour of a direct mode of painting. In part this was due to the practice of painting from nature which made swiftness of execution necessary, but it was also due to the translation of tone into colour which entailed instant decision in determining and laying down the colour with the desired effect. Oil painting, however, has remained the most responsive of media to individual treatment. Thus one might contrast the later work of Cézanne, with its application of transparent colour (almost like water-colour), to represent delicate modifications of light on the form of an object, with the heavily loaded paint of van Gogh, who used the medium with an emotional violence.

O'Keefe, Georgia (*b.* Sun Prairie, Wisconsin, 15 Nov. 1887), American painter of landscape and still life, who studied in Chicago and was later an art teacher. She first exhibited in 1916 and developed a formal linear manner with a Surrealist element, exemplified in striking paintings of animal skulls.

'Olympia', painting by Manet, signed and dated 1863 and now in

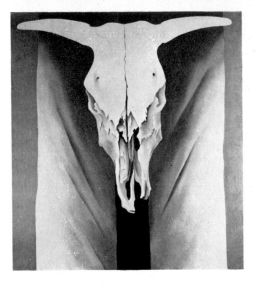

G. O'KEEFE—Cow's Skull;
Red, White and Blue—
Stieglitz Collection,
Metropolitan Museum,
New York.

the Louvre, in which, as in 'Le Déjeuner sur l'Herbe' (q.v.), he took an old master theme and treated it in a realistic modern fashion. The reclining Venus of Titian (in the Uffizi Gallery) with female attendant and pet dog distantly provided the motif. Manet's Parisienne with Negro attendant and cat caused scandal not only by her nudity but by a new and then startling insistence on light tones and their relation. The picture was the centre of controversy at the Salon of 1865.

Opie, John (*b.* nr Truro, May 1761; *d.* London, 1807), English painter of portraits and imaginative subjects. The son of a village carpenter in Cornwall, he was encouraged by Dr Wolcot ('Peter Pindar') in early efforts and coming to London in 1781 was greeted as 'the Cornish Wonder'. He became R.A. in 1787 and had a lucrative practice as portrait painter, for which he showed a natural talent. Among his best known paintings are the portraits of his wife, Amelia Opie, and Mary Wollstonecraft (National Portrait Gallery). He contributed also to Boydell's Shakespeare Gallery and attempted 'history' in his 'Murder of James I of Scotland' (Guildhall Art Gallery).

Orcagna (*b.* ? 1308; *d.* Florence, 1368), Florentine painter, sculptor and architect, whose real name was Andrea di Cione, known by his nickname, Orcagna, apparently a corruption of the Italian word for 'archangel'. He was the most eminent of Florentine artists between the periods of Giotto and Fra Angelico and to some extent a follower of Giotto, though he departed from his style in a flatter and ornamental rather than naturalistic treatment of figures and background. This reversion to a more conventional manner in religious subjects has been associated with a superstitious change in religious feeling, or a desire for the security of tradition, following the bubonic plague which beset Florence and Siena in 1348. His master work in painting, the altar-piece, 'Christ Enthroned', in the Strozzi Chapel, Santa Maria Novella, Florence, signed and dated 1357, shows all his richness of colour and decorative use of gold. His other great work, as

J. OPIE—A School—Photo: Royal Academy.

SIR W. Q. ORCHARDSON—Napoleon on Board the 'Bellerophon'—Tate Gallery.

F

A. ORCAGNA—Detail from Altar-piece Christ with the Virgin and Saints—Church of Santa Maria Novella, Florence.

architect and sculptor, is the church and tabernacle of Or San Michele, Florence, the relief on the tabernacle of 'The Death and Assumption of the Virgin' showing him a worthy pupil of Andrea Pisano. His brothers Jacopo di Cione (also known as Robiccia) and Nardo (?Bernardo or Lionardo) di Cione were also painters who are said to have completed works left unfinished by Andrea.

Orchardson, Sir William Quiller (*b.* Edinburgh, 1835; *d.* London, 13 April 1910), Scottish subject and portrait painter who studied art at Edinburgh. He wasted a genuine talent on the anecdotal themes popular in his time, though his 'Napoleon on board the *Bellerophon*' (Tate Gallery) remains one of the famous pictures of this *genre*. R.A. in 1877, he was knighted, 1907.

Orley, Bernaert (Barend) van (*b.* Brussels, *c.* 1490; *d.* there 6 Jan. 1542), Flemish painter of religious and historical subjects and designer of tapestries and stained glass, the pupil of his father Valentijn. He was a court painter of Margaret of Austria and a 'Romanist', adapting the style of Raphael in an exaggerated fashion (possibly seeing Raphael's famous tapestry cartoons at Brussels where they were woven). His works include the altar-piece 'The Trials of Job' (Brussels), tapestry designs for 'The Life of Abraham' (Hampton Court) and 'Maximilian's Hunts' (Louvre), and stained-glass windows for St Gudule, Brussels.

Orozco, José Clemente (*b.* Zapotlan, Jalisco, 23 Nov. 1883; *d.* Mexico City, 1949), Mexican painter and graphic artist, a leader in the development of Mexican mural painting. Beginning as a student of architecture, he turned to painting in 1909 and subsequently worked both in Mexico and in the United States. His art, sombre and dramatic, contains many images of death and suffering and shows that passionate concern with Mexico's history which inspired her artists after the revolution which began in 1910. In later works this feeling for humanity took a more generalized form. His frescoes include those for the Palace of Fine Arts, Mexico City, 1934, and for

[154]

SIR W. ORPEN—The Chef —Diploma Collection, Royal Academy.

the Mexican Supreme Court, 1941. He produced also many easel pictures and lithographs.

Orpen, Sir William Newenham Montague (*b.* co. Dublin, 27 Nov. 1878; *d.* London, 29 Sept. 1931), English painter, a fellow student with Augustus John at the Slade School. In portraiture he achieved a distinct style of a somewhat mannered and mechanical brilliance. He painted modern 'conversation pieces' of note, these including his 'Homage to Manet' (group of George Moore and others) and his 'Café Royal' (with portraits of its *habitués*). His many war paintings and drawings of 1914–18 culminated in his portrayal (edged with satire) of the Peace Treaty delegates at Versailles. He was knighted in 1918 and became R.A., 1919.

Ostade, Adriaen van (*b.* Haarlem, baptized 10 Dec. 1610; *d.* there, buried 2 May 1685), Dutch painter, trained at Haarlem in the studio of Frans Hals, though following the example of his fellow pupil, Brouwer (q.v.), in devoting himself to peasant, village and alehouse scenes, his 'Boors making Merry' (Dulwich Gallery) being a good instance. He made etchings and painted some delicate water-colours in the same *genre* as his oils.

Ostade, Isaack van (*b.* Haarlem, baptized 2 June 1621; *d.* there, buried 16 Oct. 1649), Dutch painter, the younger brother and pupil of Adriaen van Ostade. He worked in a vein similar to that of his brother though distinguished from him in the delicacy of his landscape, and excelling in winter scenes.

Oudry, Jean Baptiste (*b.* Paris, 17 Mar. 1686; *d.* Beauvais, 30 April 1755), French painter, pupil of Largillierre (q.v), mainly noted for his animal and still-life pictures. He was also director of the Gobelins and Beauvais tapestry works for which he made many designs.

Ouwater, Albert van (fifteenth century), Dutch painter, presumably born at Ouwater and associated with Haarlem, a follower of van Eyck in style though only two works are definitely attributed to him,

[155]

A. VAN OSTADE—A Rustic Concert—Prado.

I. VAN OSTADE—A Village Scene—National Gallery, London.

the 'Raising of Lazarus' (Berlin) and a Madonna (New York, Metropolitan Museum). He is traditionally regarded as the master of Geertgen tot Sint Jans (q.v.).

Overbeck, Johann Friedrich (*b*. Lübeck, 3 July 1789; *d*. Rome, 12 Nov. 1689), German painter, leader of the 'Nazarener' (q.v.). He studied art at the Academy of Vienna, where at the age of twenty he started a 'brotherhood of St Luke', with the aim of reviving religious art. In 1810 he settled at Rome, founding with Pforr and Vogel the Nazarener movement. He did not return to Germany like many of his associates but spent his life in Rome, becoming a convert to Catholicism. His paintings in fresco and oil, devout in intention, were lifeless imitations of Perugino and Raphael, his 'Triumph of Religion in the Arts', 1846 (Staedel Institute, Frankfurt), being typical in its defects, and like other Nazarenes he showed to better advantage in drawn designs.

Ozenfant, Amédée (*b*. 1886), French painter and theorist, who studied architecture and painting in Paris in the years before the First World War and after it was associated with Le Corbusier in propaganda for an art appropriate to a machine age. *L'Esprit nouveau* was a publication to which both contributed, verbally and pictorially, 1920–5. From 1938 onwards Ozenfant lectured and taught in the United States. The value of geometrical form, as logically developed by the machine, was the basis of a theory to which he gave the name of 'Purism'.

P

Pacheco, Francisco (*b.* Seville, 1571; *d.* there, 1654), Spanish painter and writer on art, who conducted a painting academy at Seville. Velazquez was his pupil and married his daughter. He was not a painter of great note but had an influential position in Seville, then a centre of Spanish culture. From about 1625 he devoted himself mainly to literature, and his *Arte de la Pintura* is of value for its account of Spanish art and artists. He was Velazquez's first biographer.

Pacher, Michael (*b.* Neustift, nr Brixen, *c.* 1430; *d.* Salzburg, 1498), German painter and wood-sculptor who from about 1467 was active at Bruneck in the Tirol, one of the principal late-Gothic masters of the carved and painted altar-piece, a major work being the altar-piece of St Wolfgang, Upper Austria. He had some contact with Venice, Padua and Mantua, where Mantegna was his contemporary, though Italian influence appears mainly in the concentration of perspective on a focal point and in some details of ornament. He executed altar-pieces at Gries, Neustift, Salzburg and other places in his native region and a fine 'Coronation of the Virgin' is in the Pinakothek, Munich.

Padovanino, Il (Alessandro Varotari) (*b.* Padua, 1590, *d.* 1650), Italian painter, son of a painter, Dario Varotari. He worked both at Venice and Padua, showing a great admiration for Titian, whose works he assiduously copied. Though not an original artist, he had a number of disciples and preserved the tradition of a grand decorative style to which Tiepolo was to give fresh life.

M. PACHER—Funeral of St Thomas à Becket— Landesmuseum, Graz.

[158]

Padua, centre of painting in the fifteenth century with considerable influence on the cities within range, Ferrara and Venice. It became important in art education and training with Francesco Squarcione (q.v.), who had numerous pupils, the greatest of them being Andrea Mantegna (q.v.), including also the Ferrarese Cosimo Tura and the Venetian Crivelli (qq.v.). A certain austere dignity characteristic of the Paduan School has been attributed to the influence of Donatello's great equestrian statue of Gattemalata.

Page, William (*b.* Albany, New York, 3 Jan. 1811; *d.* Tottenville, Staten Island, 1 Oct. 1885), American painter, once known as 'the American Titian'. He studied art with Samuel Morse (q.v.) and in the schools of the National Academy of Design, and from 1849 to 1860 lived in Rome where he painted the portraits of his friends, Robert and Elizabeth Barrett Browning. He was president of the National Academy of Design, 1871–3.

Palma Giovane (Jacopo Palma) (*b.* 1544; *d.* Venice, 1628), Italian painter, a leader of the Venetian School after the death of Tintoretto. He was the grand-nephew of Palma Vecchio (q.v.). After studying in Rome he worked mainly in Venice, his art owing much to that of Titian, Tintoretto and Veronese. The patronage of the architect, A. Vittorio, helped him to secure a very large number of commissions, mainly for religious and historical subjects. Many were executed for Venice, such as his frescoes for the Doge's Palace, but a number of his works were ordered from abroad.

Palma Vecchio ('the Elder'), Jacopo (Giacomo) d'Antonio de Negreti (*b.* Serinalta, nr Bergamo, *c.* 1480; *d.* Venice, 30 July 1528), Italian painter of the Venetian School, whose work shows the influence of Giorgione and Titian. He painted both religious subjects and portraits, and a voluptuous blonde type of woman, characteristic

PALMA VECCHIO—Portrait of a Poet—National Gallery, London.

[159]

in his work, is said to have inspired the similar type appearing in the art of Titian. Among his principal works are the Santa Barbara altarpiece in the Santa Maria Formosa, Venice, and 'The Holy Family with Saints' (Venice, Accademia), one of a number of 'Sacre Conversazioni'. Formerly ascribed to Titian, his 'Portrait of a Poet' (probably Ariosto) in the National Gallery is a fine example of his male portraiture. He adopted the name Palma and was later called the elder to distinguish him from his grand-nephew, Palma Giovane (q.v.).

Palmer, Samuel (*b*. London, 27 Jan. 1805; *d*. Redhill, 24 May 1881), English painter, largely self-taught though given some instruction by John Linnell (q.v.), whose daughter he married. Greatly inspired in his early work by a meeting with William Blake and the latter's engravings for Thornton's *Virgil*, he lived for a while at Shoreham, Kent, with other young enthusiasts, known as 'the Ancients', producing small pastoral scenes in oil, water-colour and sepia of

S. PALMER—The White Cloud—Ashmolean Museum, Oxford.

G. PANINI—Roman Capriccio with Column of Trojan—Ashmolean Museum, Oxford.

P. DE LA CRUZ—Doña Isabel—Prado.

remarkable beauty and intensity of feeling. These early works, now highly regarded, have had a distinct influence on the imaginative treatment of landscape in modern English art, and fine examples are in the Tate Gallery, Victoria and Albert Museum and Ashmolean Museum. Neither a visit to Italy, 1837–9, nor a later life spent at Redhill under the aegis of his father-in-law benefited his art, which declined into garishness and mediocrity.

Pamphilos (early fourth century B.C.; *b.* Amphipolis, Macedonia), Greek painter of the Sicyon School, noted as the master of Apelles (q.v.). He obtained an edict that painting should not be taught to slaves.

Panini (Pannini), Giovanni Paolo (*b.* Piacenza, *c.* 1692; *d.* Rome, 21 Oct. 1765), Italian painter of architectural subjects and views of Rome, his work comprising 'caprices'—imaginative combinations of ruins—and views of actual places, such as his versions of the interior of St Peter's. He produced also decorative works for Roman villas and palaces. He was a member of both the Academy of St Luke (president, 1754–5) and the French Academy at Rome. The record of the city's aspect left by him and his contemporary, Piranesi (q.v.), is comparable with that of Venice made by Canaletto and Guardi (qq.v.), and it seems likely that the example of Panini helped to direct Canaletto (after an early visit to Rome) to a similar specialization.

Pantoja de la Cruz, Juan (*b.* Madrid, 1551; *d.* there, 26 Oct. 1608), Spanish painter, the pupil of Sánchez Coello (q.v.), whom he succeeded as court painter to Philip II. Like his master he was influenced by Titian and Mor, and painted in Coello's formal style a number of stately portraits with much highly finished detail of costume.

Paréja, Juan (*b.* Seville, *c.* 1606; *d.* 1670), Spanish painter, a mulatto and bound servant of Velazquez. The example of his master caused him to take up painting.

Paris, *see* SCHOOL OF PARIS.

Paris Psalter, The, Byzantine manuscript, perhaps of the ninth century, now in the Bibliothèque Nationale, Paris, containing remarkable examples of painting in the Hellenistic style. They include graceful allegorical figures such as that of Night with a gauze veil studded with stars and a series of nobly antique compositions illustrating the life of David.

Parma, centre of art in the fifteenth and sixteenth centuries under the rule of the Farnese family. Its leading master was Correggio (q.v.) and his pupil Parmigianino (q.v.), one of the early Mannerists, had much influence. See (illustration of the sixteenth-century school, p. 166.)

Parmigianino, Girolamo Francesco Maria Mazzola (*b.* Parma, 1503; *d.* Casal Maggiore, Cremona, 1540), Italian painter of the Lombard School, sometimes called Parmigiano. A member of an artist family and taught by his uncles, he became one of the most distinguished of the Mannerist followers of Correggio, exaggerating the height and

NYΞ   ΗϹΑΙΑϹ   ὁ ορθρος

PAINTER OF THE PARIS PSALTER—The Prophecy of Isaiah—Bibliothèque Nationale, Paris.

slenderness of his figures with graceful effect. His early work was done in Parma, where he decorated the south transept of the cathedral in 1522. In 1523 he went to Rome, being employed by Clement VII, and is said to have been painting his 'Vision of St Jerome' (National Gallery) when imperialist troops burst into his studio during the sack of the city in 1527. He was able to escape without harm to Bologna and returned to Parma in 1531. From then on he was ostensibly occupied with frescoes in the church of Santa Maria della Staccata, but delayed so long in their execution that he was finally thrown into prison for breach of contract. On his release he fled to Casal Maggiore, where he died soon afterwards. His drawings were numerous and much prized by English collectors in the seventeenth and eighteenth centuries, and he also produced original etchings and designs from which chiaroscuro woodcuts were made.

Parrhasios (fl. late fifth century B.C.; b. Ephesus), Greek painter, the contemporary and rival of Zeuxis (q.v.). He worked at Athens and legend tells of a vanity which led him to wear a crown and call himself the king of painters. He is said to have outrivalled Zeuxis in *trompe l'œil* illusionism by the painted curtain over one of his pictures which Zeuxis mistook for a real one. He was considered to excel in rendering emotion. An anciently famous work was his allegorical representation of the Athenian Demos and his painting of Theseus adorned the Capitol in Rome.

Pascin, Jules (b. Widdin, Bulgaria, 1885; d. Paris, 1930), painter born in Bulgaria of a Spanish-Jewish father and Italian mother, associated with the School of Paris (q.v.). His real name was Julius Pincas. He first studied art in Munich and then in Paris, having some early success as an illustrator. During the First World War he was in America but returned to Paris in 1920. He made portrait studies and painted biblical and mythological compositions but is best known for the delicate art with which he drew and painted female types, rather in the spirit of Lautrec though with more sympathy. After some years of dissipation he committed suicide on the eve of a one-man exhibition.

Pasmore, Victor (b. Chelsham, Surrey, 1908), English painter and designer, self-taught. He was one of the founders of the Euston Road School, 1937–9, and first became of note for landscapes, still lifes and figure studies which might be called 'late-Impressionist' in the sense the term is applicable to the art of Bonnard. About 1947 he abandoned representation and turned to the abstract, 'the most revolutionary event in post-war British art' (Sir Herbert Read). He has since worked on Constructivist lines using linear motifs and reliefs of wood and plastic. In 1954 he became Master of Painting, Durham University, and as consulting designer for Peterlee New Town has given an instance of the sympathetic alliance between the abstract artist and the architect.

Pastel, method of painting and drawing with dry pigments in the form of soft chalk or crayon, which like charcoal requires a fixative to

SCHOOL OF PARMA (Sixteenth Century)—Portrait of a Girl—Galleria Nazionale, Naples.

M. Q. DE LA TOUR—Head
of Joseph Vernet (Pastel)—
Musée de Dijon.

be made permanent.
The use of coloured
chalks has a long history
and many European old
masters used them to
heighten the effect of a
drawing (e.g. Holbein
in his portrait draw-
ings). Red, black and
white chalks were used
with beautiful effect
by Watteau. The more
elaborate pastel paint-
ing was popularized
in eighteenth-century
France by the Vene-
tian woman painter
Rosalba Carriera (q.v.).
Quentin de la Tour (q.v.)
is its most famous ex-
ponent, though Chardin
(q.v.) used the medium with great effect. J. E. Liotard was another
practitioner of note. In England John Riley (q.v.) was noted for
his crayon painting, but the art, as in France, was developed more
fully there in the eighteenth century, notably by Francis Cotes (q.v.).
In more modern times it has been practised by Degas, Toulouse-
Lautrec, Millet and Whistler, Degas finding pastel especially congenial in some of his most beautiful ballet scenes and in his nude
studies, on account of the swift and free handling it allowed and the
fresh and luminous effects it produced.

Pastiche (Pasticcio), patchwork of borrowings or work in imitation
of another's style. The term carries with it some deprecation though
it does not necessarily imply an attempt to deceive.

Patenier (Patinir, Patinier), Joachim (*b.* Bouvignes or Dinant, *c.*
1480; *d.* Antwerp, 5 Oct. 1524), Flemish landscape painter who
worked mainly at Antwerp, where he was a pupil or follower of
Quinten Massys (q.v.). Dürer (q.v.), who made his acquaintance at
Antwerp, mentions him as a landscape painter, and he is notable for
having developed the typical background of the early Netherlandish
altar-piece into a feature of main importance, figures being subsidiary. His characteristic river scene with rocky shores may have
some reminiscence of his native Meuse country, or, it has been
suggested, through his friend and sometimes collaborator, Massys,

J. PATENIER—Virgin and Child in Landscape—Collection of Mrs Geoffrey Hart.

may ultimately derive something from Leonardo. He had a large following, many anonymous paintings being of his 'school'.

Pater, Jean Baptiste Joseph (*b*. Valenciennes, 29 Dec. 1695; *d*. Paris, 25 July 1736), French painter who studied first at Valenciennes and then in Paris for a short time with Watteau (q.v.). They fell out, but after their quarrel was finally made up the latter gave him a little further tuition in 1721. Pater was a devoted follower of Watteau in subject and style, though the inevitable comparison bears hardly on the relative weakness and poverty of invention in his *fêtes galantes*. He is well represented in the Wallace Collection.

Peale, name of an American artist family, most notable of whom was **Charles Willson** (*b*. Maryland, 16 April 1741; *d*. Germantown, Pennsylvania, 22 Feb. 1826). He studied under Benjamin West in

J. B. PATER—Military Pleasures—Louvre.

London, 1767–70, and worked successfully as portrait painter in Philadelphia. He painted several portraits of George Washington and of other famous men of his time (Independence Hall, Philadelphia). His brother **James** (1749–1831), whom he taught, was a miniaturist, and his sons (whom he named after old masters) were also painters; **Rembrandt** (1778–1860) being a portraitist and lithographer, **Raphaelle** (1774–1825) a still-life painter and **Titian Ramsey** (1800–1885) an animal draughtsman.

Pechstein, Max (*b.* Zwickau, 31 Dec. 1881; *d.* Berlin, 29 June 1955), German painter and graphic artist of the Expressionist School. He studied at Dresden and was a member of the Die Brücke group (q.v.) in 1906. With a wide interest in all forms of art he later travelled extensively in the East and the South Pacific.

Peeters, name of a Flemish painter family of Antwerp, principal among them being **Bonaventura the Elder** (*b.* Antwerp, 23 July 1614; *d.* Hoboken, July 1652), marine painter, and **Clara** (*c.* 1590–1621+), who worked as a still-life painter at Antwerp, Amsterdam and The Hague. The brothers of Bonaventura, **Jan** and **Gillis,** were also marine painters, and the son of Gillis, **Bonaventura the Younger** (*d.* 1702) painted landscapes.

Pencil, term which until the end of the eighteenth century described the smaller brushes used by artists and in poetical language

B. PEETERS (the Elder)—Winter Landscape—The Frozen River—Collection of Mrs Geoffrey Hart.

a painter's art in a more general sense. In the alternative meaning of a drawing material, which it now has exclusively, a stick of graphite (crystallized carbon), it was known as early as the sixteenth century but did not come into use in its present form until the beginning of the nineteenth century. Though an auxiliary rather than a principal means of expression it can give exquisite effect, and the pencil portraits of Ingres may be cited as masterpieces of their kind.

Pentimento, some feature of a painting, for example a figure, part of a figure or background detail, altered and covered over by the artist on second thought in the course of his work. As paint tends to become more transparent with time, these *pentimenti* may show through.

Perino del Vaga (Pietro Buonaccorsi) (1501–47), Italian painter of the Florentine School. He first studied with Ridolfo Ghirlandaio but was later a pupil and assistant of Raphael in Rome, carrying out decorations in the Loggie of the Vatican from Raphael's designs.

Permeke, Constant (*b*. Antwerp, 1886; *d*. Ostend, 1952), Belgian painter, the most powerful representative of Expressionism (q.v.) in Belgium. He studied art in the academies of Bruges and Ghent, though his first important works were produced in England, where he stayed for a while during the First World War after being wounded when in the Belgian Army. Severe in form and sombre in colour, his paintings depicted peasants, sailors and labouring families with great force and a solidity showing the effect of the artist's practice of sculpture. Notable works such as 'La Visite de l'Étranger' and 'Les Fiancés' are in the Brussels Museum.

Perréal, Jean (Jehan de Paris) (active from *c*. 1485; *d*. 1530),

J. A. D. INGRES—The Sisters Montagu (Pencil)—Collection of Viscount Hinchingbrooke.

J. B. PERRONNEAU—Girl with a Kitten (Pastel)— National Gallery, London.

French painter and miniaturist, employed by Charles VIII, Louis XII and Francis I and court painter to Margaret of Austria. He worked at Lyons but was often sent elsewhere on various commissions, visiting Italy and England. He has been identified with the Master of Moulins (q.v.), which would make him the author of outstanding works, combining Fouquet's breadth of design with something of the realism of Hugo van der Goes. The identification is considered doubtful, however, as no works attributable to the Master of Moulins are of later date than c. 1500.

Perronneau, Jean Baptiste (b. Paris, 1715; d. Amsterdam, Nov. 1785), French portrait painter in oils and pastel, trained as an engraver. He became a member of the Académie in 1753 but later led a wandering life, working in Italy, Russia and Holland. His 'Girl with a Kitten' (National Gallery) shows the charm of his art.

Persian Painting is represented by an exquisite form of miniature painting and manuscript book decoration which dates from the thirteenth century and reached maturity in the fifteenth century under the Timurid dynasty. The miniaturist then combined with the scribe and the bookbinder in producing some of the most beautiful books in the world. Though Persia came under Moslem dominion in the seventh century and Moslem principles disfavoured the pictorial image, nevertheless in the form of illustration combined with calligraphy the artists were able to display a luxurious appreciation of landscape, flowers and animals. They were no less brilliant in depicting human beings and action, while their sense of colour was wonderfully developed. A primitive form of the art is found under the Abbasid caliphs, showing some Coptic influence, but after the Mongol conquest in 1258 a decisive factor is the impression made by Chinese artists following in the conquerors' train. Chinese conventions for rock and cloud form, etc., were adopted and the Chinese delicacy of line and accent was followed. The subjects were taken from the Shah-nama (Book of Kings), the Persian epic of Firdausi, from

PERSIAN MANUSCRIPT PAINTING (Shiraz, 1545-50)—King Iskander and his Court—
Victoria and Albert Museum.

PERSIAN MURAL PAINTING (Seventeenth Century—Young Man in a Red Robe—Victoria and Albert Museum.

Top right: PERSIAN MANUSCRIPT PAINTING (1569)—A Picnic—Bodleian Library, Oxford.

Bottom right: HERAT SCHOOL (Persian, Late Fifteenth Century)—Portrait of a Painter in Turkish Dress — Freer Gallery of Art, Washington.

books of fables and historical works. The most famous of Persian painters was Bihzad (q.v.), who worked in the early fifteenth century, superb works being the Zafar-nama (Victories of Timur) and Nizami's Khamsa (in the British Museum). A high level was maintained in the sixteenth century under the patronage of the Safawid dynasty, but thereafter Persian painting declined with the decline of the literary culture that had supported it. In the sixteenth century its influence abroad was felt in the India of the Mughal emperors (*see* INDIAN PAINTING).

Perspective, scientifically accurate representation of objects at varying distances from the eye, the main rule being that receding parallel lines converge to a point on the horizon or eye level. Its use was one of the problems which Italian artists of the fifteenth century set themselves to master, Uccello (q.v.) being famous for his devotion to its study. Both western and eastern paintings show, however, that it is not a *sine qua non* of aesthetic effect. 'Aerial' perspective, distinct from the linear perspective described above, has no mathematical basis and refers to the fact that colours tend to be lighter and forms less distinct with distance and to the relations of tone and colour that convey this effect. *See also* FORESHORTENING.

Perugino, Pietro (*b.* Città della Pieve, nr Perugia, ? *c.* 1446; *d.* 1523), Italian painter, one of the masters of the Umbrian School. His proper name was Pietro Vanucci. He is said to have been a pupil of Fiorenzo di Lorenzo and probably an assistant to Verrocchio, his style being formed at Florence. Frescoes in the Palazzo Communale at Perugia, 1475, were an early undertaking. In 1480 he was one of the artists chosen by Sixtus IV to embellish his newly finished Sistine Chapel, his fresco of 'The Delivery of the Keys to St Peter'

P. PERUGINO—Apollo and Marsyas—Louvre.

[175]

showing that sense of space he was to transmit to his pupil Raphael, who worked under him at Florence, 1500–4. Among principal works were his frescoes for the Collegio del Cambio, Perugia, the 'Crucifixion with Saints', 1496 (Florence, Santa Maria Maddalena de' Pazzi), accounted his masterpiece, and the altar-piece, 'Virgin and Child with St Michael and St Raphael' (National Gallery), in which, it has been suggested, though only speculatively, there is a trace of the young Raphael's handiwork. Its gentle and youthful human types and also its serene sky and background, receding space being emphasized by tall, thin trees, indicate clearly enough the source of Raphael's early style, though Perugino was left behind by the great onward movement of the Renaissance in which Raphael attained his full stature. He painted a ceiling for one of Raphael's Stanze in the Vatican, 1508, but otherwise his later years were spent in Florence, Perugia, Siena and other cities and in works repetitive of his simple charm. There are delightful portraits by him in the Uffizi.

Peruzzi, Baldassare (b. nr Siena, 1481; d. Rome, 1536), Italian architect, sculptor and painter. As a painter he was influenced in his early work by Pintoricchio and later by Raphael, who painted the frescoes for the Villa Farnesina which Peruzzi designed. His most celebrated painting, 'Augustus and the Sibyl' in the church of Fontegiusta, Siena, follows Raphael in style. His career at Rome was interrupted by the sack of the city in 1527, in which he lost all his belongings. He then went to Siena as city architect, though he returned to Rome in 1532. In connection with the palaces he built he developed the art of decorative painting, sometimes imitative of sculptural relief and also using grotesques in the fashion of Raphael's Loggie.

Pesarese, see CANTARINI.

Pesellino (Francesco di Stefano) (b. Florence, c. 1422; d. 1457), Italian painter of the Florentine School, to be distinguished from his maternal grandfather, Giuliano Pesello, who may have been his first teacher, though he was probably a pupil of Fra Filippo Lippi (q.v.), who finished the altar-piece, the 'Trinity of Saints' (National Gallery), left incomplete at Pesellino's death. He was one of the painters who specialized in the decoration of 'cassoni'—bridal chests.

Philoxenos (fl. 316 B.C.; b. Eretria), Greek painter of the period of Alexander the Great. He was noted for the rapidity with which he worked. He is known by his picture of the Battle of Issus, in which Alexander defeated Darius. It was commissioned by Cassander, King of Macedon, and the mosaic copy, found at Pompeii, conveys the artist's skill in handling a complex composition with a wealth of vigorous detail and a great feeling for action. The soldiers' lances are used with a sense of design that may be compared with that of Velazquez in 'The Surrender of Breda'.

Piazzetta, Giovanni Battista (b. Venice, 13 Feb. 1683; d. there, 29 April 1754), Italian painter of the Venetian School, son of Giacomo Piazzetta, a sculptor and wood-carver. He was the pupil of Molinari

and studied at Bologna under G. M. Crespi (q.v.), being also influenced by the Netherlandish painter, Jan Lys. He worked in Venice for various churches, his ceiling decoration, 'The Glory of St Dominic' (SS. Giovanni e Paolo, Venice), *c.* 1727, having much influence on Tiepolo (q.v.) and the development of the rococo style. He also painted *genre* pictures (a number of which were engraved) and portraits, and produced many drawings and book illustrations to bring in money, for he was a slow painter. The use of a dark red ground has made for a dusky effect of light and shade in some works, increasing with the passage of time, though he showed a trend towards the lighter rococo scheme of colour.

Picabia, Francis (*b.* Paris, 1878), painter of the School of Paris, son of a Spanish father and French mother. He studied in Paris at l'École des Beaux-Arts and l'École des Arts Décoratifs and subsequently passed through a series of phases, Impressionist, Cubist, Dadaist and Surrealist.

Picasso, Pablo (*b.* Malaga, 25 Oct. 1881), Spanish painter, the son of a painter and drawing master, José Ruiz Blasco, using as surname the maiden name of his mother, Maria Picasso y López. He began to paint and draw at an early age under his father's tuition and fraternized with the artists and writers of Barcelona. He first went to Paris in 1900 and settled there permanently in 1904. At the beginning his work was concerned with the social scene after the fashion of Degas, Forain and Toulouse-Lautrec, but between 1901 and 1904 he turned to austere figure studies, blue being the dominant colour. Circus pictures followed, delicate and more varied in colour ('rose period', 1905–6). An epoch-making change in his art followed when between 1907 and 1909, together with Georges Braque (q.v.), he developed Cubism (q.v.) from the study of Cézanne combined with that of Negro sculpture and primitive art. 'Les Demoiselles d'Avignon',

PICASSO—Group of Nudes, 1921 (Pastel)—Staatsgalerie, Stuttgart.

1907, marks the birth of the movement to which Picasso adhered until 1914, like Braque practising successively its 'analytic' form (construction in depth) and its 'synthetic' form (more decorative and two-dimensional in effect). A feature of his Cubist still life, 1912–14, was the use of 'collage' (q.v.). He reverted to a neo-classical style, 1920–4, in painting and in outline etchings of classical themes. Meeting Diaghilev he designed the *décor* of a number of ballets, 1917–1927. A new and imaginative phase of his art began *c.* 1925, and coincided with the development of Surrealism (q.v.). The bull, traditional Spanish emblem of conflict and tragedy, began to appear in paintings and etchings and the 'Guernica', painted in 1937 during the Spanish Civil War (New York, Museum of Modern Art), was a fierce pictorial comment on a deplorable bombing incident, making use of this symbolism. Further images of violence and horror produced during and after the Second World War provoked much criticism. A Surrealistic practice in works after 1938 of combining two different views of a head in the same 'double image' often produced a monstrous distortion which also caused protest. In other works, however, a certain humour appears, and Picasso has gone freely from one style and one medium to another, using all with

[178]

PICASSO—The Three
Musicians—Philadelphia
Museum of Art.

astonishing freedom and
virtuosity. He has prac-
tised sculpture, devised
metal constructions, de-
signed pottery (from
1946 at Villauris near
Antibes) and produced a
great number of prints,
etchings, aquatints and
lithographs. His graphic
art is one of his most
distinctive achieve-
ments, including his illustrations to Ovid and
Balzac, his Minotaur
etchings and his aquatints for Buffon's *Natural History* (published
in 1942). His prodigious facility was shown in the 180 drawings
of artist and model produced between Nov. 1953 and Feb. 1954.
His restless energy has been impressively conveyed by a film
showing him at work. Picasso has affected the whole course of
modern art and no later artist of the School of Paris has rivalled him
as an international influence, though the non-figurative art of today
has found other sources of inspiration. His paintings are widely
distributed in the world's principal public galleries and in many
private collections.

Picturesque, strictly speaking that which is suitable for conversion
into a picture, though as a theory developed in the later eighteenth
century it implied a reference to already existing works of art and
their value in at least three respects: as a stimulus to the appreciation
of certain aspects of nature; as a guide to the 'improvement' of
nature represented by landscape gardening or the layout of a rural
estate; and as a guide to pictorial composition. It was based on the
idea that roughness and irregularities of form had a special aesthetic
value. Thus mountains, rocks, ruins and wild landscape in general
were picturesque, though a tumbledown cottage or old-fashioned
farmyard might also answer to the description. Such theorists as
the Rev. William Gilpin consequently distinguished an 'ideal' or
sublime Picturesque and a 'rural' Picturesque. Claude Lorraine and
Salvator Rosa were taken as models of the former, Ruisdael and
Hobbema of the latter. Richard Wilson, Alexander Cozens and many
English water-colourists represent the one tradition, George Morland
the other. A favourite butt of satirists, including Rowlandson, Jane
Austen and Thomas Love Peacock, the Picturesque is not a negligible

[179]

phase of landscape art and heralds the Romantic movement which added to it sentiment and emotion.

Piero della Francesca (*b.* Borgo San Sepolcro, *c.* 1416; *d.* 1492), also known as Piero del Borgo or Borghese but preferring the name Francesca in recognition of his widowed mother's devotion to him. He was the pupil of Domenico Veneziano (q.v.) and is first mentioned in 1439 when he was an assistant of Domenico, then painting frescoes in Sant' Egidio in Florence. He returned to his native town, no doubt with a valuable store of Florentine science, including that of perspective, and was much employed there on pictures and frescoes. He worked also at Urbino, where he had the patronage of the Duke Federigo Montefeltro, of whom and his wife he painted famous portraits (Uffizi). He visited Rome, though nothing remains of his work there, also Ferrara, Rimini and Arezzo, where he painted his masterpieces of fresco between 1452 and 1460. He returned regularly, however, between his journeys, to Borgo, to which he seems to have been much attached. He gave up painting when about sixty, when it would seem his sight was failing, and devoted himself to mathematical and philosophical studies, two written treatises remaining on perspective and mathematical figures. His great works include the profoundly impressive fresco at Borgo, 'The Resurrection', and the frescoes at Arezzo of the Legend of the True Cross, the 'Flagellation of Christ' (Urbino Cathedral) and the 'Madonna with the Duke of Urbino as Donor' (Milan, Brera). The two famous paintings in the National Gallery, the 'Baptism of Christ' and the 'Nativity', though closely related in style, are considered to be, respectively, an early and late work. The oil method of his Urbino portraits suggests some acquaintance with Netherlandish painting, but in general the art of Piero is strongly individual in its poetry and contemplative spirit and the feeling of intellectual force conveyed by its abstract treatment of space and form.

Piero di Cosimo (*b.* Florence, *c.* 1462; *d.* there, *c.* 1521), Italian painter of the Florentine School. The son of Lorenzo di Piero, he was the pupil of Cosimo Rosselli (q.v.), whose Christian name he adopted. Though influenced by Signorelli and Leonardo, he had a personal and whimsical imagination which gives a vivid life to his representations of the satyrs and centaurs of classical fable and shows itself also in the various animals he introduced into his pictures. His 'Perseus and Andromeda' (Uffizi) presents a typically fantastic dragon, and his mythological picture, formerly known as 'The Death of Procris' (National Gallery), faintly like the work of his contemporary Botticelli in its delicate pathos, introduces as well as its famous dog the strangest of fauns. Another distinctive masterpiece is the 'Venus, Mars and Cupid' (Berlin). He assisted Cosimo Rosselli in his frescoes in the Sistine Chapel, 1481–2. He was also the author of some strongly characterized portraits that have an element of Leonardesque caricature. He was the master of Andrea del Sarto (q.v.).

Pietà (It. 'pity'), in painting or sculpture a representation of the dead Christ supported on the lap of the Virgin

SCHOOL OF AVIGNON—Pietà—Louvre.

P. DI COSIMO—Perseus and Andromeda—Uffizzi, Florence.

P. DI COSIMO—Battle of Centaurs and Lapiths (detail)—National Gallery, London.

Pinacoteca Nazionale, Siena, collection of works of the Sienese School, including Duccio, Simone Martini, Pietro and Ambrogio Lorenzetti, Lippo Memmi and others.

Pinacotheca (Gr. 'picture repository'), name given to the picture-gallery of the Propylaea in the Acropolis of ancient Athens and applied by the Romans to the galleries of private collectors. In modern times the name has been reapplied to public galleries, e.g. the Pinakothek of Munich and the Pinacoteca of Siena.

Pinakothek, The Old, Munich, the Bavarian State Gallery, built early in the nineteenth century by Ludwig I, housing the existing ducal collections to which Ludwig added a fine collection of altar-pieces. It is rich in examples of old German painting and early Netherlandish and Flemish painting. Grünewald's 'Christ Mocked', Rembrandt's 'Entombment' and Botticelli's 'Pietà' are among its many masterpieces.

Pintoricchio (Pinturicchio), Bernardino di Betto (b. Perugia, c. 1454; d. Siena, 11 Dec. 1513), Italian painter of the Umbrian School,

PINTORICCHIO—Scene from the Odyssey—Penelope at her Loom (Fresco)—National Gallery, London.

the diminutive form of the nickname by which he is known referring to his small size. He assisted Perugino in Rome with the frescoes in the Sistine Chapel, 1481–2, and was much influenced by him in style. His chief works were decorations for a series of chapels in Santa Maria del Popolo and frescoes in the Borgia apartments in the Vatican, 1492–5, at Rome; and the frescoes in the library of Siena Cathedral executed for Cardinal Piccolomini, representing the history of Pope Pius II. Though somewhat lacking in substance his art was animated and elaborately decorative.

Piranesi, Giovanni Battista (*b.* Mestre, 4 Oct. 1720; *d.* Rome, 9 Nov. 1778), Italian engraver who studied at Rome and devoted himself to recording the architectural aspect of the city, ancient and modern, to which he gave appropriate majesty by massive effects of shadow and perspective. His engraved and etched views of Rome, often reprinted and imitated, form the most impressive portrayal of the city that has been made, though the free etchings of h s *Carceri d'Inven'ione*, 1745–1761, in which he created fantastic prison-like interiors, are a uniquely imaginative product of his art. He also repaired and restored some Roman churches under the direction of Pope Clement XIII. Preliminary drawings for his plates were made in pen, red chalk and bistre wash, some being etched by his son, Francesco (1758/9–1810), who collaborated with him and collected and preserved his works to the number of about 2,000.

Pisanello, Antonio (*b.* Pisa, *c.* 1395; *d.* Naples, *c.* 1455), Italian painter and medallist. His early life was spent at Verona, where he was trained in the 'International Gothic' style (q.v.) which flourished there. He was associated with one of the main Italian practitioners of the style, Gentile da Fabriano (q.v.), completing frescoes (now destroyed) by Gentile, both in Venice and Rome. As a painter and producer of portrait medallions he made a triumphal progress from one Italian court to another, working for the Gonzagas at Mantua, the Visconti at Pavia, Sigismondo Malatesta at Rimini, Lionello d'Este at Ferrara and from 1448 for Alfonso of Aragon at Naples. Of the few examples of his frescoes that remain, the 'Annunciation' in the church of San Fermo, Verona, 1423–4, and the 'St George' at Santa Anastasia, Verona, 1437–8, show his ornate manner, and on a small scale 'The Legend of St Eustace' and 'Virgin with St Anthony and St George' (National Gallery) are exquisite examples of his art. He excelled in relief portraiture, and his drawings from nature, especially his beautiful animal studies, show an observation surpassing the conventions of the belated Gothic style. The most important collection of his drawings is that of the 'Codex Vallardi' of the Louvre, and the Victoria and Albert Museum has a notable collection of the medals.

Pissarro, Camille (*b.* St Thomas, Antilles, 10 July 1830; *d.* Paris, 12 Nov. 1903), French painter and graphic artist, one of the mainstays of Impressionism. After showing a desire to paint in the Danish West Indies where he was born, he made a definite start in Paris at the age of twenty-five, working at the Académie Suisse, where he met Claude

PISANELLO—The Vision of St Eustace—National Gallery, London.

Monet (q.v.), and being influenced, like most young painters of the time, by Corot and Courbet (qq.v.). His early work, subdued in tone and simple in composition, already showed the feeling of open air which he developed in country retreat at Pontoise and Louveciennes before 1870. His house was occupied and most of his pictures destroyed in the German invasion, and 1870–1 he was in England with Monet, living in south London and painting pictures of the Crystal Palace, Sydenham and Upper Norwood. On his return he pursued a course parallel with that of Monet in the rendering of light by colour, blues, purples and greens prevailing, producing works of great beauty and exhibiting at all the Impressionist exhibitions. He settled at Eragny in 1884 but made frequent visits to Le Havre, Rouen and Paris, excellent views of the boulevards of the capital and of the waterfronts being results, though his most typical paintings represent the quiet countryside and its peasantry. He was consistent in style, though between 1886 and 1888, influenced by Seurat, he practised a systematic division of colour. His own influence on others was beneficent and by introducing both Cézanne and Gauguin to Impressionism he set them on their respective paths to maturity. His son, Lucien (1863–1944), who settled in England, pursued in painting the divisionist method his father had adopted for a while, but was

G   [185]

C. PISSARRO—Boulevard Montmartre—National Gallery of Victoria, Australia.

diverted, in his Eragny Press, for which he made many designs and engravings, to the post-William Morris style of English fine book production.

Pitti Gallery, Florence, art collection formed by members of the Medici family and housed in the Pitti palace. The paintings belong largely to the period of the High Renaissance. Among the famous works it contains are Raphael's 'Madonna del Granduca', 'Madonna della Sedia' and 'La Fornarina'; Giorgione's 'Concert', sometimes attributed to Titian; Titian's portrait of a young Englishman (said to be the Earl of Arundel); Fra Bartolommeo's 'The Deposition', and notable paintings by Andrea del Sarto and Filippino Lippi. Foreign artists represented include Rubens and van Dyck.

Pittoni, Giovanni Battista (*b.* Venice, 1687; *d.* 1767), Italian painter of the Venetian School. He studied with his uncle Francesco Pittoni and was a facile painter of religious and other subjects in the rococo manner, influenced by Sebastiano Ricci and Tiepolo. He was President of the Venetian Academy in 1765 and supplied paintings to a number of foreign clients.

Planes, element of geometric construction in painting, either as a series of flat surfaces imagined in depth as parallel with the surface of a canvas and in perspective, giving relations of size and distance between objects depicted and the eye of the spectator; or as the series of flat surfaces set at an angle one to another of which any solid, even a round object, is composed. Closely studied by Cézanne, this aspect of pictorial construction was emphasized and turned to fresh use by the Cubists.

Plastic, primarily referring to the sculptor's art of modelling in some malleable material, is a term often used to describe the painter's appreciation of solid form and ability to translate it into two-dimensional terms. *See also* MODELLING.

Plein Air, painting from nature in the open with the special purpose of catching transient atmospheric effect and studying the diffused effect of light. The oil sketches of Constable give an example and it was extensively practised in France by the Impressionists. *See* IMPRESSIONISM.

Pleydenwurff, Hans (*b.* ? Bamberg; *d.* 1472), German painter active at Nuremberg after 1450. A notable work is his altar-piece 'Crucifixion', *c.* 1460 (Munich), the influence of Netherlandish art appearing in its rich detail and elaborate landscape background.

Polidoro da Caravaggio (Polidoro Caldara) (*b.* Caravaggio, 1495; *d.* Messina, 1543), Italian painter. He was a pupil of Raphael and specialized successfully in fresco painting on the façades of Roman houses in imitation of the antique. After the sack of Rome in 1527 he

A. POLLAIUOLO—David Victor—Staatliche Museum, Berlin.

A. POLLAIUOLO—The Martyrdom of St Sebastian —National Gallery, London.

fled to Naples and then settled at Messina, where, after working profitably for some time, he was robbed and murdered. One of his best-known pictures is 'Christ bearing the Cross' (Naples).

Pollaiuolo, popular name of the Italian artist brothers, Antonio and Piero di Benci, who collaborated in Florence as painters, sculptors, goldsmiths, engravers and designers of textiles. **Antonio,** the elder of the two (*b.* Florence, *c.* 1432; *d.* Rome, *c.* 1498), was a pupil of the goldsmith Bartoluccio, father-in-law of Ghiberti, and assisted the latter in modelling the gates for the baptistery of Florence, completed in 1452. The monuments of Popes Sixtus IV and Innocent VIII in St Peter's are by him. He is assumed to have been the more creative and the better painter, energetically pursuing the study of anatomy and the anatomical effect of changes of position and movement with a science that had its influence on Signorelli and even Michelangelo. Paintings in which he had a dominant part are 'The Martyrdom of St Sebastian' (National Gallery) and the panels of 'Hercules slaying the Hydra' and 'Hercules slaying Antaeus' (Uffizi), and his engraving, the 'Battle of Nude Men', is another anatomical *tour de force*. **Piero** (*b.* Florence, *c.* 1441; *d.* 1496), who may have been the pupil of Andrea de Castagno (q.v.), seems distinct from his brother as a painter in the 'Adoration of the Virgin', 1483 (San Gimignano), and figures of the Virtues (Uffizi). While it is still assumed that they collaborated in the 'St Sebastian' of the National Gallery and other works there is a certain presumption that Piero's part was secondary.

Pollock, Jackson (*b.* Cody, Wyoming, 1912; *d.* 11 Aug. 1956), American abstract or abstract-Expressionist painter, the first of American artists to have exerted an international influence. He grew up in the west, and studied art at Los Angeles, 1925–9, and

A. POLLAIUOLO—Hercules slaying the Hydra (Pen and Ink) — British Museum.

under Thomas Hart Benton in New York, 1929–31. He was influenced successively by Albert Ryder (q.v.), by the modern Mexican painters, Orozco and Siqueiros (qq.v.) and by Picasso (q.v.), but a symbolic and fantastic element in his work gave way after 1946 to an outburst of radical energy in paint and sheer delight in its employment as a form of physical action (*see* ACTION PAINTING). He painted on a huge scale in oil or enamel paint on canvas or synthetic board, sometimes dripping paint in swirling lines or patches on the surface from above, 'as', it has been said, 'a skilful cowboy twirls his lariat'. Some have seen in these processes the destruction of painting as an art, but though its dangers as an influence are obvious (and it is easy to parody its absence of method), Pollock's painting shows an artist's gift and more control of his media than his theory would suggest, his later work, in colour or limited to black and white, being highly decorative.

Polygnotos (fl. 500–425 B.C.; *b.* island of Thasos), Greek painter who settled in Athens in the time of Cimon. At Athens he executed mural paintings of the 'Sack of Troy' in the Stoa Poecile and of the 'Rape of the Leucippidae' in the shrine of the Dioscuri. His most famous works were the 'Sack of Troy' and 'Ulysses in the Underworld' at Delphi. He excelled in the delineation of character in the human face and this quality of his work receives unqualified praise from Aristotle and other ancient critics. Something of his mode of composition may be gathered from the figures (placed at different levels) in the contemporary vase-painting of the Argonaut krater from Orvieto (Louvre). He had numerous pupils and followers.

Polyptych, altar-piece consisting of a number of hinged panels, presenting a series of paintings to view when opened or folded.

J. DA PONTORMO—Joseph in Egypt—National Gallery, London.

Pompeii, *see* GREEK PAINTING; ROMAN PAINTING.

Ponte, da. *see* BASSANO.

Pontormo, Jacopo da (*b.* Pontormo, 1494; *d.* 2 Jan. 1557), Italian painter of the Florentine School, the most brilliant pupil of Andrea del Sarto (q.v.). He was an early Mannerist, his admiration for Michelangelo leading to strange contrasts and exaggerations of proportion and in composition. Such may be seen in his 'Martyrdom of the Forty Saints' (Florence, Pitti), 'Joseph in Egypt' (National Gallery) and 'The Deposition', 1525, painted as an altar-piece in Santa Felicità, Florence. Many of his works in fresco have been destroyed, including those for the church of San Lorenzo on which he worked for more than eleven years. He was noted for his portraits and produced many drawings. Bronzino (q.v.) was his pupil.

Pordenone (Giovanni Antonio Sacchi) (*b.* Pordenone, Friuli, *c.* 1483; *d.* 12 Jan. 1539), Italian painter called after his birthplace, who painted religious frescoes and altar-pieces in various cities of northern Italy. It is assumed that he visited Rome from the traces of the influence of Raphael and Michelangelo which have been detected in his style, but he is associated with the Venetian School and was, according to Vasari, a would-be rival of Titian. His work shows the Mannerist tendency towards exaggeration.

Portraiture, the art of producing an individual likeness in painting or drawing was practised in ancient Greece (Apelles being portrait painter to Alexander the Great), but the earliest existing examples are the mummy cases painted in encaustic by Hellenised artists found in Egypt and dating from A.D. 40 to 250. Portraiture became extinct during the period of barbarian invasions and the early phases of Christian art but revived in the fourteenth century when the practice grew up of including the portraits of patrons and donors (and sometimes of the artist) in the groups of religious compositions. The portrait complete in itself was produced both in Italy and the Netherlands in the fifteenth century, Italian artists favouring the profile (adaptation of the medallion), as in Piero della Francesca's portraits of the Duke of Urbino and his wife. The oil medium gave the great artists of the Renaissance the means of imparting a more lifelike aspect to the features, especially by means of light and shade (e.g. Leonardo's 'Mona Lisa'), and this development extending into the seventeenth century made that period perhaps the greatest age of European portraiture, as exemplified by Rembrandt, Velazquez, Rubens and Van Dyck.

The secular spirit of art after the Reformation and the establishment of settled monarchies in Europe both contributed to give portraiture special importance from the sixteenth century onwards, Hans Holbein the younger in England and the Clouets in France giving outstanding early examples. A long tradition in England found its greatest expression in the eighteenth century with Hogarth, Gainsborough, Reynolds, Romney, Ramsay, Raeburn, Lawrence and others. A special growth was the intimate 'conversation piece'. The decline of portraiture began in the nineteenth century, two contributory factors being the rivalry of the camera and the divergence of many artists to a preoccupation with ideas and styles which paid a decreasing attention to likeness or at all events the requirements of the sitter—the portraits of Cézanne being an instance.

Poster, Art of the. As a form of graphic art, the modern poster has its ancestor in the handbills with woodcut illustrations of the past, posted up in public places and one of the first English posters by a distinguished artist, Frederick Walker's design announcing *The Woman in White* (1871), was engraved on wood. An entirely new prospect, however, as regards both scale and colour resulted from the use of colour lithography, and by his brilliant exploitation of its pictorial possibilities the French artist, Jules Chéret, may be called the 'father of the poster'. Influenced by him and by the simplified designs of Japanese prints, Toulouse-Lautrec (q.v.) achieved his great artistic triumphs in the colour lithographs he himself executed for various Parisian resorts. The purposes of art and propaganda coincided in the production of pictorial design simple and powerful enough to convey an immediate impact, a problem which it delighted

'BEGGARSTAFF BRO-
THERS'—Poster design for
Sir Henry Irving.

artists to solve in the classic age of the poster, the 1890's. Aubrey Beardsley gives an example and also the 'Beggarstaff Brothers' (William Nicholson and James Pryde, qq.v.), whose telling simplicities of design were evolved from pieces of coloured paper cut to shape and subsequently lithographed. Many famous artists since have designed posters for travel and commercial and industrial organizations, in England, for instance, E. McKnight Kauffer, Sir Frank Brangwyn, Duncan Grant, Graham Sutherland, Paul Nash and John Minton, such organizations as London Transport and Shell-Mex showing themselves enlightened patrons.

Post-Impressionism, phase of art immediately following Impressionism represented by the painters who in various ways modified, or reacted against, its guiding principles. Thus Cézanne reintroduced a sense of underlying structure as distinct from atmospheric effect, Gauguin brought back a decorative and simplified treatment of colour and form, van Gogh added a personal and emotional character to a perception of colour derived from the Impressionists and Seurat. The term was applied to the famous exhibition organized by Roger Fry at the Grafton Galleries in London in 1911, which caused much controversy, and a parallel in America was the Armory Show of 1913. *See also* CAMDEN TOWN GROUP.

Pot, Hendrik Gerritsz (*b.* Haarlem, *c.* 1585; *d.* Amsterdam, 16 Oct. 1657), Dutch painter, the pupil of Karel van Mander and friend of Frans Hals. He worked at Haarlem and Amsterdam, visiting London in 1632, when he painted the portrait of Charles I. He was the master of Willem Kalf (q.v.) and his *genre* scenes helped to inspire those of Dirck Hals.

Potter, Paulus (*b.* Enkhuizen, baptized 20 Nov. 1625; *d.* Amsterdam, buried 17 Jan. 1654), Dutch animal and landscape painter trained by his father, Pieter Simonz Potter. He worked at The Hague, Delft and Amsterdam, where he died at the early age of twenty-eight. His 'The Young Bull' (The Hague, Mauritshuis) is one of the most famous of animal pictures.

H. G. POT—A Carnival Party—National Gallery, London.

P. POTTER—Cattle in a Stormy Landscape— National Gallery, London.

Pourbus, name of a Flemish painter family which included **Pieter** (*b*. Gouda, *c*. 1510; *d*. Bruges, 1584), painter of religious and allegorical subjects and portraits. He was the pupil of Lancelot Blondeel and eminent at Bruges, where he mainly worked. **Frans the Elder** (*b*. Bruges, 1545, *d*. Antwerp, 19 Sept. 1581) was the son of Pieter and his pupil at Bruges, also studying under Frans Floris (q.v.) and working at Antwerp. Like his father he painted religious subjects and portraits. **Frans the Younger** (*b*. Antwerp, 1569–70; *d*. Paris, 1622) was the son of Frans the Elder. He painted portraits, was employed at the court of Mantua and from 1611 by Marie de' Medici in Paris. The family history throws its light on the decline of Bruges, the rise of Antwerp and the change in Flemish art due to Italian influence.

Poussin, Nicolas (*b*. Villers, nr Les Andelys, June 1594; *d*. Rome, 19 Nov. 1665), French painter and the most eminent representative of French classicism in art. Born of country folk in Normandy, he had some lessons in painting from a travelling artist, Quentin Varin, in 1611, and in the following year went to Paris, where he stayed until 1624. Information is scanty about this period, but he seems to have worked with a Flemish painter, Ferdinand Elle, to have been allowed to copy prints in the royal collection after Raphael and Giulio

N. POUSSIN—Diogenes throwing away the Cup—Louvre.

N. POUSSIN—The Inspiration of the Poet—Louvre.

Romano, to have been on friendly terms with Philippe de Champaigne (q.v.) and to have had a modicum of patronage. He was thirty when at last he attained his desire of going to Rome, where his genius reached fruition. At first he was much influenced by the Mannerist and baroque painting of the day, especially admiring Domenichino (q.v.), with whom he worked, but broadly speaking his sources of inspiration can be reduced to three: antiquity as represented by Graeco-Roman sculpture; Raphael in religious and storytelling paintings; and Titian in Bacchanalian and similar themes. From Raphael he learned how to convey the meaning of a subject by gesture, from Titian, whom he studied closely between 1636 and 1640, the value of warmth and richness of colour, Poussin's intense blue and its foil of warm orange reflecting the Venetian influence. He returned to Paris in 1640 at the request of Louis XIII to decorate the Long Gallery of the Louvre, but this proved an unhappy episode. He could no longer stand the colder climate, was unused to employing pupils and was disturbed by the intrigues and jealousies of the art world of Paris. He went back to Rome in 1642 and did not leave it again. His later work shows a growing austerity, apparent in the

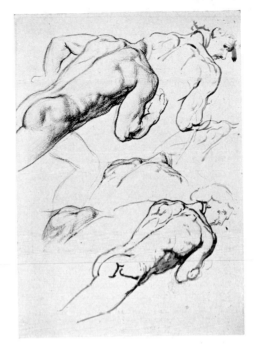

monumental calm of religious subjects, and also a growing concentration on landscape. Among his great works are 'The Inspiration of the Poet', 1636 (Louvre), 'Bacchanalian Festival', painted for Richelieu before 1641 (National Gallery), 'The Arcadian Shepherds', 1638–9 (Louvre), 'Diogenes throwing away the Cup', 1648 (Louvre), and 'The Entombment' (National Gallery of Ireland). A superb self-portrait at the age of fifty-six is in the Louvre. The beauty of ordered thought in his work places it in spiritual relation with that of Corneille, of Descartes and of Pascal.

Poynter, Sir Edward John (*b*. Paris, 20 Mar. 1836; *d*. London, 26 July 1919), English painter and official, born in Paris, son of the architect Ambrose Poynter. He studied art in Rome, where he met and was influenced by Leighton (q.v.), and in Paris. First engaged in decorative design, he turned with success to paintings of ancient history and fable, e.g. 'Visit to Aesculapius' (Tate Gallery), and was a notable draughtsman. He was first Slade Professor in London, 1871–5, Director of Art, South Kensington, 1875–81, Director of the National Gallery, 1894–1905, P.R.A., 1896–1918.

Pozzo, Fra Andrea (*b*. Trento, 30 Nov. 1642; *d*. Vienna, 31 Aug. 1709), Italian baroque painter, trained in Milan, Venice and Rome, who became a Jesuit lay brother in 1665 and a virtuoso of illusionist church decoration, the ceiling of the Jesuit church of San Ignazio, Rome, being one of his remarkable efforts. Going to Vienna in 1702, he was one of the means by which the baroque style was transmitted to Austria and south Germany.

Prado, Museo del, Madrid, established in 1819 by Ferdinand VII and Isabella of Braganza and comprising many great works accumulated by the monarchs Charles V, Philip II and Philip IV and by the religious houses of Spain. It is unquestionably the greatest collection

[197]

of Spanish masters, Velazquez, El Greco, Zurbarán, Ribera, Murillo and Goya being superbly represented. The Spanish connection with the Netherlands helps to account for the especial richness of the Flemish School, and the attachment of the Hapsburgs to Venetian art is evidenced by the wealth of paintings by Titian, Tintoretto and Veronese. It has been added to in the nineteenth and twentieth centuries by a number of bequests and by the museum's own plan for filling in gaps in the collection, though no pictures painted after 1850 are held to be eligible for inclusion.

Predella, base of an altar-piece, often painted with religious incident connected with the subjects of the main panels.

Prehistoric and Primitive Art, overlapping terms of wide and somewhat imprecise application. Thus 'prehistoric' refers to any peoples who have no history, either in the principal form of writing or in such a sequence of buildings and other material evidence as enables us to gain a coherent picture of their development. The duration of the historic period is, on this ground, some 5,000 years, and of course we accurately call 'prehistoric' the art produced in earlier times than this by people of whom otherwise we know nothing. The cardinal instance is that of the cave-dwellers of palaeolithic Europe who lived by hunting and left remarkable paintings and drawings of animals (*see* CAVE ART). On the other hand certain nomadic and hunting folk who have existed in historic and even recent times belong in effect, as far as their mode of life is concerned, to the Old Stone Age and

CAVE DRAWING—Woolly Rhinoceros (Copy by Abbé Breuil)—Musée de l'Homme, Paris.

provide a later parallel with its art. Aesthetically the most notable similarities are to be found in the naturalistic engraving on ivory of the Eskimoes of Alaska and the rock paintings and engravings of the aboriginal bushmen, found in various parts of South Africa, in which antelopes, elephants, giraffes and other animals are depicted with amazing skill and truth (*see* BUSHMAN PAINTING). The naturalistic outline art of the Australian aborigines of the northern territories in the form either of rock engravings or paintings on bark also shows some affinity with the Aurignacian art of the earlier palaeolithic period. In North Africa, rock pictures in the Atlas region of Algeria and the Hoggar mountains of the central Sahara seem to show evidence of a truly prehistoric naturalism merged with an art of later date, though no actual connection has been established between the prehistoric arts of Europe and Africa.

The advent of agriculture and a settled tribal life and the end of exclusive dependence on the hunter's quarry for food are signalized in art by the disappearance of the astonishing prehistoric realism in the depiction of animals and the development of decorative forms associated with crafts and of magic symbols reflecting the need to propitiate the gods, whose action might favourably or adversely affect the harvest. The Neolithic, Bronze and Iron Age cultures mark this development from about 3000 B.C. The term 'primitive art' may be applied to the art of any rural or coastal society at this stage, e.g. in Oceania or among the Pueblo Indians of New Mexico. This may also be distinguished from the art of cities, which represents a wider and more advanced range of needs and ideas, though primitive art is often to be called 'utilitarian' rather than necessarily 'crude'. The 'peasant art' or, as it has come to be called, 'folk art', of various European countries, in painting decorative rather than representational, is a late and diluted form of the 'primitive'. Children's art in its directness of observation and seizing of essentials has something

ANONYMOUS AMER-
ICAN PRIMITIVE (Early
Nineteenth Century) —
Portrait of Eliza Welch
Stone—Garbisch Collection.

ANONYMOUS AMERICAN PRIMITIVE (Nineteenth Century)—Meditation by the Sea—
M. and M. Karolik Collection.

in common with the art of primitive peoples and perhaps represents a transitory folk-memory. In modern usage 'primitive' has acquired some special meanings, some of these confused and confusing. 'Italian' or 'Flemish' primitive is an instance—a misleading description of the greatly accomplished art of the pre-Renaissance or early Renaissance periods in the Netherlands and Italy. The term is also applied to the work of the untutored artist, simple and uncomplicated in vision, who is to be found even in the sophisticated society of the twentieth century, Appreciation of the work of Henri Rousseau (q.v.) has led to interest in such modern primitives in France as Bombois and Bauchant (qq.v.) and in the 'primitives' of America, from the early colonial days onwards (see AMERICAN PAINTING).

Prendergast, Maurice Brazil (b. Roxbury, Massachusetts, 27 Oct. 1861; d. New York, 1 Feb. 1924), American painter of landscape and everyday life in oil- and water-colour. His early youth was spent in Boston but in 1886 he went to Paris, studying at the Académie Julian and being influenced by Impressionist painting. He also worked in Italy for some time before settling in New York. In his use of colour he advanced towards the Post-Impressionist standpoint and is of note among the pioneer observers of city life.

Pre-Raphaelite, term first applied to the German Nazarenes (q.v.), but adopted by a group of young English artists, D. G. Rossetti, Holman Hunt and J. E. Millais (qq.v.) (together with Rossetti's brother Michael, a man of letters, James Collinson, an obscure painter, Thomas Woolner, sculptor and poet, and F. G. Stephens, who became an art critic), who formed the Pre-Raphaelite Brotherhood in 1848. A reaction against the triviality of early Victorian academic art, it was based partly on Ruskin's doctrine of 'truth to nature' and partly on the idea of return to pre-Renaissance ideals. The Brotherhood (P.R.B.) did not last long, but in spite of its complexity of aim Pre-Raphaelitism in a more extended sense had immense influence. The early pictures, painted with great minuteness of detail and brilliance of colour, aroused the enthusiasm of many followers and added a new realism to the art of the 1850's. Pre-Raphaelite disciples who produced notable works are W. H. Deverell, W. L. Windus, John Brett, W. S. Burton and Robert Martineau. A second development and separate phase, stimulated by Ruskin and Rossetti, was towards the revival of handicraft and the arts of design. It was first suggested by the abortive effort to decorate the Oxford Union with 'frescoes' in 1857, in which Rossetti was assisted by William Morris, Burne-Jones and others. The firm subsequently founded by Morris carried Pre-Raphaelite art into many fields of useful design. On painting the effect of the movement was limited, and Rossetti, Hunt and Millais in various ways all showed a decline in their later work, but in the useful arts Pre-Raphaelitism, as interpreted by Morris, was the basis of much admirable effort both in England and on the Continent of Europe.

Preti, Mattia (b. Taverna, 1613; d. Malta, 1669), Italian painter of the Neapolitan School, also known as the Cavaliere Calabrese. His style was formed on that of Guercino and Caravaggio. He painted in a number of cities, Bologna, Modena, Naples and Rome, retiring finally to Malta.

Previtali, Andrea (*b*. Bergamo, *c*. 1470; *d*. there, 1528), Italian painter of religious subjects and portraits, also known as Andrea Cordeliaghi. He was a pupil of Giovanni Bellini at Venice, where he worked for some time, returning to Bergamo in 1511. His later work seems to have been influenced by Lotto.

Primary Colours, colours from which theoretically any other colour can be produced by mixing them in proper proportions, usually taken to be red, yellow and blue. A secondary colour is that obtained by the mixture of two primaries. In practice painters who have sought to translate light into colour, e.g. the Impressionists and Neo-Impressionists, have used a wider range of pigments suggested by the spectrum, violet, blue, green, yellow, orange, red. Such painters excluded black from the palette as the total absence of colour.

Primaticcio, Francesco (*b*. Bologna, 30 April 1504; *d*. Paris, 1570), Italian painter, sculptor and architect, famous as the virtual founder of the first School of Fontainebleau in France. He was the pupil of Giulio Romano (q.v.), with whom he worked, 1526–32, on the Palazzo del Tè in Mantua. He was invited to France by Francis I for the decoration of the palace of Fontainebleau, where he produced a delightful combination of painting and slender Mannerist figures in stucco. He was assisted by another Italian artist, Niccolò dell' Abbate (q.v.). Though going back to Rome and Bologna for short intervals he retained his position in France. In 1559 he became chief decorative artist to Catherine de' Medici and set up his workshop in Paris.

'Primavera', famous so-called 'Allegory of Spring' by Botticelli, painted about the same time as his 'Birth of Venus' (q.v.), *c*. 1478, for the villa at Castello near Florence belonging to Lorenzo di Pier-francesco de' Medici. It passed from the *guardaroba* of the Grand Duke into the Accademia in 1853 and thence to the Uffizi Gallery in 1919. It is a compound allegory, representing the procession of the seasons; right to left Winter, Spring, Summer and Autumn. At the same time Venus, for whom Giuliano de' Medici's favourite, Simon-etta Vespucci, provided the model, is the central figure, while other figures are Flora, the Three Graces and Mercury. (Colour, *see* list.)

Procaccini, Ercole (*b*. Bologna, 1520; *d*. Milan, 1591), Italian painter, head of a family of considerable influence in the development of painting in Milan, where Ercole founded a teaching academy. His three sons, Camillo (1546–*c*. 1629), Giulio Cesare (1548–1626) and Carlo Antonio (1555–*c*. 1605), were painters who also trained numerous Milanese artists.

Provost (Prevost), Jan (*b*. Mons, *c*. 1465; *d*. Bruges, 1529), Flemish painter of religious subjects. He studied at Valenciennes with Simon Marmion, whose widow he married, worked at Antwerp and in 1494 settled at Bruges, where he had a successful career. A painter of

P. P. PRUD'HON—The Empress Josephine—Louvre.

P. P. PRUD'HON—Portrait of Mlle Constance Mayer (Chalk Drawing)—Louvre.

transition, he followed Gerard David and Quinten Massys (qq.v.) in his early work, though with a somewhat coarse effort towards realism in facial expression. After 1521 he modelled his style on that of Dürer (q.v.), who stayed with him at Bruges.

Prud'hon, Pierre Paul (*b.* Cluny, 4 April 1758; *d.* Paris, 16 Feb. 1823), French painter educated by the monks of Cluny, and trained in art at Dijon. In 1784 he won the Prix de Rome of Burgundy and in Italy seems to have been influenced by Correggio and Pietro da Cortona (qq.v.). He exhibited frequently at the Salon from 1791 to 1822 and his work comprised portraits, allegorical, historical and amorous subjects, illustrations and decorative design. In classical subjects he was voluptuous rather than sculptural, this causing David to describe him as the 'Boucher of our time'. He was patronized by the imperial family (and designed the cradle of the King of Rome), but his seems a sad life, an early and unfortunate marriage causing him years of misery, while his attachment to his pupil, Constance Mayer, ended, to his inconsolable grief, in her suicide. Notable works are his portrait of the Empress Josephine at Malmaison, 1805 (Louvre), 'Psyche transported by the Zephyrs', 1808 (Louvre), and 'Justice and Divine Vengeance pursuing Crime', 1808, commissioned for the hall of the criminal court in the Palais de Justice and now in the Louvre. An artist of the transition from the eighteenth to the nineteenth century, he seems a Romantic in his emotionalism.

Pryde, James (*b.* Edinburgh, 30 Mar. 1866; *d.* London, 24 Feb. 1941), Scottish painter. He studied art in Edinburgh and Paris and with William Nicholson (q.v.) produced the famous 'Beggarstaff Brothers' posters, 1894–6. Esteemed as an imaginative painter, he painted pictures of Romantic gloom in which, to echoes of Guardi, Hogarth or Piranesi, he added an urban fantasy of his own.

[204]

PUVIS DE CHAVANNES—The Poor Fisherman—Louvre.

A. PYNACKER—By the Lake—Rijksmuseum, Amsterdam.

Psalter, term applied to medieval illuminated manuscripts the text of which is taken from the Book of Psalms.

Puvis de Chavannes, Pierre-Cécile (*b.* Lyons, 14 Dec. 1824; *d.* Paris, 24 Oct. 1898), the most eminent mural painter of France in the nineteenth century. He was a pupil of Henri Scheffer and Couture (q.v.) and worked for a long time in obscurity until in 1862 the panels 'Peace' and 'War', now in the museum at Amiens, attracted attention. There followed a long series of decorative works, for the Panthéon at Paris ('Life of St Genevieve'), the Hôtel de Ville, the Sorbonne and the Boston Library. He worked in oil paint on canvas cemented to the wall, developing a serene style in which forms were simplified and areas of colour were flat and delicate, thus not breaking but becoming harmoniously associated with the plane of the wall. This simplification impressed artists at the end of the century in revolt against Impressionism, and its effect is to be seen in the work of Gauguin as well as others such as Maurice Denis (q.v.) and Paul Sérusier.

Pynacker, Adam (*b.* Pynacker, nr Delft, baptized 13 Feb. 1622; *d.* Amsterdam, buried 28 Mar. 1673), Dutch landscape painter and engraver who worked in Italy and was successful on his return to Holland with decorative paintings of wooded hills with figures and animals, in a glowing light reminiscent of Claude.

Pynas, Jan (*b.* Amsterdam, *c.* 1580; *d.* there, buried 27 Dec. 1631), Dutch painter who worked with his brother Jacob in Rome, acquiring an Italianate style. His warm tones and massing of light and shade had some influence on the young Rembrandt in imaginative composition.

Q

Queen Mary's Psalter, famous example of fourteenth-century English illumination now in the British Museum. It gains its name from having been intercepted at the customs in 1553 when being sent abroad, and it was subsequently presented to the Tudor Queen Mary. It contains illustrations of biblical history from the Creation to the death of Solomon, the drawings being lightly treated with colour. There are also miniatures of New Testament scenes and figures of saints and representations of medieval life and work.

QUEEN MARY'S PSALTER (Early Fourteenth Century) — Occupations of the Months — September, Treading Grapes.

R

Raeburn, Sir Henry (*b.* Stockbridge, Edinburgh, 4 Mar. 1756; *d.* Edinburgh, 8 July 1823), most famous of Scottish portrait painters. Largely self-taught, he began by painting miniatures, married a widow of some fortune, went to London, *c.* 1778, and on the advice of Reynolds to Italy in 1785, returning to Edinburgh in 1787 to take a foremost place as portrait painter. A Doric equivalent of Reynolds, he painted the notabilities of literature and law in the great period of Edinburgh's intellectual eminence, also the chieftains of the Highland clans. He excelled rather in male than female portraits, his broad brush-stroke being well adapted to convey rugged dignity of feature. He made the most of a limited range in composition and colour and his full-lengths have dramatic force, as in the 'Macdonell of Glengarry' of the National Gallery of Scotland (a main repository of his art). He exhibited regularly at the Royal Academy in London, 1792–1823, and, as well as being President of the Royal Scottish Academy (1812), was R.A., 1815, and knighted by George IV on his visit to Edinburgh, 1822, being also appointed His Majesty's Limner for Scotland.

Raffaellino del Garbo (**Raffaelle Capponi**) (*b.* Florence, *c.* 1470; *d. c.* 1526), Italian painter of the Florentine School, probably the pupil of Filippino Lippi (q.v.), whom he is said to have assisted in the frescoes of Santa Maria sopra Minerva, Rome.

'Raft of the "Medusa", The', painting by Géricault exhibited in the Salon of 1819 as 'Scène de Naufrage', now in the Louvre under the title of 'Le Radeau de la *Méduse*. He depicts a tragic episode of 1816 after the wreck of the frigate *Medusa*—the moment when its raft, which had drifted helplessly for twelve days, with fifteen dead or dying left of its original complement, was sighted by the brig *Argus*. In its emotional expression it is one of the major products of French Romanticism. It was acquired for the collection of Charles X after the artist's death in 1824.

'Rain, Steam and Speed; the Great Western Railway', painting by Turner in the National Gallery exhibited at the Royal Academy in 1844, one of the most impressionist and atmospheric of his later works. It interprets the feeling of travel by rail in the 1840's and, though nothing is precisely defined, the scene was apparently between Taplow and Maidenhead. (Colour, *see* list.)

Ramsay, Allan (*b.* Edinburgh, 1713; *d.* Dover, 10 Aug. 1784), Scottish portrait painter, the eldest son of the poet of that name. Unlike his younger contemporary and rival, Reynolds, he sought for grace rather than grandeur in European models, acquiring in his earlier work a baroque elegance from his studies in Naples and Rome

SIR H. RAEBURN—Colonel Alastair Macdonell of Glengarry—National Gallery of Scotland.

GÉRICAULT—The Raft of the 'Medusa'—Louvre.

and profiting by the example of Solimena and Batoni; later delighting in the rococo delicacy of the French, Nattier, Perronneau and Quentin de la Tour. This European cultivation made him highly esteemed when he returned from Italy in 1736, and in 1761 he was appointed Painter-in-Ordinary to George III in preference to Reynolds. He is noted for the charm of his female portraiture, especially between 1754 and 1766, as in his masterpiece, the portrait of Margaret Lindsay, his second wife, 1755 (National Gallery of Scotland). He was devoted to drawing and the value of this study can be seen in his admirable full-lengths, e.g. of Lady Mary Coke (Collection, Marquess of Bute). After the 1760's he delegated much to assistants and 'drapery men', such as Joseph van Haeken, taking up literary pursuits and being one of the Johnsonian circle.

Raphael (Raffaello Santi or **Sanzio)** (*b.* Urbino, 6 April 1483; *d.* Rome, 6 April 1520), great Italian painter of the Roman School and the Renaissance at its height, the son of Giovanni Santi, a painter of some note. The family house still stands and a wall-painting of the Madonna and Child is thought to be a portrait of his mother Magia di Battista Ciarla and her little son. His mother died when he was eight and his father two years later, though Raphael as a child may have had early lessons from him. He was then apprenticed to the painter Timoteo Viti at Perugia and subsequently entered the studio of Perugino (q.v.) there, where he also came under the influence of Pintoricchio (q.v.). The gentle beauty of Perugino's compositions was his ideal during this first period, from about 1500 to 1504. It is

ALLAN RAMSAY—Portrait of Lady Mary Coke—Collection, Marquess of Bute.

most probable that parts of Perugino's pictures are attributable to Raphael, who also absorbed the best qualities of his master and exemplifies them in his independent early productions. His first important commission was an altar-piece for Città di Castello, 1500-1, carried out in collaboration with Evangelista di Meleto, a pupil of his father. Other works of the first period are the 'Vision of a Knight' and 'Crucifixion' (National Gallery), the 'St Michael' and 'St George' (Louvre), the 'Three Graces' (Chantilly) and the 'Coronation of the Virgin' (Vatican); the period culminating in 'Lo Sposalizio' ('The Marriage of the Virgin') of 1504 (Milan, Brera). During the four years in Florence which followed he came under new influences, those of Leonardo, Michelangelo and Fra Bartolommeo, and this was a time of readjustment, fresh assimilation and enlargement of knowledge. He studied and made drawings after the great Florentines. His art went through a transitional phase, examples of which are the 'Madonna del Granduca' (Pitti), the 'Madonna del Cardellino' (Uffizi), the 'Belle Jardinière' (Louvre), the 'Entombment' (Rome, Borghese) and the 'Ansidei Madonna' (National Gallery). Transition can be seen in the style of his portraits of the art collector, Angelo Doni, and his wife Maddalena (Pitti), the latter being modelled on Leonardo's 'Mona Lisa', though with Peruginesque detail. The Roman period following, 1508-20, saw the full expansion of his genius, stimulated not only by the example of Michelangelo but by the grandeur of the city and its classical antiquities. He began his great series of decorations in the Vatican for Pope Julius II in 1509, and the amount of work he produced after this date was prodigious. In the series of apartments and offices known as the Stanze he and his

RAPHAEL—The Miraculous Draught of Fishes (Cartoon)—Victoria and Albert Museum.

assistants produced the frescoes which are one of the supreme
Renaissance achievements, unrivalled except by Michelangelo, who
was painting the ceiling of the Sistine Chapel at the same time. The
frescoes of the Stanza della Segnatura (a court-room) came first, with
representations of Religion, Poetry, Philosophy and Justice, the
'Disputà' (in which the Glory of Christianity is the theme), the
'Parnassus' and the so-called 'School of Athens' (the development of
human knowledge) being its superb conceptions. The Stanza d'Eliodoro, 1512–14, commemorating the achievements of Julius II,
included the serene perfection of the 'Mass of Bolsena'. The Stanza
dell' Incendio was painted by assistants from Raphael's designs; so,
after his death, were the Sala di Costantino and the Loggie of the
Vatican, 1517–19. In the last decade of his short life Raphael was
overwhelmed with work. It included responsibility as architect to
St Peter's and supervisor of antiquities; the designs for tapestries in
the Vatican for Leo X; frescoes in the Farnesina, Rome; and numerous
easel paintings. The seven of the ten cartoons for tapestry from the
lives of St Peter and St Paul (Victoria and Albert Museum) are
second only to the Stanze in magnificence. Other masterpieces are the
'Galatea' (Farnesina), the Sistine Madonna, c. 1513 (Dresden), the
portraits of Leo X and of Baldassare Castiglione, and his last

RAPHAEL—Portrait of Baldassare Castiglione—Louvre.

work, left unfinished, the 'Transfiguration' (Vatican). Raphael's immediate followers included such able decorative painters as Giulio Romano, Giovanni da Udine and Perino del Vaga, but his work after his death continued to make a wide and profound impression on what artists produced, and its influence was disseminated by the engravings of Marcantonio Raimondi (q.v.). It was a force that could either make or mar, splendidly utilized by Correggio, Rubens, Poussin, Rembrandt, though with lesser artists turning into an empty religiosity or academicism, as in the nineteenth century. Such deviations of course do not detract from his own lofty eminence and richly creative power.

Realism in art may be considered generally the antithesis of idealism, that is the representation of things as they are and not in some imagined perfection. As a doctrine or theory, however, it had its origin in the 1840's and was maintained by Gustave Courbet (q.v.), to the extent that it was his aim to 'interpret the manners and customs, ideas and aspect of my own time'. It was an inevitable development of the nineteenth century when both classical and romantic subject-matter had lost significance. Manet redefined it as 'contemporanéité'—and the aim of being contemporary became a dominant motive in French art as regards both subject and style. Impressionism in both respects may be looked on as an extension of Realism. A distinct shade of meaning attaches to Social Realism, the art which reflects a critical attitude to society and reveals its shortcomings and abuses. It is found in a phase of English painting and illustration of the 1870's and 1880's and again in America during the Depression of the 1930's. This again is distinct from the Socialist Realism of Soviet art which is a form of illustrative propaganda.

Redon, Odilon (*b.* Bordeaux, 22 April 1840; *d.* Paris, 6 July 1916), French painter and lithographer of imaginative and literary mind. He studied art in Bordeaux and Paris, 1862–9, painted for some years in Brittany and at Fontainebleau, but first made his mark by lithographs (which occupied him almost exclusively from 1879 to 1890), fantastic and dream-like and inspired by Poe, Baudelaire, Huysmans and the graphic work of Goya. From 1890 onwards he entered a new phase in oil and pastel, using brilliant colour, iridescent flowerpieces being typical. A friend of Mallarmé, he is associated with the Symbolist movement, though he was always an independent spirit. He wrote much on art, and his journal *À Soi-Même* and his letters are expansive on his thoughts and beliefs. He may be looked on as one of the precursors of Surrealism.

Rembrandt Harmenz van Rijn (*b.* Leyden, 15 July 1606; *d.* Amsterdam, buried 8 Oct. 1669), Dutch painter and graphic artist, one of the greatest European masters in imaginative power, profound human insight and the range and variety of his work as oil painter, draughtsman and etcher. The fourth son of a prosperous miller, he first studied painting in the studio of Jan van Swanenburgh at Leyden, in which he spent three years, then for some six months under Pieter Lastman (q.v.) at Amsterdam, through these two painters, especially Lastman, and other contemporaries who had visited Italy, such as Honthorst (q.v.), acquiring the dramatic use of light and shade they had learned from Caravaggio. It appears already in his early works when set up as a painter in Leyden, 'The Philosopher' (National Gallery) being a remarkable example. In 1631 he

REMBRANDT—The Anatomy Lesson of Dr J. Deyman—Rijksmuseum, Amsterdam.

REMBRANDT—The Philosopher—National Gallery, London.

settled at Amsterdam and there followed ten brilliant and happy years. In 1632 he became celebrated by his group portrait of the Amsterdam Guild of Surgeons round an opened corpse, 'The Anatomy Lesson of Dr Tulp' (The Hague, Mauritshuis). In 1634 he married the daughter of wealthy parents, Saskia van Uilenburgh, who became the centre of his life and art. A joyous work is the portrait of the two together (Dresden) and he painted Saskia in various roles (as 'Flora' in the National Gallery portrait of 1635). Rembrandt prospered in portrait painting. He spent lavishly on an art collection and personal finery. In 1641 his son Titus was born.

The year 1642, however, saw a change of fortune. Saskia died. The famous group known as 'The Night Watch' (the Company of Captain Frans Banning Cocq and Lieutenant Willem van Ruytenburch—Rijksmuseum) marked the beginning of a decline in popularity, being unconventional in arrangement and not giving the equal importance to each person portrayed that his clients wished for. The years which followed seem sombre. The widower became bankrupt. His peasant housekeeper Hendrickje Stoffels, however, took care of him and Titus and acted as model, and his industry remained intense. In spiritual quality his work increased in power, including such superb late masterpieces as 'The Syndics of the Cloth Guild' and 'The Jewish Bride' (Rijksmuseum). Between 600 and 700 paintings, 300 etchings and nearly 2,000 drawings show the development of his genius, His self-portraits, from youth to old age, are a wonderful analytic study of his appearance and state of mind, most moving being those of his last years; in general Rembrandt is greatly inspired in the representation of the aged. In landscape (taking some hints from Hercules Seghers and van Goyen) he could produce such a magnificent work as 'The Stone Bridge' (Rijksmuseum). In biblical subjects he progressed from the theatrical magnificence of 'The Woman taken in Adultery' (National Gallery), with its small

REMBRANDT—Saskia as 'Flora'—National Gallery, London.

figures and immense background, to an intensely human interpretation of Christian story. Rembrandt's technical resource matches
his thought. In oils his rich impasto creates living substance and
solids. In many etchings and in his drawings another faculty comes
into play; he is swift, free and fresh, though in etching he also achieves
such elaborate triumphs as the 'Hundred Guilder' print ('Christ healing the Sick') and the 'Three Trees'. Rembrandt was buried in the
Wester Kerk at Amsterdam and his house in the city is now a
Rembrandt museum.

Renaissance, in art a change of outlook, marking the end of the
Middle Ages and reaching its climax at the beginning of the sixteenth
century. It had its origin and main triumphs in Italy. It is related to
literature and archaeological study in so far as it signalized a revived
interest in the classic past, though this may be considered an aspect
of the emancipation of the mind from medieval restrictions and conventions and was combined with the new desire for knowledge and
the free exercise of creative ability. The fall of Constantinople in 1452
and the discovery of the New World are often regarded as important
factors in creating this attitude, though the steady progress of

Italian art from Giotto
in the fourteenth cen-
tury indicates a gradual
evolution. One can
distinguish a 'proto-
Renaissance' extending
from Giotto's time to
the fifteenth century,
somewhat influenced by
Greek sculpture and
Roman narrative sculp-
ture but mainly by a
desire to gain a com-
mand of means, i.e. in
perspective, anatomy
and the representation
of space and dramatic
action. Antonio and
Piero Pollaiuolo, Andrea
del Castagno, Masaccio
and Paolo Uccello (qq.v.)

A. DEL CASTAGNO—
Portrait of Dante Alighieri
—Convent of Santa Appol-
lonia.

[218]

illustrate these tendencies. Botticelli is an instance of the great artist torn between science and poetry, sensual expression and the remaining medieval tradition. What is known as the 'High' Renaissance is the fruition of this period in which, from the end of the fifteenth century to the early years of the sixteenth, technical advance and intellectual freedom were combined in the works of a remarkable series of great men: the Florentines Leonardo da Vinci and Michelangelo; Raphael; Correggio of Parma; and in Venice Giorgione and Titian. The Renaissance ideal was in one sense that of the 'complete man' of whom Leonardo, painter and scientist, and Michelangelo, painter, sculptor, architect and poet, furnish unique examples. It may be said that the Renaissance ended with the sack of Rome in 1527, though as gradual steps have to be noted in its decline or change as in its beginnings. Mannerism and baroque art (qq.v.) stem from it. It was not limited to Italy, and Dürer, the contemporary of Raphael, represents it in Germany. What is called 'French Renaissance', however, is an aspect of the Mannerism which followed the great period. The later effects of the Renaissance in Italy are now represented by the terms Mannerism and baroque. While Shakespeare may in one aspect be considered a Renaissance genius, visual art in England was unaffected by the Renaissance style or spirit.

Reni, Guido (*b.* Calvenzano, nr Bologna, 4 Nov. 1575; *d.* Bologna, 18 Aug. 1642), Italian painter of the Bolognese School. He first studied at Bologna under the Flemish painter Denis Calvaert (q.v.), but afterwards entered the academy of the Carracci and became one of the principal adherents of Annibale Carracci (q.v.). He went to Rome about 1600, where, though belonging to an opposite camp, he seems to have been influenced to some extent by Caravaggio. He was, however, more greatly impressed by Raphael and antique sculpture. It is a Raphaelesque grace that characterizes his most celebrated work, the ceiling painting of 'Aurora preceding the Chariot of Apollo' in the Casino Rospigliosi, Rome, 1610. Apart from a visit to Naples in 1621 he worked mainly in Bologna. He was esteemed among the great masters for his skill in composition and the silvery colour of his later manner until the nineteenth century, when the

G. RENI—Aurora preceding the Chariot of Apollo—Galleria Rospigliosi, Rome.

predecessors of Raphael replaced his successors in favour. Guido was then and has since been criticized for sweetness of sentiment and empty theatricality. He had many pupils and his historical importance in the development of the baroque style is unquestionable.

Renoir, Pierre Auguste (*b*. Limoges, 25 Feb. 1841; *d*. Cagnes, 2 Dec. 1919), French painter, one of the greatest nineteenth-century masters. One of the five sons of a poor tailor (and himself pursued by poverty for forty years), he began his career in a porcelain factory painting designs on china, then earned a little money by copying eighteenth-century pictures on fans and similar work, in 1862 entering the *atelier* of Gleyre, where he made friends with Monet, Sisley and Bazille. With them he worked at Fontainebleau, and in company with Monet on the Seine near Paris, a favourite subject with both being the bathing place, 'La Grenouillère'. His early pictures show the influence of Courbet (q.v.), e.g. the portrait of Sisley and his wife, 1868 (Cologne), but after the Franco-Prussian War (in which he served as cuirassier), with Monet at Argenteuil, he produced riverscapes completely Impressionist in their atmospheric colour, such as the 'Regatta, Argenteuil', 1874. Thus associated with Impressionism and exhibiting at the Impressionist exhibitions in the 1870's, Renoir was never a theorist or addicted primarily to landscape, and many beautiful works show his main delight to be in human life and the female model, 'The Loge', 1874 (Courtauld

P. A. RENOIR—Dancing at the Moulin de la Galette—Louvre.

Gallery)—a work painted in the studio—'Dancing at the Moulin de la Galette', 1876 (main version, Louvre), and 'Madame Charpentier and her Daughters', 1879 (New York, Metropolitan Museum), being examples. A reaction against impressionism began in the 1880's after he had visited Italy, where he was influenced by the Graeco-Roman paintings from Pompeii at Naples and by a stay at L'Estaque with Cézanne (also concerned with solid and permanent qualities in painting). A harder, linear manner resulted, as in 'The Umbrellas', c. 1884 (National Gallery), and 'The Bathers', 1887. This gave way to his later style in which figures were treated loosely but plastically with colour of Mediterranean warmth. Severely affected by arthritis from 1902, he continued to paint, and in 1913, though entirely crippled, he guided assistants in the production of sculpture, e.g. 'Venus Victrix' (Tate Gallery). His vast and splendid output is widely distributed, but many important works are in America, where his genius was early and enthusiastically recognized.

Repin, Ilya Efimovich (b. Chuguyev, Ukraine, 1844; d. Kuokkala, Finland, 29 Sept. 1930), Russian painter of portraits, historical and genre subjects. He studied at the Academy of Fine Arts, St Petersburg, then travelled in France and Italy. In 1894 he was appointed professor of historical painting at the St Petersburg Academy. He was noted for his portraits of Tolstoi and such scenes of Russian life as his 'Volga Boatmen', 'The Return from Siberia' and 'The Cossacks' Jeering Reply to the Sultan Mahomet IV'.

Retable, architectural frame or screen behind the altar of a church, decorated with painting, carving or other ornament, taking a distinctive form and elaboration in Spain (Sp. *retablo*), in the fifteenth and sixteenth centuries.

Rethel, Alfred (b. Diepenbend, nr Aix-la-Chapelle, 15 May 1816; d. Düsseldorf, 1 Dec. 1859), German painter and graphic artist. He studied at the Academy of Düsseldorf and was commissioned when twenty-five to paint the frescoes in the Kaisersaal at Aix (Aachen), but is mainly remembered by two series of designs engraved on wood, 'Hannibal's Passage over the Alps' and his versions of the traditional Dance of Death theme, 1848. The latter are masterpieces of powerful macabre design, the style of which had an appreciable influence on English illustration of the 1860's. In his later years he became insane.

Reymerswael, Marinus van (? 1497–1570), Flemish subject painter, whose name indicates he was born at Reimerswaal (a town subsequently swallowed by the sea) in Zeeland, the pupil of a glass painter at Antwerp but mainly an imitator of Quinten Massys (q.v.). Most of his paintings (e.g. in Uffizi and National Gallery) were free adaptations of Massys's subject, the Banker (or Money Changer or Usurer) and his Wife, with an addition of caricature, though the popularity of this subject perhaps depended as much on the carefully painted detail, parchments, candle, inkhorn, piles of coin, etc. He also adapted Dürer's St Jerome. Dated works are from 1521 to 1560.

M. VAN REYMERSWAEL
—Two Bankers or Usurers
—National Gallery, London.

For his part in the iconoclastic riots at Middelburg it seems he was sentenced in 1567 to public penitence and exile.

Reynolds, Sir Joshua (*b.* Plympton, Devon, 16 July 1723; *d.* London, 23 Feb. 1792), English portrait painter and aesthetician, the son of the Rev. Samuel Reynolds (master of Plympton Grammar School and sometime fellow of Balliol). He spent three years as apprentice to Hudson in London, painting both in London and Devonshire until in 1749 Commodore Keppel took him on H.M.S. *Centurion* to the Mediterranean. The three years' stay in Italy thus made possible was an important turning-point in his career. While painting portraits of visitors (and some of the caricature groups then popular) he made an intelligent and careful study of Renaissance art both in Rome and Venice. There were two results: the infusion into his own painting of that learning and dignity which distinguish it and the stimulation of those ideas of the 'Grand Style' and a European hierarchy of art which he was to expound so well in his discourses to the students of the Royal Academy, 1769–90. Settled in London in 1753 he quickly became the most eminent portrait painter of his day and, with the formation of the Royal Academy in 1768, the first and greatest of its presidents. He was knighted in 1769 and succeeded Allan Ramsay as Painter-in-Ordinary to George III. though never enjoying so much royal favour as Ramsay or Gainsborough. Yet the procession of aristocratic and other sitters to his house in Leicester Fields was endless and his learning and personality made him the centre of a brilliant group, president of the famous Literary Club and friend of Johnson, Burke, Goldsmith, Sheridan and Garrick. His keen intelligence is apparent in his judiciously eclectic art, which owes as much to Rembrandt as to the Florentines or Venetians (e.g. in the noble self-portrait—Royal Academy), and reinforces by variety of pose and composition the psychological insight and sympathy of his portraiture. Portraits of men of letters, e.g. his 'Dr Johnson' and 'Sterne', are among his best; children too

[222]

SIR J. REYNOLDS—Nelly O'Brien—Wallace Collection.

have a special place in his work. While he is noted less for portraits of women, his 'Nelly O'Brien' (Wallace Collection) is a masterpiece of charm. Here his colour can be appreciated, though too often his experimental taste and desire for richness led to such errors as the use of bitumen which has disfigured many of his canvases. The 'Grand Style' has only a frustrated and experimental place in his own art, but his written exposition of it remains lucid and inspiring, and as a teacher Reynolds was far from deserving mockery such as that of Blake. He is justly regarded as a leader and formative power of the English School.

Ribalta, Francisco (b. Solsona, Catalonia, 1565; d. Valencia, 1628), Spanish painter who worked in his youth in Madrid, where he seems to have been influenced by the paintings of such Italian Mannerists as Sebastiano del Piombo (q.v.). After 1599 he lived and worked in Valencia, developing those 'tenebrist' effects of dark shadow in which he was the first of artists in Spain to express a sombre fervour (distinct from the spiritual exaltation of El Greco) appropriate to scenes of torture and martyrdom. He has sometimes been supposed to have derived his style from the study of Caravaggio, though he had begun to cultivate it before Caravaggio started to paint. 'The Crucifixion' (Leningrad, Hermitage), 'Christ embracing St Bernard' (Prado), 'The Last Supper' (Valencia) and 'The Vision of Father Simón' (National Gallery) are among his principal works. Ribera (q.v.) is said to have first studied with him. Ribalta's son, Juan (b. Valencia, 1596; d. 1628), was his pupil and collaborated with him.

Ribera, Jusepe de (b. Jativa, nr Valencia, Feb. 1591; d. Naples, 2 Sept. 1652), Spanish painter and etcher who may possibly have studied under Ribalta (q.v.) in his early days but by 1616 had settled in Naples, where his life was mainly spent. Naples was then under Spanish rule, and Ribera, known as 'Lo Spagnoletto', often emphasized his Spanish origin by adding 'Jativa' or 'Valencia' to

J. DE RIBERA—The Boy
with a Club Foot—Louvre.

his signature, but his
style was derived from
Caravaggio and his Nea-
politan followers. Like
Ribalta and in the
spirit of his time and
country he painted
gloomy religious sub-
jects of martyrdom and
torture, though these
were varied by realistic
studies of common
types in which the
'naturalism' derived
from Caravaggio was
opposed to the 'idealism'
of the School of Bologna.
He enjoyed great favour
with the Spanish vice-
roys of Naples, though
he is said to have terror-
ized such rivals as Guido
Reni and Domenichino
with threats and acts
of violence. Many of
his works went back
to Spain and he may be
directly credited with having introduced into his native country
the Caravaggesque light and shade and attitude to art. Though
he never abandoned his brown shadows he made some progress
towards richness and luminosity of colour in his mature work, of
which the 'Martyrdom of St Bartholomew', ?1639 (Prado), is an
example. One of his last paintings, the 'Boy with a Club Foot', 1652
(Louvre), is a masterpiece of realism, while such studies of types
(represented as celebrities of antiquity) as his 'Aesop' and 'Archi-
medes' (Prado) are in a vein which Velazquez pursued.

Ricci, name of two Italian artists of the eighteenth-century
Venetian School. **Sebastiano** (*b*. Belluno, 1 Aug. 1660; *d*. Venice, 15
May 1734) studied at Venice and Bologna and worked in a number of
Italian cities, Florence, Parma, Modena, Milan, as well as visiting
Rome and Vienna, where he worked in the Schönbrunn Palace. In
1712 he went to England with his nephew Marco Ricci, both leaving
in 1716, when Sir James Thornhill was preferred as decorator of the
dome of St Paul's and for other work at Hampton Court. The

S. RICCI AND M. RICCI—The Adoration of the Kings—Royal Collection, Buckingham Palace.

'Resurrection' (Chelsea Hospital Chapel) is by Sebastiano. He was noted for the skill with which he imitated Veronese and his lighter touch is intermediary between Veronese's decorative style and that of Ticpolo, whom he influenced. **Marco** (*b.* Belluno, 1676; *d.* Venice, 1730), his nephew and pupil, worked in Turin, Rome, Florence and Milan as well as England and Holland, visiting London for the first time in 1708, when he painted scenery for the Italian Opera. He initiated a style of rococo landscape, often with fanciful architecture, a number of such landscapes being painted in *gouache* on kid-skin. Works by both Riccis are numerous in the Royal Collection.

Ricciarelli, Daniele, *see* VOLTERRA.

Rigaud, Hyacinthe (*b.* Perpignan, 18 July 1659; *d.* Paris, 29 Dec. 1743), French portrait painter who first studied at Montpellier and Lyons and went to Paris in 1681. Though he won the Prix de Rome in 1685 he was advised by Le Brun (q.v.) to stay in Paris instead of going to Italy, becoming a successful court painter to Louis XIV, after Louis's death to the regent, Philippe d'Orléans, and later to Louis XV. The style of his earlier portraits, formal and grandiose, culminates in the pomp of his 'Louis XIV' (Louvre). Afterwards he developed a more intimate and natural approach, some works showing the influence of Rembrandt, seven paintings by whom were in his possession in 1703. Many replicas were required of him and he had a busy studio, few works being entirely the product of his own hand.

Rijksmuseum, Amsterdam, national gallery of Holland, built in the late nineteenth century, the nucleus of the collection consisting of pictures belonging to the House of Orange and Netherlandish art having pride of place. All the Dutch masters are abundantly represented, Rembrandt's 'Night Watch' and Vermeer's 'The Letter' and 'The Little Street' being among its great treasures. A series of rooms is designed to show the changes and developments of Dutch culture.

H. RIGAUD—Louis XIV—
Louvre.

Riley (Ryley), John (*b.* London, 1646; *d.* there, 1691), English portrait painter, son of the Keeper of Records in the Tower and a pupil of Gerard Soest. He had a large practice in succession to Lely, painted portraits of Charles II and James II and his queen and with Kneller was appointed court painter to William and Mary. He was not above painting minor domestic members of the royal household and his portrait of Charles II was candid enough to have evoked, it is said, the royal comment: 'Odd's fish, I'm an ugly fellow.' Pepys was among his sitters. Works by him are in the National Portrait Gallery, Royal Collection and at Oxford.

Rivera, Diego (*b.* Guanajuato, 8 Dec. 1886; *d.* 1957), Mexican painter and graphic artist, a leader in the renaissance of Mexican art that followed the revolution of 1910. He studied and worked in Europe between 1907 and 1921, being somewhat influenced by Cubism and by the 'classical' period of Picasso, but on his return to Mexico devoted himself to depicting Mexican life and history, developing a bold, narrative style and often showing a strong revolutionary or anti-capitalist bias in subject. He painted murals in Mexico and also, 1930–4, in the United States at San Francisco, Detroit and New York. Disagreement with the sponsors led to the replacement of his work at Rockefeller Center, New York, by a mural painting by Sir Frank Brangwyn. He used both the true fresco method and a form of encaustic wall painting. Notable among his wall-paintings in Mexico are those for the National Preparatory School, the Ministry of Education, the chapel at Chapingo, the Governor's Palace, Cuernavaca, the Palace of Fine Arts and the Institute of Cardiology.

Robert, Hubert (*b.* Paris, 22 May 1733; *d.* there, 15 April 1808), French painter and garden designer, also known as 'Robert des

DIEGO RIVERA—Flower Festival: Feast of Santa Anita, 1931—Museum of Modern Art, New York.

Ruines'. He studied drawing with the sculptor Slodtz and when twenty-one was taken to Italy by his patron, the future Duc de Choiseul. Influenced by Panini and Piranesi (qq.v.), he painted in Rome many pictures of classical ruins real and imaginary, with eighteenth-century figures. He became friendly with Fragonard (q.v.), with whom he painted in the gardens of the Villa d'Este for the dilettante Abbé de Saint Non, each having some influence on the other in style. Returning to Paris in 1765, he made prolific use of his Italian studies in pictures, decorative panels and in a classical-romantic style of garden design. He was garden designer to the king, 1778, and in 1784 was made keeper of the royal art collection and lodged in the Louvre. Imprisoned during the Revolution (when he sketched prison scenes), he was released after the fall of Robespierre and later painted a number of pictures of Paris.

Roberti, Ercole d'Antonio de (b. Ferrara, c. 1450+ ; d. there, 1496), Italian painter, one of the founders of the Ferrarese School. He seems to have been a pupil of Francesco Cossa (q.v.), with whom he may have worked at Bologna, and to have been influenced by Cosimo Tura and also by Jacopo Bellini (qq.v.). An altar-piece of 1480 now in the Brera, Milan, is a principal work, others being the 'Pietà' (Liverpool, Walker Gallery), two panels at Dresden of scenes from the Passion and 'The Israelites gathering Manna' (National Gallery). He worked for the Este court at Ferrara.

Rococo (Fr. *rocaille*, shell-work, grotto decoration), decorative eighteenth-century style which followed in the wake of baroque (q.v.). It emerged in France about 1700 and is associated with the relaxing of tension that followed the death of Louis XIV, and with the charm and frivolity of court life that replaced a severe and formal discipline. In painting it is marked by the choice of fanciful and amorous themes treated with a graceful delicacy of handling and a certain artificiality, impressiveness of subject yielding place to an

E. DE ROBERTI—The Israelites gathering Manna—National Gallery, London.

elegance that harmonized with the dainty curvature and ornamental furnishing of the aristocratic interior. It is represented by Watteau, Boucher and Fragonard but was to some extent an international style. Tiepolo and Marco and Sebastiano Ricci give Venetian examples, and Goya's paintings for tapestry illustrate its influence in Spain. Established late in England, it dominated decorative art in silver and porcelain between 1750 and 1760 and had some effect on painting. The French imitator of Watteau, Philippe Mercier (1689–1760), introduced a form of rococo conversation piece. The curved line of Hogarth's *Analysis of Beauty* is a rococo conception and an element of the rococo grace appears in the art of Gainsborough. In France in the second half of the eighteenth century it gave way by degrees to the new and more austere mood of Neo-Classicism (*see* CLASSICISM) and was finally swept away by the Revolution in 1789 as part of the luxury and a symbol of the failings of the *ancien régime*.

Roelas, Juan de las (*b.* Seville, 1560; *d.* 1625), Spanish painter who seems to have studied at Venice, being influenced by Tintoretto. He worked at Seville, among his principal religious paintings being the 'Death of St Isidore' and the 'Martyrdom of St Andrew'. Zurbarán (q.v.) was his pupil.

'Rokeby Venus, The', only surviving painting of a nude by Velazquez, now in the National Gallery. It was painted in 1651 or perhaps earlier at the time of Velazquez's second visit to Italy and in emulation of Titian. Its actual title is 'The Toilet of Venus' but the description by which it is popularly known refers to its having been in the Morritt collection at Rokeby Hall, Yorkshire, before its acquisition by the National Gallery. (Colour, *see* list.)

Roman Painting in imperial times was the anonymous product of the painter-decorators who were either Greek or imitators of the Greek style of painting. The principal though not the only source of our knowledge of this form of art is the wall-painting found in the Campanian cities of Pompeii, Herculaneum and Stabiae which were

GRAECO-ROMAN PAINTING—The Three Graces—Photo: Alinari.

GRAECO-ROMAN PAINT-
ING (Pompeii)—Girls play-
ing the Game of Knuckle-
bones—Museo Nazionale,
Naples.

GRAECO-ROMAN PAINT-
ING (Herculaneum)—
Theseus victorious over the
Minotaur—Museo Nazion-
ale, Naples.

GRAECO-ROMAN PAINT-
ING—Landscape with Fig-
ures—Museo Nazionale,
Naples.

GRAECO-ROMAN PAINT-
ING—Details of fresco from
the Villa of the Dionysiac
Mysteries—Pompeii.

GRAECO-ROMAN PAINTING—The Aldobrandini Marriage—Vatican Museum.

buried by the eruption of Vesuvius in A.D. 79. In these cities, then full of new buildings, it may be assumed that a large number of works were of the first century, though at least four different types of decoration have been distinguished there and in excavations of other ancient Roman buildings: (1) a painted imitation of marble wall panels, second century B.C.—Masonry Style; (2) architectural illusion with landscape or figures—Architectural Style, first century B.C.; (3) use of elaborate decorative motifs—Ornate Style; (4) renewed effort to give dimensional illusion to the wall—Intricate Style. The Pompeian paintings include copies of what were obviously Greek masterpieces if judged only by their dignity of style and composition, but the subject-matter is varied and includes still life and even comic or grotesque themes. The popular element is perhaps due to the native artist following his own bent and not reproducing Greek models. Landscape appears in the Scenes from the Odyssey, first century B.C., preserved in the Vatican. 'Graeco-Roman' portraiture is impressively represented by the heads on mummy cases painted in encaustic found in the hellenized districts of Egypt and dating from the first to third centuries A.D. Their gravity and the concentration on the eyes may perhaps be traced in Byzantine work and, in a final stylization, in the rigid formula of the icon (q.v.). The painting of the classical period left its imprint of style in the Christian art of the catacombs at Rome (*see* EARLY CHRISTIAN PAINTING), and there are later traces of the tradition (*see* ROME). The Roman codex (*see* CODEX) provides the origin of the illuminated manuscript and comparison of the Virgil fragment, third or fourth century A.D., preserved in the Vatican Library, and the Genesis (Vienna, fifth century) has pointed to the continuance of the classical style in the earliest Christian manuscripts. The Renaissance painters, notably Raphael, studied such remains of ancient painted decoration as were found in Nero's 'Golden House', and the decorations of the Loggie of the Vatican by Raphael and his assistants utilize ancient motives. The discoveries at Pompeii had a stimulating effect on the neo-classicism of the late eighteenth and early nineteenth centuries (*see* CLASSICISM).

Romanesque, term referring primarily to the architecture and sculpture of Europe in the eleventh and twelfth centuries, a great period of church, monastery and castle building, but comprising also the impressive form of wall-painting of the same period of which

[232]

Catalonia has some of the best examples, others being in France, Germany and England. Characteristic of the style was a simplified and rhythmic type of design with a strong geometrical element; and these characteristics also appear in the monastic illuminated manuscripts of the period.

Romanist, term applied mainly to the Netherlandish artists of the early sixteenth century who went to Italy to study and brought back to northern Europe in their paintings some element of the Italian Renaissance style. The Romanists include Quinten Massys, Marinus van Reymerswael, Joachim Patenier, Jan Gossart (Mabuse) and Bernaert van Orley (qq.v.).

Romano, Giulio (Giulio Pippi de Giannuzzi) (*b.* Rome, 1492; *d.* Mantua, 1546), Italian painter and architect, the favourite pupil and principal assistant of Raphael. With others he worked to Raphael's designs in the Stanza dell' Incendio and after Raphael's death carried out the composition 'Battle of Constantine against Maxentius' in the Sala di Costantino of the Vatican, as well as decorating the Loggie to Raphael's designs. He also completed Raphael's 'Transfiguration'. His early architectural works include the Villa Madama with its fresco of Polyphemus. In 1524 Federigo Gonzaga, Duke of Mantua, invited him to undertake renovations and decorations in that city. He drained the marshes, restored many buildings and reconstructed the Palazzo del Tè, adding a series of decorations, those of the Sala dei Giganti being famous. They depicted the Titans destroyed by the thunderbolts of Jove, and showed a vivid and grotesque invention. In its exaggerations, his work (influenced by Michelangelo as well as Raphael) is already Mannerist. Though he

G. ROMANO—The Infancy of Jupiter—National Gallery, London.

painted a number of religious pictures he was nearer in spirit to the Roman wall decorators of antiquity.

Romanticism, tendency to lay stress on personal and emotional expression as opposed to the systematic pursuit of formal beauty. The Romantic spirit may thus be found in any period, but the Romantic movement in specific form and as expressed in painting is part of the general artistic upheaval of the late eighteenth century, culminating in the decade 1830–40. The love of wild landscape and of violent effects in nature, of the mysterious, the exotic in any guise, a nostalgia for the past and a rebellious delight in unbridled energy and freedom dictated the painter's choice of subjects, and it is this rather than any characteristic manner that distinguishes Romantic art. It is represented in various aspects in England by Fuseli and Blake; by the landscape painters, Turner above all; by the colossal conceptions of John Martin, B. R. Haydon and James Ward; and by many others. Romanticism in Germany is represented by the revival of religious art attempted by the Nazarenes (q.v.); the melancholy of P. O. Runge; the love of legendary ancient times of Moritz von Schwind; and (best of all) by the mysterious moonlit landscapes of Caspar David Friedrich. In France it appears in J. L. David (despite his being called a classicist), in Girodet de Roucy, Prud'hon, Géricault, Delacroix, and in a decadent form in the canvases of Delaroche. The Romantic spirit in art had indeed no boundaries; it is to be found in the nightmare conceptions of Goya and in another form in the delight of American painters of the nineteenth century in the immense vistas opening out before them. *See* individual articles on artists mentioned, also BARBIZON SCHOOL; CLASSICISM; HUDSON RIVER SCHOOL; PICTURESQUE.

Rome as a centre of art in the Christian era has two aspects: (1) in an early phase as a repository of the Graeco-Roman tradition of painting never entirely extinguished, to be found, e.g., in the catacombs and in some medieval wall-paintings and mosaics (*see* EARLY CHRISTIAN PAINTING); the tradition was represented in the thirteenth century by Pietro Cavallini (q.v.), in whose work the origin of the style of Giotto and Florentine painting has been discerned; (2) as the restored and rebuilt society of an able and energetic series of popes after the sloth and schism of the 'Babylonish Captivity' at Avignon; the reconstructed Vatican and St Peter's are its symbols, and the decoration of these and other churches and palaces drew artists from every centre of Italy from the fifteenth century onwards. Thus though the art of the Renaissance was not initiated by an indigenous Roman school, but was much more the product of Florentine genius, it was at Rome that the supreme works of the High Renaissance were executed. The sack of Rome by imperial mercenaries in 1527 again dispersed artists for a time, but the impetus continued, and in the seventeenth century with the Counter-Reformation it was the centre of baroque painting (q.v.). Rome entered a new phase also as the international centre of study for artists from many different countries, a position which it retained until the end of the nineteenth century and is perpetuated in the French and English 'Prix de Rome.' The most illustrious of its foreign artist settlers in the seventeenth century were Poussin and Claude Lorraine, and it was in Rome that the style of so-called 'classical' landscape developed. In the eighteenth century the demand of visiting and other patrons for views of the city or 'Grand Tour' portraits was satisfied by such artists as Piranesi, Panini and, in portraiture, Mengs and Battoni.

Romney, George (*b.* Dalton-in-Furness, Lancs., 26 Dec. 1734; *d.* Kendal, 15 Nov. 1802), English portrait painter. After provincial training and practice in portraiture at Kendal and York he came to London in 1762, leaving behind a wife from whom he remained separated until towards the end of his life. In London he gained success, ranking next in popularity to Reynolds and Gainsborough, though far their inferior in the quality of his art. A visit to Italy, 1773–5, filled him with the ambition to paint classical and imaginative compositions, and between 1782 and 1785 he drew and painted Emma Hart (Lady Hamilton), whom he admired obsessively, in many preliminary studies for the classic themes he was ill fitted to carry out. He went back to Lancashire broken in health and spirit in 1789. His best work is to be found in the straightforward realism of 'The Beaumont Family' (National Gallery) or the unassuming charm of 'The Parson's Daughter' (Tate Gallery).

G. ROMNEY—The Beaumont Family—National Gallery, London.

Rops, Félicien (*b.* Namur, 7 July 1833; *d.* Essones, 23 Aug. 1898), Belgian painter, etcher and lithographer. Trained at Brussels, he founded the independent paper *Uylenspiegel*, to which he contributed satirical drawings. The admiration of Baudelaire and Huysmans has given him prominence as a 'decadent', though while there is macabre suggestion in his graphic art, Huysmans exaggerated its satanic and erotic peculiarity. Rops settled in France in 1878 and painted some landscapes of an Impressionist character.

Rosa, Salvator (*b.* Arenella, nr Naples, 21 June 1615; *d.* Rome, 15 Mar. 1673), Italian painter, etcher, musician and satirist. He studied art under an uncle, Paolo Greco, and his father-in-law, Francesco Fracanzo (a follower of Ribera). The painter Lanfranco (q.v.) bought his 'Hagar' and started him on a prosperous career to which his paintings lend more of an atmosphere of romantic violence than it actually contained. Whether or no he consorted with bandits he invented a type of romantic art in his rocky landscapes with ruins and brigand-like figures, inspired by southern Italy, and with Claude Lorraine (q.v.) is one of the founders of the picturesque tradition so influential in eighteenth-century Britain. Following the example of Aniello Falcone he also painted some battle scenes. Good examples of his art are 'Saul and the Witch of Endor' and 'Battlepiece' (Louvre), both from the collection of Louis XIV, and the 'Bridge' (Pitti). He worked mainly at Rome with an interval in Florence, 1642–7, being invited there by the Duke of Tuscany.

Rosselli, Cosimo (*b.* Florence, 1439; *d.* there, 7 Jan. 1507), Italian painter of the Florentine School, a pupil of Neri di Bicci. He was one of the team of painters commissioned by Sixtus IV to paint frescoes in the Sistine Chapel, contributing a 'Last Supper' and two other works. His 'Procession of the Miraculous Chalice', 1485, is in Sant' Ambrogio, Florence. His pictures are dignified, despite a hard and mannered style and a monotony of gold and ultramarine. Fra Bartolommeo and Piero di Cosimo (qq.v.) were his pupils.

Rossetti, Dante Gabriel (*b.* London, 12 May 1828; *d.* Birchington-on-Sea, 9 April 1882), English painter and poet, son of the Italian exile, Gabriele Rossetti. His art training is of little account but his poetic gift and love of medievalism were important factors in the Pre-Raphaelitism of which, with Hunt and Millais, he was one of the founders in 1848. His early oil-paintings, 'The Girlhood of Mary Virgin' and 'Ecce Ancilla Domini', 1849–50, already show mystical feeling as well as a sense of design; his best works are the water-colours of the 1850's, in which, unhampered by the technical demands of oil, he recreated the glow of medieval illumination. To this achievement must be added the beautiful series of drawings of Miss Siddal, whom he married in 1860. His subsequent work in oils, technically more competent and inspired either by Dante or a mystical idea of feminine beauty (of the same ultimate derivation), is less artistically remarkable. His influence, however, was great; the exploit of painting the Oxford Union walls, 1857, failure as it was, was a gesture towards design of which his protégés, Burne-Jones and William Morris,

S. ROSA—Landscape with Hermit—Walker Art Gallery, Liverpool.

C. ROSSELLI—St Lawrence—Walker Art Gallery, Liverpool.

D. G. ROSSETTI—The Tune of the Seven Towers (Water-colour)—Tate Gallery.

realized the import; and even Whistler was not unaffected for a period by his art.

Rossi, Francesco dei, *see* SALVIATI.

Rosso, Il (Giovanni Battista Rossi) (also known as **Rosso Fiorentino**) (*b.* Florence, 1494; *d.* Paris, 1540), Italian painter and architect. He was the pupil of Andrea del Sarto (q.v.), and friend of Pontormo (q.v.), like whom he developed a strongly Mannerist style, being much influenced by Michelangelo. He worked in Florence until 1523, when he went to Rome, staying there until the sack of the city in 1527 drove him elsewhere. From Venice he departed for France in 1530 at the invitation of Francis I to decorate the palace of Fontainebleau. He was later joined by Primaticcio (q.v.). The first School of Fontainebleau was thus founded on Italian Mannerism.

Rottenhammer, Johann (*b.* Munich, 1564; *d.* Augsburg, 1623), German painter who travelled to Venice in 1589 and spent many years there and in Rome. He painted small pictures on copper of mythological scenes in an Italianate style. Settling in Augsburg, 1606, he worked for the Count von Schaunburg at Bückeburg, executing wall and ceiling decorations.

[238]

Rouault, Georges (*b*. Paris, 27 May 1871; *d*. there, 13 Feb. 1958), French painter. He served an apprenticeship as a boy with a painter of stained glass and later studied at the École des Beaux-Arts under Gustave Moreau (q.v.). After the death of Moreau in 1898 he was made curator of the Musée Gustave Moreau. He had met Matisse at the Beaux-Arts and exhibited with him and the Fauves of 1905, though the trend of his ideas had more affinity with those of the German Expressionists than of his French *confrères*. Suffering as a personal emotion, or a sense of the existence of suffering in the world, seemed to direct him first to paintings of sad clowns and even to harsh social comment as in ' Les Noces' (Tate Gallery), and later to religious paintings tragic in spirit. This sense of tragedy was impressively conveyed by sombre tones and distortions of form, though as time went on he gave his religious themes something of the dusky richness of stained glass (with some reminiscence no doubt of his early training). He illustrated books for Ambroise Vollard, the dealer to whom all his productions were reserved for many years, the etched plates for *Miserere*, 1948 (executed 1922–7), being a notable achievement. In both etchings and lithographs he showed all the quality of his painting.

Roublev, Andrei (*c*. 1360–*c*. 1430), Russian monk, a painter of icons and frescoes, the most eminent painter of medieval Russia. He was probably the pupil at Moscow of Theophanes the Greek and Daniel Chyorny, with whom he collaborated. The two works which represent his genius are the fragments of a ' Last Judgment', 1408, in the Cathedral of Vladimir and the Icon of the Holy Trinity (now in the Moscow Museum of History), a work of majestic simplicity and feeling far transcending the conventional icon, Byzantine or Russian.

Rousseau, Henri Julien (*b*. Laval, 20 May 1844; *d*. Paris, 4 Sept. 1910), French painter known as ' Le Douanier', an official in the Paris toll department who did not devote himself exclusively to painting until he retired in 1884 to open a little shop where he sold his own pictures. Though something more than a 'modern primitive' or naïve 'Sunday painter', he might be termed the patron saint of such instinctive artists by virtue of his unsophisticated candour of vision and quaintness of outlook. His views of Paris suburbs, portraits and exotic landscapes (dream-like recollections of an early period of service in the military campaign in Mexico, 1862–7), as well as some remarkable feats of allegory, place him among the great artists of his time. He exhibited at the Salon des Indépendants, 1886–1910, and Gauguin and Pissarro knew and admired his work, though it was the applause of Alfred Jarry, Pablo Picasso and Guillaume Apollinaire which in his later years made him known. The ' Portrait of Pierre Loti' (Zürich), 'The Jungle' (Cleveland, Ohio), 'The Dream' (New York, private collection) and 'The Poet and his Muse' (Basel) are among many remarkable productions. Interest in his work undoubtedly led to the modern appreciation of the untutored ' primitive', especially in France and the United States.

Rousseau, Pierre Étienne Théodore (*b*. Paris, 15 April 1812; *d*.

H. ROUSSEAU—War—Louvre.

P. E. T. ROUSSEAU—Outskirts of the Forest, Fontainebleau—Louvre.

Barbizon, 22 Dec. 1867), French landscape painter, a pupil of his cousin, Pau de St Martin, and two other minor landscapists, but more effectively influenced by Constable, Ruisdael and Hobbema. The lack of success in the Salons which earned him the title of 'le grand refusé' caused him to withdraw to the forest of Fontainebleau, which to his romantic spirit was the essence of the wild. Joined at the village of Barbizon by Dupré, Diaz and Millet (qq.v.), he may be called the founder of the Barbizon School (q.v.). The melancholy which Baudelaire remarked on in his darkly toned pictures of forest glades was due to his own temperament and the mood caused by the mental derangement of his wife, but he is notable also for an objective devotion to nature. Success came to him late, signalized by the *salon* assigned to him at the Exposition Universelle of 1855.

Roussel, Ker-Xavier (*b.* Metz, 18 Dec. 1867; *d.* 6 June 1944), French painter, decorator and pastellist. He became associated as a student with Bonnard, Vuillard and Maurice Denis (qq.v.) and was a member of the 'Nabi' group which they formed in 1889. He was closely associated with Vuillard (whose sister he married) in stage design and decorative undertakings. He stands somewhat apart from his associates, however, in his preference for mythological subjects—sunny landscapes peopled with nymphs and fauns, these 'age-old pretexts' for painting being combined with the landscape character of the Île-de-France and a realistic ability in drawing and painting the figure.

'Rout of San Romano', series of three paintings by Paolo Uccello, (q.v.) depicting a battle or skirmish fought between Florentines and

P. UCCELLO—The Rout of San Romano—National Gallery, London.

T. ROWLANDSON—The Roadside Inn—Whitworth Art Gallery, Manchester.

Sienese in 1432 at San Romano (between Florence and Pisa), a minor incident of the long-continuing rivalry between Florence and Siena. The pictures were framed together in the palace of the Medici at Florence, and now hang in the Louvre, National Gallery and Uffizi. It is probable that the National Gallery picture hung on the left, the Uffizi in the centre and the Louvre on the right. The Florentine commander, Niccolò da Tolentino, has been identified in the National Gallery version by his device of knotted cords ('Solomon's Knot') appearing on the standard.

Rowlandson, Thomas (*b*. London, July 1756; *d*. there, 22 April 1827), English water-colour painter and etcher of *genre* and landscape. He studied art at the Royal Academy Schools, 1771, and while still a student spent some time in Paris. He settled in London, 1777, as a portrait painter but quickly found a congenial and popular vein in etched caricature prints and in humorous subjects drawn with a pen and delicately tinted with colour. They comprised scenes of London and sporting life and views of town, village and coast in various parts of England, forming in their immense total an even more comprehensive view of social life than that given by Hogarth; while in his gift of composition and endless invention he showed himself a great artist. He worked for the publisher Ackermann, his illustrations to William Combe's *Tour of Dr Syntax*, 1812–21, and *The Microcosm of London* (in collaboration with Pugin) being famous. One of his best drawings, 'Vauxhall Gardens' (previously known by an aquatint engraving), was rediscovered in 1945.

Royal Academy of Arts, superseded various attempts (*a*) to provide gratuitous teaching (e.g. the academies of Sir Godfrey Kneller and Sir James Thornhill) and (*b*) a central and periodic exhibition, that of the 'Incorporated Society of Artists', 1765–8, being the immediate forerunner. With the sanction of George III, 'The Royal Academy of Arts in London, for the purpose of Cultivating and Improving the Arts of Painting, Sculpture and Architecture' was founded, 10 Dec. 1768, Sir Joshua Reynolds (q.v.) being the first president. Its first quarters were in Somerset House, then in the National Gallery, 1836–1869. In the latter year it moved to its present quarters, Burlington House, Piccadilly. It consists of forty academicians, painters, sculptors, engravers and architects; thirty associates and honorary academicinsa (distinguished foreign artists chosen from time to time). The special title Honorary Academician Extraordinary was created for Sir Winston Churchill after the Second World War. An exhibition of works by living artists is held every summer from the first Monday in May to the first Monday in August and an exhibition of some great period or phase of art every winter from the first Monday in January for ten weeks. There are schools giving instruction in art, all persons who have passed the required examination being admissible. The Academy administers various bequests, notably in conjunction with the Tate Gallery, the Chantrey Bequest. See also ACADEMY.

Rubens, Peter Paul (*b*. Siegen, 28 June 1577; *d*. Antwerp, 30 May 1640), 'Prince of Painters and fine gentleman', as his contemporary, Sir Dudley Carleton, described him, the supreme master of northern baroque, born of an Antwerp family in Westphalia, where his father, Jan Rubens, a lawyer, had gone into exile. On the latter's death his widow returned, 1587, to Antwerp, where Peter Paul was educated at

P. P. RUBENS—The Rainbow Landscape—Wallace Collection.

P. P. RUBENS—Peace and War—National Gallery, London.

the Jesuit school, and at sixteen he was prepared for courtly life as a page of the Countess Lalaing. He studied art under 'Romanist' masters, Tobias Verhaecht, Adam van Noort (q.v.) and Otto van Veen (q.v.), and in 1598 was a member of the Painters' Guild at Antwerp. Going to Italy he worked from 1600 to 1608 as court painter to Vincenzo Gonzaga, Duke of Mantua, painting many portraits of the nobility, and in 1603 went to Spain on the duke's behalf. His study of the Italian masters, especially of Titian and Veronese at Venice, was a major factor in the development of his powers. He returned to Antwerp equipped for splendid undertakings, in 1609 being appointed painter to the Brussels court of the Archduke Albert and the Infanta Isabella, and gathering a brilliant cohort of assistants around him. A triumphant release of force appears in the great religious compositions of 1609–21 for the cathedral and the Church of the Jesuits at Antwerp, in which Rubens seems to express the essence of the Counter-Reformation, using all the compositional and theatrical devices of the baroque style. This decorative magnificence on a vast scale was applied, 1622–5, to secular use in the cycle of the Life of Marie de' Medici, at whose invitation he visited Paris. His happy marriage with Isabella Brant was ended by her death in 1626, and Rubens was now often away from the stately home he had built at Antwerp (since 1946 renovated as a Rubens museum). Diplomatic missions took him to Spain, 1628, where he painted Philip IV and met Velazquez, and to London, 1629–30, where he was knighted by Charles I, made an honorary M.A. of Cambridge University and commissioned to paint the ceiling (extant and now restored) for the

[244]

P. P. RUBENS—Susanna Fourment (Le Chapeau de Paille)—National Gallery, London.

Banqueting Hall, Whitehall. On his return to Antwerp in 1630 he married Helena Fourment, a girl of sixteen who inspired a number of portraits and appears also in various religious and mythological works. In 1635 he bought a country residence, the Castle of Steen, and during the last five years of his life was occupied with paintings for the Torre de la Parada, Philip IV's hunting lodge near Madrid, and, for his personal satisfaction, with landscapes.

No brief outline can do justice to one who must be approached at such various levels. The Olympian energy of Rubens was stupendous. In less than forty years he produced more than three thousand paintings, more than four hundred drawings. He created masterpieces in every *genre*: religious, e.g. 'The Descent from the Cross', c. 1611–14 (Antwerp); portraiture, the so-called 'Chapeaude Pailles, (q.v.), c. 1620 (National Gallery); peasant life, the 'Kermesse', c. 1622 (Louvre); allegory, 'War and Peace', c. 1629–30 (National Gallery); landscape, the 'Château de Steen', c. 1635–7 (National Gallery). As a colourist and technician he is remarkable and he devised a classic oil method of thinly painted shadow and loaded high light. His studio-factory was a model of efficient administration, his assistants so able and his own supervision so well directed that the standard of works not due to his hand alone is consistently high. He summoned into being a whole school of engravers, occupied in reproducing his works. In addition he was a great collector, of ancient marbles and gems, pictures, manuscripts and books, a classical scholar who knew and corresponded with men of learning throughout Europe, and a diplomat who spoke five languages. His influence on painters—Velazquez, Watteau, Delacroix, Constable among them—was enormous. All told, he may well be called the genius of abundance.

[245]

Ruisdael, Jacob Isaacksz van (*b*. Haarlem, 1628–9; *d*. there, buried 14 Mar. 1682), Dutch landscape painter, possibly a pupil of his uncle, Salomon van Ruisdael, and of Cornelisz Vroom. He painted many views in the region of Haarlem and of Amsterdam, where he lived from 1659 to 1681, afterwards returning to his native city. His only known journey abroad is to Caen, where he took a degree in medicine in 1676, presumably at that late stage of his career with a view to practice, but his work gives some evidence of journeys along the Rhine and on the German border, and either like Everdingen he went to Norway and Sweden or else in one phase he borrowed crags, waterfalls and pinewoods from Everdingen. He is, however, primarily an interpreter of typical Dutch landscape, of dunes, coastal gleams, low horizons over which great clouds sweep, and quiet patches of woodland, his dark greens and greys seeming to infuse a personal and romantic melancholy. He had a worthy pupil in Hobbema but posthumously was the master of both English and French landscape painters, greatly influencing Gainsborough, Constable and the Barbizon School. The large collection of his works in the National Gallery illustrates every type of subject he painted.

Runge, Philipp Otto (*b*. Wolgast, 23 June 1777; *d*. Hamburg, 2 Dec. 1810), German Romantic painter and poet. He studied at the

P. O. RUNGE—Family Group—Kunsthalle, Hamburg.

J. RUISDAEL—The Edge of a Wood—Dulwich College Picture Gallery.

Copenhagen Academy and worked in Dresden and Hamburg, producing severely grave and melancholy portraits and symbolic compositions of a fanciful kind.

Ruskin, John (*b.* London, 8 Feb. 1819; *d.* Brantwood, Coniston, 20 Jan. 1900), English writer on art, artist and social reformer, a major force in nineteenth-century England, though erratic in his enthusiasms. He recognized more fully than any of his contemporaries the genius of Turner; his exposition of 'truth to nature' in *Modern Painters* gave a watchword to the Pre-Raphaelites of 1848; his account of Gothic in *The Seven Lamps of Architecture* inspired William Morris, and his various writings on Italian painting, sculpture and architecture widened appreciation of art from Pisano to Tintoretto. Grotesquely bigoted in the attack on Whistler which led to the famous libel action, he was in other directions admirable in intention, as in his establishment of a drawing school at Oxford. His own drawings are a delicate by-product of his career.

Russian Painting. Medieval painting in Russia is most characteristically represented by the icon, a wooden panel, painted usually in tempera though sometimes in oil, and depicting sacred persons according to prescribed formulae. Early icons of the eleventh and twelfth centuries were essentially Byzantine in inspiration and limited in colour, but in the two centuries following there was a great expansion of the art. Local schools grew up in a number of towns, at Moscow, Novgorod, Pskov, that of Novgorod being noted for brilliant colour. The Moscow school reached its height in the fourteenth–fifteenth century with the genius of Roublev (q.v.). The early fifteenth century saw the development of the elaborate iconostasis of the Eastern Church, the screen separating the sanctuary from the main body of the church and adorned with icons. The tradition of Roublev was carried on to the end of the fifteenth century by the Moscow masters, notably the Greek painter Dionysos. The sixteenth and seventeenth centuries were an age of transition. The Stroganov school produced elaborate miniature icons but in the seventeenth century the art declined and by the nineteenth century had become

NOVGOROD SCHOOL (Fifteenth Century)—The Prophets Daniel, David and Solomon—Tretyakov Gallery, Moscow.

VELAZQUEZ—Venus and Cupid ('The Rokeby Venus')—National Gallery, London.

NOVGOROD SCHOOL (Late Fifteenth Century)— St. George and the Dragon —Tretyakov Gallery, Moscow.

the mass production of insipidly conventional images, a monopoly of Vladimir. The appearance of picture painting in the Western European manner may be dated from the reign of Peter the Great, though, as part of a westernizing policy, court patronage was long given preferentially to foreign artists. The foundation of the Academy of Fine Arts at St Petersburg in 1757 gave the first real impetus to Russian painting. Portraiture was a main activity, leading portraitists being D. G. Levitski (1735–1822), V. L. Borovikovski (1757–1826) and Vassily Tropinin (1776–1857). Feodor Alexeyev (1753–1824) introduced the Venetian manner of view painting and later Ivan Aivazowsky (1817–1900) was distinguished as a painter of marines. As in the West, the nineteenth century saw the cultivation of historical and domestic *genre*. Early *genre* painters of note were Alexei Venetsianov (1780–1847), with his peasant scenes, and Pavel Fedotov (q.v.). The two commanding figures in historical *genre* were Ilya Repin and Vassily Vereschchagin (qq.v.).

Dissatisfaction with academic subject painting towards the end of the nineteenth century found expression in the review and exhibiting society, the World of Art (*Mir Iskusstva*), founded by Alexander Benois (q.v.) with Serge Diaghilev. Modern in outlook, this society also aimed to encourage a native Russian art. From it stemmed the brilliant Russian phase of ballet design represented by Benois, Bakst (q.v.), Roerich, Larionov, Goncharov and others. A number of painters such as Valentin Serov (q.v.) were influenced by the World of Art, and before 1914 artists in Russia as in other countries were influenced by the Impressionism and Post-Impressionism of France, among them being Igor Grabar (*b.* 1871), Kuzma Petrov-Vodkin (1878–1939) and Alexander Gerasimov (*b.* 1885). The latter became one of the most esteemed of Soviet painters. Cubism and Futurism

F. Y. ALEXEYEV—View of the Palace Quay, St Petersburg, in 1794—Tretyakov Gallery, Moscow.

KUKRYNIKSY (pseudonym of three Soviet artists)—The End (Last Days of Hitler and his Staff in the Reichschancellery Bunker)—Tretyakov Gallery, Moscow.

A. P. RYDER—Death on a Pale Horse—J. H. Wade Collection, The Cleveland Museum of Art.

(qq.v.) had their adherents and one of the most interesting painters from a western point of view was Kasimir Malevich (q.v.), a pioneer of abstract art. Between 1917 and about 1927 an experimental and free phase of art was associated with the Revolution, Wassily Kandinsky (q.v.), Malevich and Marc Chagall (q.v.) pursuing for a while an unhindered course; but modern western art then fell into disfavour as a form of 'bourgeois decadence', and 'socialist realism', illustration with a propagandist basis of the people's life and work, became and has remained dominant. Alexander Deineka (q.v.) is a typical artist in this vein. An exhibition of Russian art at the Royal Academy in London, 1959, showed how far painting in the U.S.S.R. had returned to a late nineteenth-century academicism which the West had long discarded. As an illustrative extreme 'The End' (the Last Days of Hitler and his Staff), produced by three artists in collaboration (Tretyakov Gallery, Moscow), is of interest.

Ruysch, Rachel (*b.* Amsterdam, 1664; *d.* 1750), Dutch painter of flowers and fruit, who studied under van Aelst. She married the portrait painter Juriaen Pool and in 1708 was appointed court painter to the Elector Palatine. Her flower-pieces are comparable with those of van Huysum (q.v.).

[251]

Ryder, Albert Pinkham (*b*. New Bedford, Massachusetts, 19 Mar. 1847; *d*. Elmhurst, New York, 28 Mar. 1917), American painter, largely self-taught, of truly poetic imagination. He lived the life of a recluse in New York, painting and repainting small pictures expressive of memories and dreams, 'Moonlight Marine' (New York, Metropolitan Museum) and 'Death on a Pale Horse' (Cleveland Museum of Art) being characteristic works. His enamel-like colour and rhythm of design remain appreciable despite the faulty technique which has caused many to deteriorate.

S

Sacchi, Andrea (*b.* Rome, 1599; *d.* 1661), Italian baroque painter, a pupil of Albani and the Carracci (qq.v.). He worked in Rome for the Barberini family. He represents the more classic aspect of the baroque style, based on the art of Raphael, both in his own art and in his teaching. Principal works are the 'Vision of St Romuald' and 'Miracle of St Gregory' (the latter in mosaic) in the Vatican. Carlo Maratta (q.v.) was his pupil. He and Sacchi were called by Reynolds 'the last of the Romans'.

Sacra Conversazione, painting of the Madonna and Child with saints in which the figures form a group aware of one another's presence and all taking part in the situation presented. In fifteenth-century Italian art it superseded the type of altar-piece in which the personages were painted in individual isolation.

'Sacred and Profane Love', early masterpiece of Titian while he was still strongly influenced by Giorgione, now in the Borghese Gallery, Rome. The title by which it is generally known is later than Titian's lifetime, and in the early seventeenth century, when in the Cardinal Scipio Borghese's collection, it was known as 'Beauty Clothed and Unclothed'. The symbolism lends itself to various interpretations, but is perhaps all the better for this. The painting is eminently poetic in feeling and richly sensuous in quality.

Saenredam, Pieter (*b.* Assenfeldt, 1597; *d.* 1665), Dutch painter who worked at Haarlem, specializing in architectural views, mainly church interiors of immaculate austerity.

Saftleven (Sachtleven), Cornelis (*b.* Gorkum, *c.* 1607; *d.* there, buried

TITIAN—Sacred and Profane Love—Borghese Gallery, Rome.

P. SAENREDAM—Interior of St Bavo, Haarlem—National Gallery, London.

4 June 1681), Dutch painter and engraver of *genre* subjects in the style of Brouwer and Teniers. His brother Herman (*b*. Rotterdam, 1609; *d*. Utrecht, 5 Jan. 1685) was a landscape painter and engraver, the pupil of van Goyen (q.v.).

Salon usually refers to the yearly exhibitions in Paris organized by the Société des Artistes Français, which was given an official State Commission for this purpose in 1882. What is considered the first Salon, however, was held by the Académie Royale in the courtyard of the Palais Royal in 1673. It was later held in the Long Gallery of the Louvre and in 1737 in the Salon Carré of the Louvre, whence the name Salon is derived. It was then limited to academicians, a privilege abolished under the Revolution, and is now freely open to any painter to submit works. It has had unofficial counterparts, notably the Salon des Indépendants, organized in 1884 by artists of unacademic character who did not favour, or find favour with, the official body.

Salon des Refusés, the 'Salon of Rejects' set up by Napoleon III in 1863 as a result of the contentions aroused by the rejection of Manet and others from the official Salon. Manet's 'Déjeuner sur l'Herbe' was one of the principal exhibits. Other artists exhibiting were Boudin, Cézanne, Fantin-Latour, Jongkind, Pissarro and Whistler.

Salviati (Francesco dei Rossi) (*b*. Florence, 1510; *d*. Rome, 11 Nov. 1563), Italian painter of the Florentine School who took the name of his patron Cardinal Salviati. He studied under several painters in his youth, among them Andrea del Sarto (q.v.). He worked in Florence, Venice and Rome with an interval in Paris, 1554–6, and painted religious and classical subjects in fresco (the latter including the 'Story of Psyche' in the Palazzo Grimani, Venice), as well as portraits. His 'Justice' (Florence, Bargello) is a good instance of his mannered style.

Sandby, Paul (*b*. Nottingham, 1725; *d*. London, 7 Nov. 1809), English painter and engraver. He and his brother, Thomas Sandby (1721–98), came to London in 1742, being employed in the Military Drawing Office in the Tower of London. Paul was a draughtsman in the survey of the Highlands that followed the '45 rebellion and stayed in Scotland some years, making drawings and etchings of Scottish scenery and character. Subsequently he stayed often at Windsor with his brother, who was appointed Deputy Ranger of Windsor Forest, some of his best work (Royal Collection) being of Windsor Castle and environs. He also travelled widely in Britain, being one of the first to depict the beauties of Welsh scenery. His landscapes in *gouache* and water-colour have a great eighteenth-century charm. He was a founder member of the Royal Academy in 1768. His brother was an architectural draughtsman of some merit.

Sandrart, Joachim von (*b*. Frankfurt, 12 May 1606; *d*. Nuremberg, 14 Oct. 1688), German painter, engraver and art historian, pupil of the engraver, Théodore de Bry. Between 1628 and 1635 he travelled

P. SANDBY—An Ancient Beech-tree—Victoria and Albert Museum.

G. SANTI—Madonna and Child—National Gallery, London.

widely in Italy, visiting Venice, Bologna, Rome and Naples. Later he stayed at Amsterdam, Munich, Nuremberg and Augsburg. He is mainly of note for his biographical publication, the *Teutsche Academie* of 1675, which is a fund of information on seventeenth - century painting.

Sanguine, red chalk, a popular medium for drawing with many old masters. It was used by Andrea del Sarto, Michelangelo, Correggio, Annibale Carracci and Guercino among Italian artists, by Rubens and Rembrandt occasionally, and, in conjunction with black chalk, by the Clouets in France and again notably by Watteau.

Sano di Pietro (*b.* Siena, 1406; *d.* 1481), Italian painter of the Sienese School, a pupil of Sassetta (q.v.), whom he followed in style. Many of his works are preserved at Siena, one of the most highly considered being his 'St Bernard preaching.'

Santi, Giovanni (*b.* ? Urbino, *c.* 1450; *d.* 1494), Italian painter of the Umbrian School, principally of note as the father of Raphael. He shows a true artist's sensitiveness of feeling in such a work as the National Gallery's 'Madonna and Child', though the work of his great son was evidently inspired by other sources.

Sargent, John Singer (*b.* Florence, 12 Jan. 1856; *d.* London, 18 April 1925), American painter, perhaps the most brilliant academic artist of the nineteenth century. The son of American parents living in Europe, his father being Dr Fitzwilliam Sargent of Boston, he studied art in Florence and in Paris under Carolus-Duran. A visit to Spain, 1879, introduced him to Velazquez, though a native illustrative tendency appears in his 'El Jaleo', a picture of Spanish dancers, one result of the visit. He lived in Paris until 1885 when, his portrait of Mme Gautreau having incurred a storm of criticism, he moved to London, thenceforward his headquarters. He quickly became a

J. S. SARGENT—Ena and Betty Wertheimer—Tate Gallery.

successful 'society portrait painter', though not in the sense that he flattered: he brilliantly depicted a type of society, and indeed Anglo-American society in general. His paintings of the Wertheimer family (Tate Gallery) constitute a remarkable family record, and for twenty-five years he portrayed a long series of celebrities, including Roosevelt, Rockefeller, Chamberlain, Ellen Terry and many others. In various ways he reacted against the demands of portraiture: in the much criticized murals for the Boston Library, 1890; in his war pictures, e.g. 'Gassed', 1920 (Imperial War Museum); and in the water-colours in which after 1910 he found his main pleasure, his views of Venice in this medium being notable works. He may most readily be compared in portraiture with British artists, especially Sir Thomas Lawrence (q.v.). The superficiality of which he is often accused may be said to be also that of the society he depicted, and he remains one of the outstanding recorders of an age.

Sarto, Andrea del (*b.* Florence, 16 Aug. 1486; *d.* there, 29 Sept. 1530), Italian painter of the Florentine School. He was Andrea d'Agnolo, the son of a tailor, whence comes the name by which he is generally known. The pupil of Piero di Cosimo (q.v.), he also studied the works of Michelangelo and Leonardo da Vinci and the engravings of Dürer and painted in the fully developed Renaissance style, being known also as 'Andrea senza errori' from his correctness of drawing. In 1518 he went to France at the invitation of Francis I, but left after a year at the behest of his wife (who has been described as a bad influence on him), at the same time appropriating sums entrusted to him by the king. He painted a number of frescoes for the brotherhood of the Servites, his 'Madonna del Sacco' in the Church of the Annunziata, 1525, being considered his masterpiece. It is said that at the taking of Florence in 1529 the soldiers were so awestruck by his 'Last

* 1 [257]

Supper' at San Salvi that they left the building without committing any violence. 'A Sculptor' (National Gallery) is a famous example of his portraiture. Among his many pupils were Vasari and Pontormo (qq.v.).

Sassetta (**Stefano di Giovanni**) (*b.* Siena, *c.* 1392; *d.* 1450), Italian painter of the Sienese School, a pupil of Paolo di Giovanni Fei. He worked in the old Sienese tradition, his paintings being still medieval in outlook and character, though of great beauty and showing something of the fifteenth-century advance in pictorial science. Panels from altar-pieces by him are widely distributed, a dismembered polyptych, the Apotheosis of St Francis, from Sansepolcro, 1437–44 (Berenson Collection and National Gallery), being considered his masterpiece. He had many pupils, Sano di Pietro (q.v.) being the most notable.

Sassoferrato (**Giovanni Battista Salvi**) (*b.* Sassoferrato, 11 July 1605; *d.* Rome, 8 August 1685), Italian painter, the son and pupil of Torquinio Salvi. He seems to have studied also with Domenichino. In the academic spirit of the School of Bologna, he produced Raphaelesque Madonnas, so much in the style of an earlier period that he was at one time mistakenly referred to as an artist of the sixteenth century.

Savery, Roelandt (*b.* Courtrai, 1576; *d.* Utrecht, 25 Feb. 1639), Flemish painter, pupil of his brother Jacob. He worked for Henry IV in France, at Prague for Rudolph II and after the death of Rudolph in 1612 became personal painter to the Emperor Mathias. Later he worked in Amsterdam and Utrecht. He painted landscapes with mythological incident and minutely detailed flowers and animals, and was also an etcher. He died poor and, according to Houbraken, insane.

Savoldo, Giovanni Girolamo (*b.* Brescia, *c.* 1480; *d. c.* 1550), Italian painter of the School of Brescia, perhaps trained at Venice, his style being modelled on that of the Venetian Renaissance masters. He seems to have worked mainly in Venice but also at Florence and

SASSETTA—The Journey of the Magi—Metropolitan Museum, New York.

G. SAVOLDO—Mary Mag-
dalene approaching the
Sepulchre—National
Gallery, London.

Treviso. He foreshadows the realism of Caravaggio in such a masterly work as his 'Mary Magdalene approaching the Sepulchre' (National Gallery), while the landscape backgrounds of his religious subjects are also remarkable in their effects of light.

Scarpazza, *see* CARPACCIO.

Schiavone, Andrea (*b.* Zara, *c.* 1515; *d.* Venice, 1563), painter of Dalmatian origin (Andrea Meldolla—'the Slavonian') associated with the Venetian School. He settled in Venice, and painted both religious and mythological subjects. He may have been the pupil of Parmigianino (q.v.), but he was influenced by Titian and developed a Venetian richness of colour.

Schiavone, Giorgio (*b.* Sebenico, Dalmatia, 1436–7; *d.* 1504), painter of Dalmatian origin, his name being Giorgio Ciulinovi (called 'the Slavonian'). He is associated with the Italian School, and was a pupil of Squarcione (q.v.) at Padua, 1456–9, returning to Sebenico in 1463, where he settled, though he revisited Padua. He painted altarpieces and seems to have been most active in his early Paduan period.

Schmidt-Rottluff, Karl (*b.* Rottluff, nr Chemnitz, 1 Dec. 1884), German Expressionist painter who studied in Dresden, where he was one of the founders of the 'Die Brücke' group (q.v.), later working in Berlin. In paintings and woodcuts influenced by African sculpture he developed a forceful primitive style which caused his work to be banned by the Nazis. In 1947 he became teacher at the Berlin Academy.

Schongauer, Martin (*b.* ? Colmar, *c.* 1430; *d.* Breisach, 1491), German painter and engraver of the Upper Rhine School, son of the goldsmith, Kaspar Schongauer, who became a freeman of Colmar in 1455. From about 1473 he worked in Colmar, where the monastery church has his one entirely authenticated painting, 'The Madonna of the Rose-arbour'. In 1488 he became a citizen of

K. SCHMIDT-ROTTLUFF
—Woman at her Toilet—
Kunsthalle, Hamburg.

[260]

M. SCHONGAUER—The Adoration of the Shepherds—Staatliche Museum, Berlin.

Breisach. His line engravings are classics of that art which set a standard widely followed. The young Dürer admired and copied his work, sought him out at Colmar and, though Schongauer died before they could meet, worked in his studio.

School, primarily a geographical term, referring to a number of artists working in the same region, though suggesting also that they show some general likeness of style or outlook. As applied in a national sense, e.g. British School, it refers more particularly to the period in which a country excelled or had a most distinctively national character—the Dutch School referring us, for instance, to the seventeenth century. It is, however, a more precise term in further division by cities or regions, Italy providing the most remarkable example in the diverse art of its city states, Florence, Venice and so on. The School of Fontainebleau, the Barbizon School, the Norwich School are other examples of art localized for one reason or another. 'School of Paris' describes the remarkable concentration of artists from all over the world in the French capital in the first half of the twentieth century, animated by some advanced or progressive doctrine. 'Belonging to the school of' is a somewhat unsatisfactory description of the followers or imitators of a particular master.

'School of Athens', title commonly applied to the wall-painting by Raphael in the Stanza della Segnatura of the Vatican, a companion painting to the 'Disputà' (q.v.). As the latter represents the triumph of Christianity so the so-called 'School of Athens' represents the advance and splendour of philosophy and learning. In the colonnade of a stately 'Temple of Knowledge' adorned with the statues of Apollo and Minerva are the central figures of Plato and Aristotle surrounded by others symbolic of various forms of science and education. Raphael included a number of famous figures of antiquity, such as Socrates and Diogenes, though the identity of some is conjectural, and as in the 'Disputà' he introduced portraits of a later—or of his own—time. Raphael himself appears, and the architect Bramante as a geometer with compasses.

School of Paris, term denoting the internationalism of Paris as an art centre in the first half of the twentieth century and its leadership in initiating and developing new conceptions of art. It does not refer to any one style of painting but in a general way to artists infected by the prevailing atmosphere of experiment and discovery which came in the wake of Post-Impressionism (q.v.), animated Cubism and Surrealism (qq.v.), and has also been evident in abstract or non-figurative painting. While the School of Paris has included many French artists, among them Bonnard, Braque, Duchamp, Dufy, Othon Friesz, Léger, Marquet, Matisse, Rouault, Utrillo and Vlaminck, brilliant adherents came from other countries. Picasso, Spanish by origin, is its most commanding figure. Other foreign painters associated with the school were Juan Gris, Salvador Dali, Joan Miró and Francisco Borès (Spanish), Modigliani (Italian), Chagall and Soutine (Russian), van Dongen (Dutch), Pascin (Bulgarian) and Hartung (German). Many more artists, even if they worked in other countries,

[262]

felt the stimulus of Parisian example and contact. The most flourishing period of the School of Paris was between the First and Second
World Wars when artists, attracted by its prestige and such other
factors as a favourable rate of exchange and the possibility of living
more economically than elsewhere, flocked from all over the world to
the undisputed centre of art as in the past they had done to Rome. At
the present day, while Paris has many eminent painters and still
living representatives of the 'between-wars' school, the international
trend of modern art is more widely diffused and no longer seems to
depend as formerly on a geographic centre or a single source of
inspiration. The School of Paris is passing into history.

Schwind, Moritz von (*b.* Vienna, 21 Jan. 1804; *d.* Munich, 8 Feb.
1871), Austrian painter and illustrator who studied art under
Cornelius (q.v.) at Munich. He represents a late stage of German
Romanticism in his scenes of old German life and architecture.

Scorel, Jan van (*b.* Schoorl, nr Alkmaar, 1 Aug. 1495; *d.* ? Utrecht,
6 Dec. 1562), Dutch painter of portraits and religious subjects,
trained at Alkmaar and Utrecht, where he settled. He travelled to
Germany, Italy and the Holy Land (portraits by him of Dutch
pilgrims to Jerusalem being in the Utrecht Museum). Appointed
keeper of the Belvedere in the Vatican by Hadrian VI, he acquired a
deep admiration for Raphael and Michelangelo and his work was
favourably affected by
the Renaissance influ-
ence. He was the master
of van Heemskerk and
Anthonis Mor (qq.v.).

Scott, Samuel (*b.* ?
London, *c.* 1702; *d.*
Bath, 12 Oct. 1772),
painter of marine and
topographical   views,
who worked in London
and is said to have
taken up painting 'as
an amusement'. He fol-
lowed van de Velde
(q.v.) in paintings of
ships and sea fights
(fourteen are in the
National Maritime Mu-
seum) and collaborated

J. VAN SCOREL—Portrait
of a Humanist—Prado.

[263]

with George Lambert in six pictures for the East India Company of their principal settlements (now in the Ministry of Commonwealth Relations). From about 1735 he turned to views of London and the Thames, many subjects being those later painted by Canaletto, who came to London in 1746. Though Scott admired Canaletto, his style is distinct. He retired to Bath.

Scuola di San Rocco, Venice, headquarters of one of the Venetian confraternities, famous for its wall-paintings by Tintoretto (q.v.).

Sebastiano del Piombo (*c.* 1485–1547), Italian painter, whose real name was Sebastiano Luciani, called 'del Piombo' as keeper of the papal seal. He was apprenticed to Giovanni Bellini and also knew Giorgione (qq.v.), on whom he modelled his style, as in the 'Daughter of Herodias', 1510 (National Gallery). In 1511 he went to Rome to paint frescoes in the Villa Farnesina. He settled there and met Raphael and Michelangelo (qq.v.). He was helped by the latter and discarded his Venetian for a Roman style. His principal works include the 'Raising of Lazarus', 1516 (National Gallery), the 'Visitation', 1521 (Louvre), and his portraits of Clement VII (Naples) and Andrea Doria (Rome, Doria Gallery).

Seghers, Daniel (*b.* Antwerp, 1590; *d.* there, 1661), Flemish flower painter, a pupil of Jan Brueghel. He became a Jesuit in 1614 and lived for some time in Italy. He painted highly detailed garlands of flowers often enclosing a picture by some other artist, either a portrait or some devotional subject. Characteristic works are the 'Nicolas Poussin' (Warsaw National Gallery) and 'St Ignatius de Loyola' (Antwerp, Musée des Beaux Arts), both portraits being surrounded by a floral garland.

D. SEGHERS—Flowers encircling a Relief—Dulwich College Picture Gallery.

H. SEGHERS—The River Valley   Uffizi, Florence.

Seghers, Hercules Pietersz (*b.* Haarlem, 1589-90; *d.* ? 1638), Dutch painter and etcher who became a member of the Guild of Painters at Haarlem. He worked at Amsterdam and Utrecht and is said to have travelled to Italy and Dalmatia, such a painting as 'The River Valley' (Uffizi) suggesting first-hand acquaintance with mountain regions. He was a pioneer of Dutch landscape, Rembrandt admiring and learning from his sombre and dramatic works.

Sellaio, Jacopo del (*b.* Florence, *c.* 1441; *d.* 12 Nov. 1493), Italian painter of the Florentine School, a pupil of Fra Filippo Lippi (q.v.). He painted religious and mythological subjects, modelling his style on that of Botticelli. A 'Pietà', 1483 (Berlin), is one of his principal authentic works and a number of Botticellian imitations have been tentatively attributed to him. (*See* illustration, p. 266.)

Sepia, brown pigment used as a water-colour, prepared from the colouring matter secreted in the ink bags of some species of cuttle-fish. It was not in use before the eighteenth century, though it is sometimes confused with the bistre (q.v.) of earlier draughtsmen, and only came into general use in the nineteenth century.

Serov, Valentin Alexandrovich (*b.* St Petersburg, 20 Jan. 1865; *d.* 1911), Russian painter, son of the composer, A. Serov. He studied under Repin (q.v.) and was one of the World of Art (*Mir Iskusstva*) group. He was considered the best portrait painter of his day in Russia, though he also painted landscape and *genre* and produced designs for the theatre, lithographs and etchings.

Serra, family of Catalonian painters in the late fourteenth century, of whom the best known are the brothers Jaime and Pedro. They worked in the Sienese manner introduced by Ferrer Bassa (q.v.), and produced large and elaborate altar-pieces. The Altar of the Holy

J. DEL SELLAIO—The Triumph of Chastity—Museo Bandini, Fiesole.

Spirit by Pedro Serra, 1394, with its five-storeyed range of panels, is an example (Manresa Cathedral).

Sert, José Maria (*b.* Barcelona, 1876; *d.* 27 Nov. 1945), Spanish decorative painter who executed grandiose murals both in Europe and the United States, examples being his work at Geneva for the Palace of the League of Nations and in New York at the Rockefeller Center.

Sesshū, Japanese painter, a pupil of the Zen Buddhist monk Shūbun. Like his master he was greatly influenced by the landscape of the Chinese painters of the Sung Dynasty, in particular by Ma Yuan and Hsia Kuei (qq.v.). He travelled in China, 1467–9, developing an original style of brushwork and introducing a new naturalism of effect into Japanese painting.

Seurat, Georges (*b.* Paris, 2 Dec. 1859; *d.* there, 29 Mar. 1891), French painter, one of the outstanding creative artists of the late nineteenth century. At sixteen he went to the École des Beaux-Arts, where he remained for four years, showing a remarkable early proficiency in figure drawing. Masters whose work he studied were Delacroix (frescoes at St Sulpice) and Piero della Francesca, with whom he shows an affinity in his sense of formal and geometrical

SESSHU—Landscape of the 'Bridge of Heaven', near Kyoto—Japanese Commission for the Protection of Cultural Properties.

beauty. An early masterpiece was 'La Baignade' of 1884 (now in the Tate Gallery), in which the atmospheric effect of Impressionist painting was combined with a new solidity of form and composition. At this time Seurat, together with his friend Signac (q.v.), interested himself in the colour theories of various scientists, especially the 'simultaneous contrast' and interplay of complementary colours expounded by Eugène Chevreul, to the purpose of giving a new range of vibration in the rendering of light and its effect on any surface. The method of using three sets of complementaries, red and green, blue and orange and violet and yellow, in small separate touches known as 'Divisionism' (q.v.), was first systematically applied in Seurat's famous 'A Sunday Afternoon on the Island of La Grande Jatte', 1886 (Art Institute of Chicago), the final product of many oil sketches and drawings. Seurat practised Divisionism in a number of other works, including such beautiful landscapes as the 'Bridge at Courbevoie' (Courtauld Gallery), the broken colour being in a sense 'neo-Impressionist' in the term devised by his friend Felix Fénéon, though a different element was the ordered geometric scheme of composition he carefully worked out. Urban and industrial landscapes and views of the Seine and the Normandy coast were followed by compositions suggested by a ninetyish metropolitan gaiety, in which the simple opposition of verticals and horizontals characterizing his landscapes is replaced by a more lively geometry, interpreting movement as in 'Le Chahut' (Kröller-Müller Museum) and 'Le Cirque' (Louvre). As a draughtsman Seurat was no less exceptional than as a painter, his drawings executed with a greasy conté crayon on rough paper conveying a remarkable richness of light and shade. His death in his thirty-second year went unnoticed by the press but his art has since been appreciated as a great achievement.

G. SEURAT—Bridge at Courbevoie—Courtauld Institute Gallery, London.

Severini, Gino (*b.* Cortona, 1883), Italian painter, a pupil of Giacomo Balla in Rome, at first influenced by the Divisionism of Seurat, but becoming in 1910 one of the leading painters in the Futurist movement, with a leaning towards Cubism. Later he turned to mural decoration in fresco and mosaic for churches and secular buildings in Switzerland and Italy. *Du Cubisme au Classicisme,* 1921, was one of several critical works.

Sezession, name given to groups of artists and the exhibitions they organized in Munich, Berlin and Vienna during the 1890's in revolt against official and academic art. They were influenced partly by Impressionism (q.v.), represented at Munich by such artists as Slevogt and Corinth and at Berlin by Liebermann (qq.v.); also by the work of the Norwegian painter Edvard Munch (q.v.), who between 1892 and 1898, after a first exhibition which aroused much controversy, gained wide recognition and exerted great influence in Germany; and by the Art Nouveau (q.v.) currents of the decade, alternatively known as Jugendstil. The German 'Secessions' represent a stage of revolt and development which took a more distinct form in the Expressionist movement. *See* EXPRESSIONISM.

[268]

G. SEVERINI—The Boulevard—Estorick Collection.

B. SHAHN—Handball—Museum of Modern Art, New York.

Sfumato (It. 'vaporous'), term describing delicate gradations of shadow like smoke or mist, as used with subtle effect by Leonardo da Vinci.

Sgraffito (It. 'scratched'), linear method of decoration in which a light surface is scratched through to reveal a darker layer underneath or vice versa. There are prehistoric examples of its graphic use in the Pyrenean caves, and the scraper-board of the modern commercial artist who scratches a white line on a prepared black ground to simulate the effect of a wood-engraving is a variant.

Shahn, Ben (*b*. Lithuania, 12 Sept. 1898), American painter, son of immigrant parents, a commercial lithographer until 1930. He studied art at the National Academy of Design and in Paris and became noted in the 1930's for works embodying social criticism in harshly defined figure groups, e.g. 'The Passion of Sacco and Vanzetti' (New York, Whitney Museum), 'The Death of a Miner' (New York, Metropolitan Museum). He has also produced a number of murals.

Sheeler, Charles (*b*. Philadelphia, 16 July 1883), American painter, trained at the Pennsylvania Academy, who after a period of Cubist experiment found a vein of his own in views of American industrial works and architecture treated as forms of severely geometric and

C. SHEELER—Modern Classic—Collection of Mrs Edsel Ford, Detroit.

linear construction. Pictures made at the Ford works were good examples of this commentary on modern design and technology.

Siberechts, Jan (*b.* Antwerp, 29 Jan. 1627; *d* in England, *c.* 1703), Flemish painter of landscapes with rustic figures and animals, the pupil of his father (also Jan), a sculptor, Going to London in 1672, he settled in England, and has a place among the forerunners of eighteenth-century English landscape.

Sickert, Walter Richard (*b.* Munich, 31 May 1860; *d.* Bath, 22 Jan. 1942), painter and etcher, eldest son of the Danish painter, Oswald Adalbert Sickert, and a naturalized Englishman. The family moved to London in 1868, and as a young man Sickert worked with Whistler in Chelsea, taking, like his master, to etching. He met Degas in Paris in 1883, and on him rather than Whistler founded his style and attitude to art. Often called an Impressionist, he was only so to the same limited extent as Degas, constructing a picture with deliberation from swift notes made on the spot and never painting in the open air. He worked at Dieppe, 1885–1905, with occasional visits to Venice, and to this period belong music-hall paintings and views of Venice and Dieppe executed in dark, rich tones. From 1905 to 1914 was his 'Camden Town' period, in which he explored the little back rooms, shabby lodging-houses and dingy streets, his zest in urban life and his personality gathering a group of younger artists about him. Though

W. R. SICKERT—The Piazzetta and Doge's Palace, Venice—Collection of the Hon. Mrs Henry Cubitt.

W. R. SICKERT—Little Dot Hetherington at the Old Bedford—Collection of H. Emmons, Esq.

the modern art that may be dated from Cézanne was a closed book to him, he thus rallied together in 1911 the English Post-Impressionists of the Camden Town Group (q.v.). His later work became broader in treatment and lighter in tone, a late innovation being the 'Echoes', in which he freely adapted the work of Victorian illustrators. His verve and quality as an artist claim general modern respect, though the prejudices expressed in his writings (collected in 1947 under the title *A Free House*) date both in substance and style of wit. His third wife, Thérèse Lessore, whom he married in 1926, was also a painter.

Siena, great centre of painting from the thirteenth to fifteenth centuries, for a time rivalling, though eventually outstripped by, its near neighbour, Florence. The general characteristics of the Sienese School were its charm and decorative beauty of line and colour, though its artists did not show the intellectual and scientific power of the Florentine masters. It first shows a Byzantine influence in the work of Guido da Siena and Duccio. Duccio's follower Simone Martini (q.v.) was one of the most eminent painters of the fourteenth century, reflecting the Gothic style of northern Europe but exercising an influence outside Italy by his stay at Avignon. His brother-in-law, Lippo Memmi, worked with him. In the same line of development in the fourteenth century were Pietro and Ambrogio Lorenzetti, Barna di Siena and Bartolo di Taddeo. They were followed in the fifteenth century by Taddeo di Bartolo, Domenico di Bartolo, Sassetta, Vecchietta, Giovanni di Paolo, Pietro di Sano, Neroccio, Matteo di Giovanni and Girolamo. Siena played a small part in the Renaissance, though Beccafumi was a pleasant Mannerist. Painters from other districts who worked there included Spinello Aretino and at the beginning of the sixteenth century Sodoma and Pintoricchio.

Signac, Paul (*b.* Paris, 11 Nov. 1863; *d.* Marseilles, 15 Aug. 1935), French painter associated with Seurat (q.v.) in the development of 'neo-Impressionist' theory. When twenty-one he exhibited in the first Salon des Indépendants, with which exhibiting body he was associated until 1934, and in 1886 he joined with Seurat in the

SPINELLO ARETINO—Death of the Virgin—Accademia, Siena.

D. BECCAFUMI—St
Catherine receives the Stig-
mata—Accademia, Siena.

P. SIGNAC—St Tropez—Leaving the Harbour (1901)—Private Collection.

scientific use of spectrum colour. He painted with separate mosaic-like blocks of pure colour, as distinct from the dots or so-called 'Pointillism' of Seurat, and remained the practitioner and propagandist of this method throughout his life. Without the individual genius which makes Seurat unique he produced many striking landscapes and seascapes of the Normandy and Brittany coasts and in the Mediterranean, his love of ships and the sea finding expression in many admirable water-colours as well as oils. In his well-known book *D'Eugène Delacroix au Néo-Impressionisme*, published in 1899, he acclaimed Delacroix as the precursor of the new art of colour he and Seurat pursued.

Signatures. In signing their work painters and engravers have made use of the following (mainly Latin) technical terms and their abbreviations:

Pinxit (pinx.), *pictor:* Painted, painter
Delineavit (delin., del.): Drew
Fecit (fec., f.): Made (painting or print)
Invenit (inv.): Designed
Sculpsit (sculp., sc.), *sculptor:* Engraved, engraver
Incidit (incid., inc.): Engraved or etched
Excudit (excud., ex.) } Printed
Impressit (imp.) }
Lith.: Lithographed (either artist or lithographic printer)

[274]

Signorelli, Luca (*b*. Cortona, *c*. 1441; *d*. there, 16 Oct. 1523), Italian painter, associated with both the Umbrian and Florentine Schools. He was the pupil of Piero della Francesca (q.v.), but was also much influenced by the Florentine, Pollaiuolo (q.v.), and the latter's study of anatomy and physical movement. He was one of the group of painters chosen to decorate the Sistine Chapel, 1481–3. His most famous work is the series of frescoes in the Brizio chapel of the cathedral of Orvieto, 1499, an undertaking begun by Fra Angelico in 1447. The Overthrow of Antichrist, the Destruction of the World by Fire, the Resurrection of the Dead and Punishment of the Damned and the Blessed ascending to Heaven were the themes painted with tremendous force and unusual effects of colour, the frescoes being noted above all for figures in an expressive violence of action which gave inspiration to Michelangelo for his 'Last Judgment'. A masterpiece on canvas was his 'Pan' (Berlin), destroyed during the Second World War. His later years were spent at Cortona in less ambitious effort.

Silhouette, term applied to small portraits, either solid black on a white ground or white on a black ground, popular in the late eighteenth and early nineteenth century until superseded by the daguerreotype. The word originally had reference to the exactions of Étienne de Silhouette (1709–67), comptroller-general of France, and thus satirically to any 'reductions to a minimum'. In general as regards painting and graphic art it refers to any area defined by a flat colour.

Silverpoint, now obsolete method of drawing with an instrument pointed with silver on paper coated with a special ground. The effect resembled that of a pencil drawing but was more delicate. It was much used in the fifteenth and sixteenth centuries in Italy, the

LEONARDO DA VINCI—
Bust of a Warrior (Silver-
Point)—British Museum.

[275]

L. SIGNORELLI—Last Judgment—The Fate of the Damned—Cathedral, Orvieto.

L. SIGNORELLI—Pan (formerly at Berlin, now destroyed).

Netherlands and Germany. The ground was composed of powdered bones and gumwater, giving an ivory finish, though in Italy and expecially in Florence tinted grounds were favoured. Being indelible and not liable to smudge, the silverpoint was convenient for the sketch-book, as in that which Dürer took with him on his visit to the Netherlands. Points of other metals, e.g. lead, were also employed in the same period with similar effect.

Siqueiros, David Alfaro (*b*. Chihuahua, 1898), Mexican painter and graphic artist. Like Diego Rivera and Orozco he was much influenced by the Mexican Revolution, in which as a boy he took part. He studied in Europe, 1921–3, and subsequently executed many mural paintings in Mexico, Uruguay and Argentina and also in the United States. His work has a strong patriotic, political and revolutionary character which shows itself both emotionally and technically. Harking back to the spirit of Aztec art, he has also used experimental modern techniques, e.g. the employment of the spray-gun for mural painting and modern industrial paints.

Sisley, Alfred (*b*. Paris, 30 Oct. 1839; *d*. Moret-sur-Loing, 29 Jan. 1899), painter of English parentage, linked with the French Impressionist School. His father was a wealthy business man in Paris and the boy was sent to England at eighteen and destined for a commercial career, but was afterwards allowed to study art and

A. SISLEY—The Floods at Port-Marly—Louvre.

RAPHAEL—The Sistine Madonna—Dresden Gallery.

M. SLEVOGT—In the Jungle—Kunsthalle, Hamburg.

worked under Gleyre with Monet and Renoir. He devoted himself exclusively to landscape, exhibited at the first Impressionist exhibition of 1874 and is a close partner of Monet in atmospheric colour. He began virtually as an amateur, but the loss of the family fortune compelled him to paint in earnest for a living. Despite a lifelong struggle with financial difficulty his art shows an admirable consistency and quality. Apart from two short stays in England, when he painted on the Thames, he lived and worked in the valley of the Seine and near Paris, settling finally in a small dwelling at Moret. 'The Floods at Port-Marly' (Louvre) and 'Bridge at Sèvres' (Tate Gallery) are beautiful examples of his art, which figures in many galleries.

Sistine Chapel, Vatican, Rome, erected, 1473–81, under Pope Sixtus IV, contains (1) a series of frescoes, executed c. 1481–3 by Florentine and Umbrian masters, Perugino, Pintoricchio, Botticelli and others, (2) the great ceiling decoration by Michelangelo, 1508–12, and (3) the 'Last Judgment' (q.v.) on the altar-wall by Michelangelo, painted 1534–41 under Paul III. *See* MICHELANGELO.

'Sistine Madonna', most famous of all Raphael's Madonnas, painted c. 1513 for the Benedictines of San Sisto and purchased from them by Francis III, Duke of Modena. It is one of the great treasures of the

[279]

Dresden Gallery, from which it was removed by the Soviet administration after the Second World War but returned with other pictures in 1955. In ampler and more remote splendour than the early Madonnas, e.g. 'La Belle Jardinière' (q.v.), the Virgin rises among clouds.

Slevogt, Max (*b*. Landshut, Bavaria, 8 Oct. 1868; *d*. Neukastell, 20 Sept. 1932), German painter, like Liebermann (q.v.) and Corinth an exponent of Impressionism. He studied at Munich and in Paris and painted landscapes, still life and portraits, his fondness for music and the opera leading him to paint a number of musicians and singers.

Sloan, John (*b*. Lock Haven, Pennsylvania, 2 Aug. 1871; *d*. Hanover, N.H., 8 Sept. 1951), American painter of city life. He studied at the Pennsylvania Academy and was one of the 'Eight', American painters who in 1908 declared the right of the artist to depict American life with freedom and zest. He painted and drew New York streets, interiors and crowds with an observant eye.

Smet, Gustave de (*b*. Ghent, 1877; *d*. Deurle, 1943), Belgian Expressionist painter who lived in Holland during the First World War, when he seems to have made some contact with German Expressionist art. He worked in Belgium at Laethem Saint-Martin with Permeke (q.v.) and others of sympathetic tendency, producing emphatically stylized paintings of popular life.

Smith, Sir Matthew Arnold Bracy (*b*. Halifax, 22 Oct. 1879; *d*. London, 29 Sept. 1959), English painter. He studied at the Slade School and in Paris, working, 1911, for a short while in Matisse's school and being much influenced by Fauvism. His mature style developed in the 1920's and in a series of nudes, landscapes (Cornwall and South of France) and flower and still-life paintings he displayed a sumptuousness of colour in which he had no modern British rival. He was knighted in 1954.

SIR MATTHEW SMITH—
Jeune Femme (1930)—Photo
Tooth Gallery.

[280]

CÉZANNE—Curtain,
Jug and Fruit-dish—
Whitney Collection.

F. SNYDERS—Cat and Dog—Musée de Grenoble.

Snyders, Frans (*b.* Antwerp, Nov. 1579; *d.* there, 19 Aug. 1657), Flemish painter whose parents kept the tavern in Antwerp, De Groote Bruckoftscamere, frequented by artists. He was the pupil of Pieter Brueghel the Younger (q.v.) and Hendrik van Balen, and settling at Antwerp after the customary visit to Italy, 1608–9, was employed as assistant by Rubens especially for the still-life and animal detail in which he excelled. An instance of his collaboration is in the paintings commissioned from Rubens by Philip IV for his hunting lodge. He married, 1611, the sister of the animal painter, Paul de Vos, with whom he also worked. He painted vigorous hunting scenes of his own conception and some battle pieces.

Social Realism, *see* REALISM.

Sodoma, Il (Giovanni Antonio Bazzi) (*b.* Vercelli, 1477; *d.* Siena, 1549), Italian painter of the Milanese School. He was a pupil of a minor painter, Martino Spanzotti, at Vercelli, but on going to Milan was strongly influenced by Leonardo da Vinci. He settled in Siena, 1501, and much of his best work consists of frescoes of religious subjects in that city. He completed a series of frescoes depicting the life of St Benedict begun by Signorelli (q.v.) in the Benedictine monastery of Monte Oliveto, 1505–8, and in 1508 visited Rome, where he painted in the Camera della Segnatura of the Vatican, though Julius II, dissatisfied with his work, replaced him by Raphael. He also painted at Rome the 'Marriage of Alexander and Roxana' in

the Villa Farnesina,
1512. He did some
work in other Italian
cities, Mantua, Volterra,
Florence and Pisa. 'The
Vision of St Catherine',
1526 (Siena, San Dom-
enica), represents his
graceful and ornate
style at its best. His
sneers at the *Lives* of
Vasari are said to have
provoked the latter's
unfavourable account of
his art and life.

Soest, Konrad von
(active fifteenth cen-
tury), German painter of
the Westphalian School,
who was active in Dort-
mund from about 1394.
His principal works are
the altar-piece 'Crucifixion', at Niederwildungen, 1404, and
'Madonna', Dortmund, 1420.

Soft Style, term applied to German painting and sculpture of the
late Gothic period, early fifteenth century, referring to its gentle
harmonies of composition and the mild beauty and innocence of the
types represented. It was mainly characteristic of the painters of the
Cologne School, Stefan Lochner (q.v.) being a notable exponent. It
was followed in the fifteenth century by a sharper realism which has
been termed the 'hard style' and is exemplified by Konrad Witz (q.v.).

Solario, Andrea da (*b.* probably Milan, *c.* 1460; *d. c.* 1520), Italian
painter whose style was formed on Alvise Vivarini and Antonello da
Messina during a stay in Venice, 1490–3, and on Leonardo da Vinci in
Milan. He went to France in 1507 and may have visited Flanders,
which would account for Flemish influence discernible in his work,
but he was back in Italy by 1515. His 'Venetian Senator' (National
Gallery) shows a masterly ability in portraiture.

Solario, Antonio da (called **Lo Zingaro**) (active 1502–*c.* 1518),
Italian painter, a gipsy by origin, though signing himself a Venetian.
He was a follower of Bellini and Carpaccio. Principal works by him
were frescoes illustrative of the life of St Benedict in the convent of
San Severino, Naples.

A. DA SOLARIO—A Venetian Senator—National Gallery, London.

Solimena, Francesco (called l'Abbate Ciccio) (*b*. Nocera de' Pagani, 4 Oct. 1657; *d*. Barra, nr Naples, 5 April 1747), Italian painter of the Neapolitan School, one of the most famous and successful of the later baroque artists. In style he may be compared with his friend Luca Giordano (q.v.), and he decorated many churches in Naples. Among his best works are frescoes in San Paolo Maggiore and his 'Last Supper' (Assisi).

Sotto in sù, foreshortening in a ceiling painting, so devised as to give a convincing illusion of figures and objects in space when seen from below.

Soulages, Pierre (*b*. Rodez, 24 Dec. 1919), French painter of the non-figurative school. He settled in Paris in 1946 and has since exhibited in Paris, Berlin, New York and London. Like his friend Hartung (q.v.) he has exploited the effect of dark near-monochrome abstractions, interstices of light between black pillars of paint giving an effect of space.

South African Art first emerges in the early nineteenth century, though at a much earlier date English marine painters had painted views of the Cape, e.g. George Lambert and Samuel Scott (1720). Art in the early colonial period was documentary and is represented by Thomas Baines (1820–75) artist and explorer, the first to see and paint the Victoria Falls; Thomas William Bowler (1813–69), watercolourist at Cape Town; Samuel Daniel (1775–1811), noted for his illustrated work, 'African Scenery and Animals'; J. C. Poortemans (1776–1870), Dutch artist-lithographer, and a few others. A new phase of development began *c*. 1900, when boundaries were fixed and the country became settled and prosperous. Pieter Wenning (1874–1921), who came to South Africa in 1906 and produced many paintings and drawings, is regarded as a founder of contemporary South African art. Jacob Hendrik Pierneef (*b*. 1886) is a leader in decorative landscape; Walter Battiss (*b*. 1906) has been influenced by Bushman

THOMAS BAINES—Hunting Hippo by Makoba in Canoe—Africana Museum, Johannesburg.

art, of which he has made a special study. A number of artists have been trained and have worked both in South Africa and Europe: Graham Bell (1910–32), Enslin Du Plessis (*b.* 1894), Merlyn Evans (*b.* 1910), Gwelo Goodman (1871–1939), Neville Lewis (*b.* 1895), Le Roux Smith le Roux (*b.* 1914). A series of murals in South Africa House, London, well represents Pierneef and others. A large collection of pictorial works of South African interest is now in the Africana Museum, Johannesburg.

Soutine, Chaim (*b.* Smilovitch, nr Minsk, 1894; *d.* Champigny-sur Vende, 9 Aug. 1943), painter of Lithuanian origin, associated with the School of Paris (q.v.). Escaping from the misery of the ghetto, he worked for a while in the art school at Vilna and then found his way to Paris, where he lived a poverty-stricken Bohemian life among the painters and poets. He was driven by poverty to attempt suicide in 1912. He was the close friend of Modigliani, on whose death he retired for a while to Céret, painting tormented canvases that seemed to reflect despair. After 1923, however, when Zborowski, the dealer to whom Modigliani introduced him, arranged an exhibition, he had a measure of success in Paris. The Expressionist distortion of his work recalls van Gogh and in his still life (a plucked fowl being a characteristic subject) he shows a remarkable intensity of colour.

Spanish Painting first developed in Catalonia, which was furthest removed from the sphere of Islamic influence and dominion, and remarkable paintings in the Romanesque style (*see* ROMANESQUE)

[284]

SPANISH PAINTING (Fifteenth Century)—Virgin and Child in a Gothic Embrasure—Victoria and Albert Museum.

were produced at such places as Tahull, Pedret and Urgel in the twelfth century. In the fourteenth century Sienese influence appears in the work of Ferrer Bassa, Luis Borrassa and Jaime and Pedro Serra, but in the fifteenth century the influence of Netherlandish art comes into prominence in the production of altar-pieces. In Castile there are Juan de Flandes and Fernando Gallego and in Aragon Luis Dalmau, Jaime Huguet, Bartolomé Bermejo and the Vergos family (*see* GOTHIC PAINTING). In the Spanish Kingdom, united in 1472, art entered a new phase marked by (1) the development of royal and aristocratic portraiture, with the internationalized Dutch painter Anthonis Mor (Antonio Moro), Alonso Sanchez Coello and Pantoja de la Cruz, and (2) painting influenced by the Italian Renaissance, with the Masips, father and son, Luis de Vargas, Pablo de Cespedes and the Florentine born Vicente Carducci. A great and typically Spanish period, sixteenth to seventeenth centuries, is ushered in by the genius of El Greco and the work of Luis de Morales. The seventeenth century is noted for the sombre intensity of religious painting and for a realism especially marked in the School of Seville. Painters of this age include Ribalta, Ribera, Juan de Roelas, Francisco Pacheco, Francisco de Herrera, Juan Sanchez Cotán, Francisco Zurbaran, Alonso Cano, Murillo and Valdés-Leal. The towering genius of Velazquez rises in this period, his pupils being Juan Pareja and Juan Battista del Mazo. The eighteenth century produced numerically few painters of note but a fresh individual outburst of genius in Goya. Luis Meléndez and Francisco Bayeu may also be mentioned. A decline followed in the nineteenth century, though Antonio Esquivel and

Vicente Lopez are of some little note. In recent times efforts have
been made to present the colour and local character of Spain, as in the
work of Zuloaga (q.v.), Sorolla (1863–1923), Anglada and others,
though the Spanish genius is most remarkably displayed in the
Spanish painters of the School of Paris (q.v.), Picasso, Juan Gris,
Salvador Dali and Joan Miro.

Spencer, Stanley (*b.* Cookham, 1892; *d.* Taplow, 14 Dec. 1959),
English painter, religious in inspiration, born in Berkshire at a
Thames-side village with which his life as an artist is closely linked.
He studied art at the Slade School, 1910–14, and served in the war of
1914–18 in Macedonia, this leading to a great work, the Memorial
Chapel at Burghclere, in which scenes of military life are added to
the conception of the Resurrection central in his work. 'The
Resurrection' of 1927 (Tate Gallery) was followed by a number
of interpretations of this and other Christian themes deriving their
intensity of effect from their locally particularized and contemporary
character of presentation. As a visionary and in this relation of the
particular with the sublime he may be compared with Blake. A Pre-
Raphaelite aspect of his work appearing in highly detailed landscapes (as in those of his painter brother, Gilbert Spencer, A.R.A.) was
distinct from his visionary painting, in which he was unique among
contemporary artists.

Spinello, Aretino (*b.* Arezzo, active 1373; *d.* 1410–11), Italian
painter, pupil of Jacopo Casentino, who carried on the tradition of

STANLEY SPENCER—The Angels of the Apocalypse—Photo: Tooth Gallery.

Giotto and belongs to the early Florentine School. He worked in Arezzo, Florence, Pisa and Siena successively, his frescoes including those illustrating the life of St Nicholas, church of San Niccolo, Arezzo; in the principal chapel of Santa Maria Maggiore, Florence; and in the monasteries of San Miniato, near Florence, San Bernardo, Arezzo and Monte Oliveto, near Florence. Six of the frescoes illustrating the life of San Raniero in the (war-damaged) Campo Santo, Pisa, were by him and considered by Vasari among his best works. He also painted scenes from the life of Pope Alexander III in the Palazzo Pubblico, Siena.

'Sposalizio, Lo', the 'Betrothal of the Virgin', famous early work by Raphael, painted for the Franciscans of Città di Castello. It is signed on the cornice of the temple in the background RAPHAEL URBINAS. MVIIII. Raphael adapted the composition from a painting of the same subject by Perugino in the cathedral of Perugia, though his work already has a beauty and character of its own. A French general carried the painting off in 1798 but it was later retrieved by Giovanni Sannazzaro of Milan, who left it to the hospital of that city in 1804. In 1806 it was purchased by the State and placed in the Brera Gallery, Milan.

Spranger, Barthel (b. Antwerp, c. 1546; d. Prague, c. 1627), Flemish painter of religious and allegorical subjects and portraits, trained at Antwerp. He worked in Rome for Pius V and later at Vienna and Prague for the emperors Maximilian I and Rudolph II in the Italian Mannerist style.

Squarcione, Francesco (b. Padua, 1394; d. 1474), Italian painter, a merchant in early life, who travelled extensively, especially in Greece,

B. SPRANGER—The Triumph of Wisdom over Ignorance—Kunsthistorisches Museum, Vienna.

N. DE STAËL—Still Life against Black-and-white Ground—Photo: Tooth Gallery.

whence he brought back a collection of antiques. He took to painting and became famous as a teacher, being known as the 'father of painting' and an influence in the development of the Venetian School. He used his collection in the instruction of his pupils, of whom he had as many as 137. They included Mantegna, Tura and Crivelli. A signed work by Squarcione is the polyptych 'Madonna and Saints' in the museum at Padua.

Staël, Nicolas de (*b.* Russia, 1914; *d.* Paris, 1955), Russian-born painter of the French modern school who settled in Paris in 1943. He was influenced by Georges Braque (q.v.) but developed a personal, non-figurative style about 1945. Later he showed an increasing interest in landscape, figure and still-life composition. The simplified forms and bright colour of his work were of special interest in their equivalent suggestions of abstraction and nature.

Stained Glass, one of the great medieval arts, developing with the increase of window space in the Gothic church and to some extent serving the same purpose as a wall-painting with the added richness given by translucence and the variations of light piercing through from outside. Windows of an early date consisted of a mosaic-like arrangement of pieces of brightly coloured glass stained the whole way through. Later pictorial subjects were introduced, the roughly cut pieces of glass being set in leads which arbitrarily outlined figures, drapery, etc., and were fastened to an iron tracery, slight shading and details being painted on the glass in grisaille (q.v.). In origin it is

TOULOUSE-LAUTREC—La Clownesse (Colour Lithograph).

UTAMARO—A Girl and her Reflection (Colour Woodcut)—
British Museum.

ENGLISH STAINED GLASS (Canterbury, Thirteenth Century)—The Parable of the Sower—Photo: Victoria and Albert Museum.

STAINED GLASS (German Fourteenth Century)—Christ in Limbo (detail)—Stendal Cathedral.

* K

probably related to the Byzantine use of coloured glass as mosaic. One of the earliest mentions of stained glass is that of Count Arnold's gift of a window to the abbey of Tegernsee in Bavaria, A.D. 999. Much of the most beautiful glass belongs to the twelfth and thirteenth centuries. Splendid examples are to be found in La Sainte Chapelle, Paris, Chartres, Bourges and Le Mans cathedrals, York Minster, Beverley Minster and Lincoln and Canterbury cathedrals. From the fourteenth century glass became increasingly pictorial and showed divergences of national style. The workshops of Engrand Leprince at Beauvais produced beautiful glass in the sixteenth century, examples being in St Étienne, Beauvais, and St Vincent, Rouen. In England the magnificent stained glass of King's College Chapel, Cambridge, represents a Netherlandish method. In the mid sixteenth century a new technique was introduced, the painting of glass in enamels, the method producing imitations of oil painting in which the true nature and brilliance of the art was lost. The windows by Sir Joshua Reynolds in New College, Oxford, are a later illustration of its decay and misuse. The revival conducted in the nineteenth century by William Morris and Edward Burne-Jones produced windows of interesting design though lacking the splendour of the Middle Ages. The twentieth century has seen a number of efforts to combine ancient methods with the modern sense of colour. Matisse in the chapel at Vence, Rouault and Alfred Manessier are French artists who in various ways have stimulated a fresh approach. In Britain the work of Miss Evie Hone (Eton College Chapel), and of a group of artists who have designed windows for the new Coventry Cathedral, is notable.

Stanfield, Clarkson (*b.* Sunderland, 1793; *d.* London, 18 May 1867), English marine painter. After early experience in the merchant service and navy he became a theatrical scene painter, and painter of the pictures of sea and coast, British and continental, which were very popular and praised beyond measure by Ruskin. He was made R.A., 1835, and long known as the 'English van de Velde'.

Stanze, papal state apartments of the Vatican, decorated with frescoes by Raphael (q.v.), 1508–20, at the invitation of Popes Julius II and Leo X. They comprise the Stanza della Segnatura, so called from the court of justice held there over which the Pope presided, and other rooms deriving their names from the subjects of the frescoes they contain, Stanza dell' Incendio, Stanza d'Eliodoro and Sala di Costantino.

Steel Engraving, in technique the same as engraving on copper, but replacing it in use for book illustration in the later nineteenth century, partly because as a harder metal a larger number of perfect impressions could be taken from it and also because of the fineness of line shading it allowed. A beautiful quality was obtained in early nineteenth-century steel engravings after Turner and other landscape painters, e.g. in the vignettes to Rogers's *Italy*. It was a laborious process which the steelfacing by electrolysis of copperplate or wood block later rendered obsolete.

Steen, Jan Havicsz (*b.* Leyden, *c.* 1626; *d.* there, 3 Feb. 1679), Dutch painter of popular life who studied under Adriaen van Ostade and Jan van Goyen (qq.v.), whose daughter he married. He worked at The Hague, Delft (where he had a brewery) and Leyden, where in his later years he kept an inn. He was a master of humorous *genre* which his great sensitiveness as an artist preserved from triviality. A well-known picture is 'The Prince's Birthday' (Rijksmuseum).

Steer, Philip Wilson (*b.* Birkenhead, 28 Dec, 1860; *d.* London, 21 Mar. 1942), English painter, the son of Philip Steer, a portrait painter. He studied art in Paris under Bouguereau and Cabanel but was more influenced by the French Neo-Impressionism of the 1880's, and in beauty of colour and effective simplicity of design his paintings of Walberswick and Cowes, executed between 1886 and 1892, were a signal contribution to the early exhibitions of the New English Art Club. Later he returned to English tradition, leaning towards Constable and Turner, his 'Chepstow Castle' (Tate Gallery) being a Turnerian view as Constable might have handled it. He revived the art of direct water-colour painting and also painted some able portraits and figure studies suggested by Gainsborough's 'fancy pictures', but is of note mainly as an English Impressionist in landscape. He received the Order of Merit in 1937.

Steinlen, Théophile (*b.* Lausanne, 10 Nov. 1859; *d.* Paris, 14 Dec. 1923), French graphic artist of Swiss origin. He went to Paris about 1882 and devoted himself to depicting the popular life of the city, Montmartre in particular, in works of a vivid, illustrative character. In his illustrations, lithographs and posters the influence of the

P. W. STEER—The Bridge, Étaples—Tate Gallery.

Japanese print appears and he contributed to that style of the 1890's which assumes individual greatness in the work of Toulouse-Lautrec.

Stevens, Alfred (*b*. Blandford, Dorset, 1817; *d*. London, 1 May 1875), English architectural sculptor, designer, painter and draughtsman, the son of a heraldic painter. He studied painting, sculpture and architecture in Florence and Rome and returned to England steeped in the spirit and technique of Renaissance art, applying himself to a variety of decorative tasks (including designs for stoves and fenders which won prizes at the Great Exhibition of 1851). His chief work was the Wellington Monument for St Paul's on which he spent seventeen years, 1858–75. Other works of design were the lions for the British Museum railings, the mosaics of prophets for the spandrels under the dome of St Paul's and a scheme of decoration for the old Dorchester House, Park Lane. His principal legacy as a pictorial artist is an immense number of beautiful chalk and pencil drawings, studies for his larger undertakings, fully represented at the Tate Gallery. His distinction as a portrait painter is shown by his 'Mrs Leonard Collmann' (National Gallery).

Still Life, painting which represents inanimate objects seen at close range, the purpose being either to suggest some pleasurable association (as in pictures of flowers or fruit) or to concentrate attention on form and colour without introducing the rival claims on the attention

[292]

DUTCH STILL LIFE (Seventeenth Century)—by C. de Heem—Photo: T. Agnew & Son.

represented by more elaborate subject-matter. It was not unknown in
the ancient world; the Greek painter Sosos (third century B.C.) made
a remarkable design out of the debris of a banquet, as is shown by a
mosaic copy in the Lateran Museum, Rome, and Pompeian wall-
painting gives other examples. Subsequently, however, still life as the
sole or main theme of a picture virtually disappears until the seventeenth century, though from the fifteenth century onwards it often
appears as an incidental in figure compositions on which the artist
lavishes care and skill. Caravaggio at the end of the sixteenth century
painted a basket of fruit which is complete in itself as a picture,
but generally speaking still life was little cultivated in Italy, and in
the seventeenth century was largely a speciality of Dutch and
Flemish artists. The Dutch interest in floriculture created a demand
for minutely detailed and accurately coloured flower pictures, as in the
work of Jan Davidz van Heem, Rachel Ruysch and Jan van Huysum
(qq.v.), and a delight in the appurtenances of the table encouraged
the production of works such as those of Willem Claesz Heda and
Willem Kalf (qq.v.). Flemish art produced the opulent still-life
paintings of Jan Brueghel and Frans Snyders (qq.v.). Spanish artists
also showed an intense appreciation of material substance, exemplified by the bodegones (q.v.) of Velazquez and by now lesser-known
still-life painters such as Cotán (q.v.) forming a school best known by
the work of Zurbarán (q.v.). A taste for Flemish and Dutch still

[293]

life in eighteenth-century France encouraged Chardin (q.v.) to produce his masterpieces of the *genre*. Still life was much cultivated by the great artists of nineteenth-century France, Delacroix, Courbet, Manet, Renoir, Cézanne and van Gogh providing great examples, though the interest possessed by objects in themselves gave way increasingly to the study of light and colour for which the object served as a pretext. Cubism (q.v.) carried this process a stage further in breaking through surface appearance, though the Cubist still life retains a suggestion of familiar things. While it indicates a trend towards abstract art, still life stops short of complete abstraction.

Stipple, in painting, drawing and engraving, a method of obtaining effect by means of dots instead of solid areas of colour or tone or of continuous lines. In **Stipple Engraving,** etching and line engraving are combined to produce the effect, while an instrument called the roulette with a toothed wheel provides a dotted line. Special types of roulette are used in the associated process of crayon (or chalk) engraving to produce a grain like that of a chalk drawing.

Stothard, Thomas (*b.* London, 17 Aug. 1755; *d.* there, 27 April 1834), English painter and illustrator. He studied at the Royal Academy Schools and was made R.A., 1794. His graceful drawings, of minor interest in themselves, had some little influence on Flaxman and Blake. He is remembered for his popular painting of the Canterbury Pilgrims, in which, at the suggestion of the dealer Cromek, he unwittingly forestalled Blake.

Strigel, Bernhard (*b.* Memmingen, 1460; *d.* there, 1528), German painter who studied at Ulm and later worked in Augsburg with Hans Burgkmair (q.v.). He worked principally at Memmingen in Bavaria, also as portrait painter to the Viennese court and late in life was court painter to the Emperor Maximilian. He imitated the Milanese, da Predis, in his profile portraits. His 'Sybilla von Freyberg' (Munich) is a work of note.

Strozzi, Bernardo (called **Il Cappucino**) (*b.* Genoa, 1581; *d.* Venice, 2 Aug. 1644), Italian painter and engraver. He was a Franciscan friar for some time in early life but left the Order when he was twenty-nine

G. STUART—George Washington, Vaughan Portrait—National Gallery of Art, Washington.

to support his aged mother and sister. On the death of his mother and the marriage of his sister he refused to obey the order to return and was sentenced to three years' imprisonment. He escaped to Venice, however, and there spent his later life as a painter, producing many religious pictures with a Venetian richness of colour. He also painted a number of portraits in the style of Caravaggio.

Stuart, Gilbert (*b.* Rhode Island, 3 Dec. 1755; *d.* Boston, 27 July 1828), American portrait painter, who first studied at Newport, Rhode Island, but went to England in 1755, becoming a pupil of Benjamin West (q.v.). He assimilated the methods of English portraiture and was successful in London, though he got into debt and his financial embarrassments caused him to retreat to Ireland. He worked, 1778–93 (again with success), in Dublin. He returned to America to paint George Washington, three versions resulting in the ' Athenaeum ' portrait of which he made many replicas. His freshness of colour and the calm dignity of his heads make him outstanding. He painted many distinguished Americans besides Washington, and among his artist sitters were Copley, West and Reynolds.

Stubbs, George (*b.* Liverpool, 25 Aug. 1724; *d.* London, 10 July 1806), English painter, largely self taught. As a young man he practised portrait painting at York and elsewhere in the north of England while studying human and animal anatomy. He visited Italy, *c.* 1754. In 1759 he moved to London, where he worked on the plates and text for his celebrated treatise *The Anatomy of the Horse*, 1766, finding also much employment among the sporting aristocracy for paintings of racehorses. He was elected A.R.A., 1780. Not only an expert animal painter, he has come to be regarded as one of the major English artists of the eighteenth century in power of design and composition and all-round ability. Examples are the spacious ' Gimcrack with a Groom, Jockey and Stable-lad on Newmarket Heath ', painted for Viscount Bolingbroke, and his beautiful pictures

G. STUBBS—Gimcrack with a Groom, Jockey and Stable-lad on Newmarket Heath—
Collection of Major and the Hon. Mrs R. Macdonald-Buchanan.

of haymakers and reapers. He painted some works in enamel colours
on Wedgwood plaques. One of the pictures most popular during his
lifetime (in several versions) was his 'Lion Devouring a Horse'
(Royal College of Surgeons), a memory, according to his biographer,
of a scene witnessed in Morocco, where he made a halt on his return
voyage from Italy.

Suardi, Bartolommeo, *see* BRAMANTINO.

Sully, Thomas (*b.* Horncastle, Lincs, 5 Nov. 1783; *d.* Philadelphia,
5 Nov. 1872), American painter, born in England but taken to the
United States as a child. He became an American citizen in 1809. He
studied the works of Stuart, Trumbull and other American painters
and with the help of patrons went to England, where he was helped
and advised by Benjamin West. He returned in 1810 to Philadelphia,
where he mainly worked, and became of note as a portrait painter in
a facile style recalling that of Sir Thomas Lawrence. A prolific artist,
he produced a great number of portraits, miniatures and subject
pictures.

Suprematism, theory of art devised by the Russian painter Malevich (q.v.) in 1913 proclaiming that the true reality of art was to be
found in geometric form and colour absolutely divorced from the
representation of objects or the conscious attempt to convey ideas.
He had a small following in Russia and a decided influence on the
course taken by Kandinsky (q.v.) in abstract art and the protagonists
of the Dutch de Stijl movement (q.v.).

Surrealism, twentieth-century movement, influential in literature,
painting and sculpture, which as an attempt to restore the imaginative faculty to a place of importance may be compared with the
Romantic movement (*see* ROMANTICISM). In its visual aspect it was a

revolt against the purely aesthetic and abstract values of modern art, laying stress on the value of instinctive expression (sometimes referred to as 'automatism') and seeking to interpret the workings of the subconscious mind. Fantastic and unusual relations of form and imagery acquired a special significance as suggesting the dream world of the mind and stimulating the sense of wonder. The movement took some impetus from the iconoclastic outburst of Dadaism (q.v.) in the later stages of the First World War and the years immediately following, was the subject of much theoretical debate in Paris in the 1920's, when it was fostered by the poets André Breton and Paul Eluard, but reached its zenith in the 1930's and with the International Surrealist Exhibition of 1936. Surrealism claimed a long ancestry in art, reaching back to the fantasy and symbolism of Jerome Bosch (q.v.), and apparent in such masters of the weird as Henry Fuseli and Odilon Redon (qq.v.). Outstanding as a precursor in this century was Giorgio de Chirico (q.v.), while Paul Klee and Marc Chagall (qq.v.) were hailed as kindred spirits. A strongly Surrealist element is to be found in the post-Cubist work of Picasso (q.v.), and other artists closely connected with the movement were Hans (Jean) Arp, Salvador Dali, Marcel Duchamp, Max Ernst, Alberto Giacometti, René Magritte, Joan Miro, Man Ray, André Masson and Yves Tanguy. There was no specifically Surrealist style in painting. The smoothly finished, curiously detailed fantasies of Dali (q.v.) are often regarded as typical, but the collages of Max Ernst (q.v.) present a different development. The irrational impulse and the 'anti-art' character of the movement appear in the cultivation of the 'found object' (q.v.). While it did not survive the Second World War in any coherent shape, Surrealism had a liberating influence on a number of artists of the present time, among them Graham Sutherland (q.v.), Henry Moore and the younger school of sculpture.

'Surrender of Breda, The' ('Las Lanzas'), famous masterpiece by Velazquez painted c. 1635 for the Buen Retiro Palace, Madrid, as one of a series of 'victory pictures'. It shows the surrender of the Dutch city by Justin of Nassau to the Spanish general Ambrose Spinola, Marqués de los Balbases, in June 1625. Velazquez never visited the Low Countries but he had travelled to Italy on the same ship as Spinola, and though the latter died in 1630 would no doubt recall his appearance and perhaps Spinola's description of the event. The Spanish title refers to the serried row of lances which completes the original character of this great composition.

Süss, Hans (von Kulmbach) (b. Kulmbach, c. 1480; d. Nuremberg, Sept.–Dec. 1522), German painter, first influenced by the Venetian Jacopo de' Barbari (q.v.) (who worked in Germany under the name of Jacob Walch) and later the pupil and friend of Dürer (q.v.). He acquired a Venetian richness of colour and pursued Dürer's linear style with effect in the portraits for which he is best known, an outstanding work being his portrait of the Margrave Casimir von Brandenburg, 1511 (Munich).

Sutherland, Graham Vivian (*b.* London, 24 Aug. 1903), English painter and designer. He first studied engraving and etching, his early prints showing some affinity with the work of Samuel Palmer (q.v.), but began to paint from 1930 onwards and during that pre-war decade acquired a Surrealist appreciation of the strangeness and metaphorical suggestion of natural form. This developed into the characteristic thorns, sinister tree shapes and distillations of landscape of the 1940's. As official war artist from 1941 the sense of strangeness found vivid expression in paintings of bomb devastation. The 'Crucifixion', 1946, for the church of St Matthew, Northampton, the 'Origins of the Land' (for the Festival of Britain, 1951, now in the Tate Gallery), the excursions into portraiture, among which the 'Somerset Maugham' is especially striking, and his designs for the tapestry of Coventry Cathedral are varied aspects of his art, the essence of which, however, is the imaginative symbolism that has gained him international repute. Awarded the Order of Merit in 1960.

Sutterman (Sustermans), Justus (*b.* Antwerp, 28 Sept. 1597; *d.* Florence, 23 April 1681), Flemish painter of religious and historical subjects, the pupil of Willem de Vos and in Paris of Frans Pourbus the Younger (q.v.). He worked in Florence as court painter to the Medicean Grand Dukes of Tuscany, Cosimo de' Medici II, Ferdinand II and Cosimo III, and met Van Dyck in Florence in 1624. Subsequently he painted at Rome, Genoa, Modena, Parma and Piacenza, also at Innsbruck for the emperor.

Swedish Painting may be considered, together with that of Norway and Denmark, as representing Scandinavian tendencies in which a northern character and the effect of contact with France and Germany are both to be found. A demand for painting grew in the eighteenth century, portraitists of note being Carl Gustaf Pilo (1711–93) and Alexander Roslin (1718–93). Topography is represented by Elias Martin (1739–1818), who worked in both Sweden and

England. Romantic influences appear in the landscapes of Marcus Larson (1825–64) and the historical pictures of J. F. Höckert (1826–1880). Outdoor scenes and native landscape were cultivated in the later nineteenth century, Carl Larsson (1853–1919), Anders Zorn (1860–1920), Karl Nordström (1855–1923), Carl Wilhelmson (1866–1928) and Bruno Liljefors (1860–1939) being notable.

A Nordic intensity of expression appears in Carl Josephson (1851–1906) and Carl Fredrik Hill (1849–1911), though the principal exponent of Expressionism (q.v.) was the Norwegian Edvard Munch (q.v.). Early years of the twentieth century, however, saw a strengthening of links with Paris and colouristic developments, represented by Isaac Grünewald (1889–1946), Sigrid Hjertén (1885–1948), Karl Isakson (1878–1922), who worked in Denmark, and Leander Engstrom (1886–1927). Outstanding colourists also are Carl Kylberg (1878–1922) and Ragnar Sandberg (b. 1902). A primitive strain is to be seen in Bror Hjorth (b. 1894) and Sven Erixson (b. 1899), but abstract painting of an Expressionist kind is more characteristic of the present day in Scandinavia, as represented, for example, by the Swedish artists Evert Lundquist (b. 1904) and Lennart Rodhe (b. 1916) and the Danish artists Asger Jorn (b. 1914) and Richard Mortensen (b. 1910).

Swiss Painting is related by various threads to French, German and Italian art. It is represented by such notable artists of the fifteenth and sixteenth centuries as Konrad Witz, Nicolaus Manuel Deutsch and Urs Graf (qq.v.). Switzerland has nurtured Holbein, a citizen of Basel, and Füssli (Fuseli), a native of Zürich. In modern times the Bernese painter Ferdinand Hodler stands out as a distinctive national figure not without European influence. Felix Vallotton of Lausanne had a distinguished association with art in France. Paul Klee, though much of his work was done in Germany, had a Swiss mother and grew up and spent his later years in Bern. Other modern artists of note are Cuno Amiet, Augusto and Giovanni Giacometti and Sophie Taeuber-Arp, while the sculptor, painter and draughtsman Alberto Giacometti is widely known at the present day.

Symbolism, movement in painting towards the end of the nineteenth century connected with the literary Symbolism of the French poets, Mallarmé in particular, and endeavouring to express ideas by associations of form and colour. Odilon Redon (q.v.) was acclaimed one of its leaders and Gustave Moreau and Puvis de Chavannes (qq.v.) may be considered on its perimeter, but Gauguin and his disciples of Pont-Aven give its clearest pictorial interpretation of what was described as an 'ideational, synthetic, subjective, decorative' aim. Thus local colour was once more emphasized, given an emotional value of suggestion and substituted for the Impressionist effects of light. Decided black outlines stressed the decorative and symbolic character of such a work as Gauguin's 'Le Christ Jaune'. These Symbolist methods were alternatively known as 'Synthetism' and 'Cloisonnism'. The invention and propagation of these theoretic descriptions seem to be largely due to Gauguin's followers, Émile Bernard and Paul Sérusier.

T

Tachisme, name given to the method used by some contemporary artists of exploiting the quality of freely flowing oil paint for its own sake; one aspect of a tendency to seek new effects in paint substance and colour without representation and formal design pursued both in Europe and America. Sam Francis (*b.* California, 1923) is one of its noted exponents. *See also* ACTION PAINTING.

Taddeo di Bartolo, *see* BARTOLI, TADDEO.

Taeuber-Arp, Sophie (*b.* Davos, 1889; *d.* Zürich, 1943), Swiss painter who studied in Munich and Hamburg, was professor at the Kunstgewerbeschule, Zürich, 1916–29, and afterwards lived in France. She married the sculptor Jean Arp in 1921. One of the earlier painters of geometric abstractions, she was among the founders of the 'Abstraction-Création' group in Paris, 1931.

Tanguy, Yves (*b.* Paris, 5 Jan. 1900; *d.* Waterbury, Conn., early in 1955), French Surrealist painter, self taught, who began to paint after seeing one of de Chirico's pictures and joined the Surrealist group in 1926, contributing to many of their group shows. With a smoothly finished technique he produced compositions in which amoeba-like shapes filled extensive and mysterious plains with phantom effect. He went to the United States in 1939 and later became an American citizen.

TACHISME—Sam Francis —British Council Collection.

YVES TANGUY—Mama, Papa is Wounded! (1927)—Museum of Modern Art, New York.

Tate Gallery, London, contains the national collection of British painting from the sixteenth century to the present day, of modern foreign painting from the Impressionist period onwards, and of modern sculpture, British and foreign. It was opened at Millbank in 1897. It has unique collections of the work of Turner and Blake, one of the best Pre-Raphaelite collections, and since the Second World War has been extensively rearranged and added to in pursuance of its dual function as the National Gallery of British Art and the National Gallery of Modern Art. *See* Appendix, British Artists in the Tate Gallery.

Tempera, form of painting anciently practised in which powdered colour is mixed with some gelatinous or albuminous substance, usually the yolk of egg or the yolk and white together, diluted with water as required. It is applied to a surface, usually a wood panel, coated with gesso (q.v.). The paint dries quickly and somewhat lighter than when first applied, the result being opaque and permanent. It is necessary to use a special technique of shading or hatching with the brush to complete the effect of modelling and detail without disturbance to the paint already laid on and dry. Tempera was the universal means of picture painting in Europe (as distinct from fresco, q.v.) until the fifteenth century, when it gradually gave way to oil painting (q.v.). An intermediate method between the two was that of completing a picture laid in in tempera with a transparent film of colour mixed with oil. The greater richness and adaptability of oil painting led to its superseding tempera and since the Renaissance period it has been little used. *See also* DISTEMPER.

'Tempest, The' (or 'Storm'), one of Giorgione's few fully authenticated works, described as his by a contemporary, Michiel, painted about 1503 and now in the Accademia, Venice. It has never been restored and is presumably as it left the artist's hand, though radioscopic examination indicates that he substituted the figure of a soldier for that of a second nude girl washing her feet in the brook. The picture in either case, however, is without a story and defies explanation in that respect; what clearly appears is the contrast between the seemingly placid and immobile figures and the ominous background of lightning and approaching storm. The strange feeling of tension and drama thus produced makes more vividly appreciable the detail and sumptuous quality of paint and colour. Vasari, though he does not mention 'The Tempest', confessed himself puzzled by Giorgione's absence of 'meaning' in other works, but it is possible to regard this as a deliberate sacrifice to attain that poetic mystery which makes. 'The Tempest' a masterpiece. (Colour, *see* list.)

Tenebrist, name given to the seventeenth-century painters of various countries, Neapolitan, Netherlandish and Spanish, who intensified darkness of shadow in imitation of Caravaggio.

Teniers the Younger, David (*b*. Antwerp, Dec. 1610; *d*. Brussels, 25 April 1690), Flemish painter of *genre*, still life, landscape and portraits, who also made a number of etchings. Trained by his father, David Teniers the Elder (1582–1649—a painter mainly of religious subjects), he was more directly influenced by Rubens and Brouwer (qq.v.). He became court painter to the Archduke Leopold at Brussels and keeper of his art collection, and was extremely popular for his portrayals of small figures in landscape, rustic interiors, fairs and fêtes and odd characters such as alchemists, also for his 'Temptations

D. TENIERS (the Younger)—A Music Party—National Gallery, London.

G. TER BORCH—The Letter—Royal Collection.

of St Anthony', conceived in a gay, vivacious style. His painting shows great skill and sensitiveness of touch, if less penetrating in observation than that of Brouwer. Though Louis XIV disdained him, saying ' Éloignez-moi ces magots' when shown Teniers's work, Philip IV of Spain admired him so much that the Prado is especially rich in his pictures. His country seat at Perck (appearing in 'Teniers's Château at Perck', National Gallery, No. 817) was the resort of Spanish and Flemish connoisseurs and nobles. Notable works are 'The Smoker' (Louvre), 'Village Fête' (National Gallery) and 'Meeting of the Civic Guards' (Leningrad).

Ter Borch (Terburg), Gerard (*b*. Zwolle, 1617; *d*. Deventer, 8 Dec. 1681), Dutch painter, taught by his father and the elder Pieter Molyn at Haarlem. He travelled to England, Italy, Germany and Spain (where he studied Velazquez) and settled in 1654 at Deventer. He is noted for his portraits and above all for interiors with figures representing the social life of wealthy Dutch citizens, painted with great skill and feeling for light and material textures, 'The Letter' (Royal Collection) being an excellent example. His 'Peace of Munster', 15 May 1648 (National Gallery), is a famous portrait group of the conference that marked the end of the Thirty Years War.

Terbrugghen, Hendrick (*b*. Deventer, 1588; *d*. Utrecht, 1629), Dutch painter of religious subjects, the pupil of Bloemaert (*q.v.*) at Utrecht, where he settled in 1616 after ten years spent in Rome and Naples. Impressed by Caravaggio, he was a leader of the Utrecht School and the hybrid Italianate style it propagated.

Theophanes the Greek (active late fourteenth century), eminent Byzantine painter. Trained, it seems beyond doubt, at Constantinople, he was one of the Greek artist emigrants to Russia. He produced both icons and wall-paintings, the latter including his decorations for the cathedral of the Transfiguration, Novgorod, 1378, and his 'Last Judgment' in the cathedral of the Dormition, Vladimir, *c*. 1408. He worked also at Moscow, where Roublev (*q.v.*) collaborated with him.

Another Theophanes of later date (sixteenth century) was a leading artist of the Byzantine school of Crete which had flourished in its monasteries from the beginning of the fourteenth century.

Thoma, Hans (*b*. Bernau, Black Forest, 2 Oct. 1839; *d*. Karlsruhe, 7 Nov. 1924), German painter who studied at Karlsruhe and in Paris, where he was somewhat influenced by Courbet. Though he painted some symbolic works he was at his best in realistic studies of German landscape. He became Academy Professor and Museum Director at Karlsruhe in 1899.

Thornhill, Sir James (*b*. Melcombe Regis, Dorset, 1676; *d*. Thornhill, Dorset, 4 May 1734), English baroque painter, pupil of Thomas Highmore, whom he succeeded in 1720 as serjeant-painter to Queen Anne. He modelled his style on Italian baroque (studying prints though he did not visit Italy) and on Le Brun, whose work he saw in France, and had a number of large decorative commissions. They

TRÈS RICHES HEURES DU DUC DE BERRY—The Month of May—Musée Condé, Chantilly.

SIR J. THORNHILL—Ceiling of Painted Hall, Greenwich—Royal Naval College.

included chiaroscuro designs for the interior of the dome of St Paul's, and the great hall at Blenheim, but his masterpiece is the wall and ceiling paintings of the Painted Hall, Greenwich, admirably restored in 1960. Other works were altar-pieces for All Souls and Queen's College, Oxford, and portraits (e.g. Sir Isaac Newton, Trinity College, Cambridge). He made proposals for a royal academy (on the French model) and set up his own drawing school in Covent Garden, Hogarth, who married his daughter Jane, being one of his pupils. Thornhill's son, also James, became serjeant-painter to George II.

Tiepolo, Giovanni Battista (*b*. Venice, 5 Mar. ? 1696; *d*. Madrid, 27 Mar. 1770), Italian painter and etcher of the Venetian School, unsurpassed in decorative brilliance and the last of the great Venetian fresco painters. He studied under the minor painter, Gregorio Lazzarini, but the source of his light and fanciful rococo style may be found in Sebastiano Ricci (q.v.). Influenced also by Crespi and Piazzetta (qq.v.) in such early works as the 'Sacrifice of Isaac', *c*. 1715–16 (Venice, Ospedaletto), and his paintings in the church of the Scalzi, he shed their dark effects of chiaroscuro to attain a luminous and aerial atmosphere in which he rivals Veronese, who also led him to cover vast wall spaces with sumptuous effects of architecture and splendidly attired groups of figures. Until 1750, with immense virtuosity and a quality of brush-stroke and colour entirely his own, he covered the walls and ceilings of many villas and palaces in Venice and elsewhere in northern Italy, the series of 'Antony and

G. B. TIEPOLO—The Banquet of Cleopatra—National Gallery of Victoria, Australia.

Cleopatra' (Palazzo Labia) being a culminating achievement. The decoration of the Villa San Sebastiano at Malmarana, near Vicenza, 1737, with scenes from the *Iliad*, *Orlando Furioso* and *Gerusalemme Liberata* was another of many notable works in Italy. He went to Würzburg, 1751–3, to decorate the Prince Bishop's Palace, being assisted by his sons, Giovanni Domenico and Lorenzo. In 1755 he was elected president of the Venetian Academy and in 1762 was invited to Spain by Charles III, there carrying out a scheme of decoration for the Palacio Real and painting altar-pieces for San Pasquale at Aranjuez. These were later replaced by pictures by Mengs, his competitor and opponent in style. Tiepolo's drawings (well exemplified in the Victoria and Albert Museum) are also of exceptional brilliance. He married the sister of Francesco Guardi (q.v.) in 1719 and of his two sons the more notable as an artist was Giovanni Domenico (1727–1802). As a painter he assisted and imitated his father, and in his later years produced some original and satiric scenes of Italian comedy and Venetian life. Like his father he was a facile and able draughtsman.

TINTORETTO—The Origin of the Milky Way—National Gallery, London.

TINTORETTO—The Miracle of St Mark—Accademia, Venice.

Timomachos of Byzantium (1st century B.C.), last great painter of antiquity, who sought to interpret Greek tragedy in painting. Copies of his impressive 'Medea' were found at Pompeii and Herculaneum.

Tintoretto, Jacopo Robusti (*b.* Venice, Sept. or Oct. 1518; *d.* there, 31 May 1594), Italian painter of the Venetian School. The name by which he is known refers to his father's occupation as dyer (*tintore*). He is said to have been a pupil of Titian for a short time and perhaps also of Schiavone, with whom he worked. According to a famous story he wrote on the wall of his studio 'the drawing of Michelangelo and the colour of Titian' as a precept to follow, and he did in fact make a number of drawings from casts of Michelangelo's sculptures. Except for a visit to Mantua he never seems to have left Venice, where unremitting labour produced a vast output of religious paintings, portraits and a number of allegorical and mythological subjects. They include his great 'Miracle of St Mark', 1548 (Venice, Accademia), his decorations for the Scuola di San Rocco (including the vast 'Christ before Pilate' and 'Last Supper'), 1560, and the overwhelmingly impressive 'Paradise' for the Doge's Palace, 1590. These great works show a never-failing imagination, a wonderfully dramatic sense of movement, space and lighting in composition, and superb use of colour. The effects he observed (and utilized in his painted

[308]

compositions) from focusing light on small wax models grouped inside a box had a considerable influence on later painters. His originality in portraiture can be appreciated in the 'Doge Mocenigo' (Venice, Accademia), Self-Portrait (Louvre) and 'Vincenzo Morosini' (National Gallery). Masterpieces, apart from his religious works on a decorative scale, are his 'Susanna and the Elders' (Vienna), 'St George and the Dragon', with its sense of rushing movement (National Gallery), and the 'Origin of the Milky Way', one of the most beautiful of painted allegories. The Scuola di San Rocco works inspired a famous panegyric by Ruskin, who, in *The Stones of Venice* and other writings, did much to rescue his fame from neglect. His art may be looked on as a foundation of that of El Greco. His son Domenico was his assistant in his later works and carried on his workshop, in which another son, Marco, and his daughter, Marietta, were also trained.

Tischbein, Wilhelm (*b.* Hayna, Hesse, 1751; *d.* Eutin, 1829), German painter of historical subjects, portraits and still life who made a long stay in Italy, 1779–89. He is remembered mainly by his portrait of Goethe among classical ruins in the Roman Campagna which earned him the nickname of 'Goethe Tischbein'.

W. TISCHBEIN—Goethe in the Campagna—Staedel Institute, Frankfurt.

J. J. TISSOT—The Picnic—Tate Gallery.

Tisio, Benvenuto, *see* GAROFALO.

Tissot, James (*b.* Nantes, 15 Oct. 1836, *d.* Buillon, 3 Aug. 1902), French painter and etcher, notable mainly for the *genre* pictures painted during a prolonged stay in London after the war of 1870, a good example being 'The Picnic' (Tate Gallery). Later he produced illustrations for the New Testament, spending ten years in Palestine for this purpose.

Titian (Tiziano Vecellio) (*b.* Pieve da Cadore at uncertain date between 1480 and 1490; *d.* Venice, 1576), Italian painter of the Venetian School and one of the greatest masters of the Italian Renaissance. He was born in a mountainous district of the Venetian Alps (from which his landscape backgrounds seem often to derive) and was apprenticed as a boy of nine to mosaicists (Zuccati) in Venice, afterwards being the pupil of Giovanni Bellini (q.v.), like Giorgione (q.v.), with whom he worked. It is assumed they collaborated, 1507–8, on the decoration of the Fondaco de' Tedeschi (now destroyed). Titian seems to have finished pictures left incomplete at Giorgione's death in 1510 (e.g. the 'Concert'—Pitti Gallery), though there is still controversy as to the extent of this posthumous collaboration. From the sensuous and poetic suggestion of Giorgione he quickly developed a personal style. The most famous of his early works are the so-called

TITIAN—Portrait of a Man
—National Gallery, London.

'Sacred and Profane Love' (Rome, Borghese), 'L'Homme au Gant' (Louvre), 'Christ and the Tribute Money' (Dresden) and 'Flora' (Uffizi). After about 1518, the expansion of his powers and his rise to European eminence were steady and continuous. The masterpiece 'Bacchus and Ariadne' was painted in 1522, and the great religious works, the 'Assumption' (Church of the Frari, Venice) and 'Entombment' (Louvre), belong to this period. In 1533 he was introduced to the Emperor Charles V, who sat to Titian for his portrait, rewarding him by making him a Count Palatine and a Knight of the Golden Spur. The admiration of Charles V and his successor, Philip II, for Titian accounts for the presence of so many of his masterpieces in the imperial collections and the Prado, Madrid. Titian was now international in fame, rulers competing for his 'poetical compositions' or 'poesie' (as he termed his mythological scenes with their sumptuous nude figures), and for his portraits. He worked in a number of centres: in Venice, where in 1537 he painted his 'Battle of Cadore' (destroyed by fire in 1577); in Milan, where in 1541 he was with the emperor; in Rome, 1545, at the invitation of the Pope; in Augsburg, 1548, where he painted Philip of Spain. From this time onwards he painted mainly at Venice, the splendid Indian summer of his art producing works profound in feeling and characterized by remarkable developments in technique. His method was complex and deliberate. On a solid foundation in a red earth colour the cooler tones were laid and films or glazes of transparent colour applied at intervals, the artist sometimes softening the effect with finger rather than brush and adding crisp touches of definition. In this way he achieved his inimitable depth of colour and feeling of rich material texture. In the style of his old age a broken richness of colour and a preoccupation with effects of light might be called 'impressionist'. His quality as a portrait painter may be appreciated in many works, the 'Portrait of a Man', formerly called 'Ariosto' (National Gallery), the 'Charles V'

TITIAN—Bacchanal—Prado.

(Munich), the delightful portraits of his daughter Lavinia (as Salome —Prado, as Pomona—Berlin, also in the three-quarter-length at Vienna), the magnificent self-portrait in old age (Prado). In pictorial fable and painting of the nude one may group together as masterpieces the three paintings intended for the palace of Alfonso I of Este at Ferrara, the 'Bacchus and Ariadne' (National Gallery) and the 'Bacchanal' and 'Worship of Venus' (Prado); the several versions of 'Venus and Adonis' (Prado, National Gallery, Metropolitan Museum, New York); and the 'Danae' (Prado and Naples). In addition to the religious subjects already mentioned, the 'Presentation in the Temple' (Venice, Accademia) is superb in its concentration of dramatic effect. The 'Pietà' (Venice, Accademia), left unfinished and completed by Palma Giovane (q.v.), has been well described as a 'mournful hymn to Death'. Titian died of the plague; how near to a hundred years of age is still a matter of debate. His son, Orazio, his painter assistant, died in the same epidemic. Velazquez, Rubens and Poussin are among the many great artists inspired by his achievement.

Tobey, Mark (*b*. Centerville, Wisconsin, 1890), American abstract painter who has developed an original and personal style of 'brush writing'. He spent a number of years in both Europe and the Far East before going to live at Seattle in 1939, and the Pacific orientation of America may be considered an influence in his art, which owes something to oriental calligraphy as well as to Paris.

Tone, in painting the gradations from light to dark. Tonality refers to the general effect of the tones of a painting. Values are the relations of tone established between one part of a painting and another.

Toulouse-Lautrec, Henri de (*b*. Albi, 24 Nov. 1864; *d*. Château de Malromé, Gironde, 9 Sept. 1901), French painter and graphic artist, descendant of the ancient counts of Toulouse, son of Comte Alphonse de Toulouse-Lautrec and the Comtesse Adèle. He broke both legs in boyhood, as a result of which he was stunted in growth and turned perhaps by way of compensation to art. At eighteen he entered the studio of Bonnat and later of Cormon, but abandoned academic tuition in 1884 and took his own studio in the rue Tourlaque, where he remained thirteen years. His main activity as an artist belongs to the decade 1885–95, when his life revolved round Montmartre. At home in society of every grade and in the haunts of gaiety or vice, he drew and observed in the cafés, cabarets and *maisons closes*, giving in total a wonderful picture of what has been called 'midnight civilization'. Detached in outlook, he shared physically in the excesses of the 1890's which brought him broken in health to a sanatorium in 1899. There he drew and painted from memory the series 'Au Cirque'. In 1901, nearing final collapse, he joined his mother at the family château, where he died, aged thirty-seven. He was impressed by Degas, owes something also to Forain and brilliantly adapted the

L [313]

design and technique of the Japanese print to his own purpose in colour lithography, his posters for the Moulin Rouge and other resorts being classics of their kind. The usual oil method of painting does not seem to have been congenial to him, and he was interested neither in light nor form as such but in the intensity of mood and expression, which he conveyed with the utmost mastery. His *peinture à l'essence*, a favoured medium, oil diluted with petrol and used on board, giving a matt effect, enabled him to sketch swiftly and vividly in paint, but it is in drawings and lithographs that he is unique. Yvette Guilbert, La Goulue, Valentin, Chocolate the Negro dancer, Jane Avril, have become his characters and are immortal in his portrayal. (Colour, *see* list.)

Towne, Francis (*b. c.* 1740; *d.* London, 17 July 1816), English water-colourist, esteemed for his spaciously simplified quality of design. He exhibited landscapes at the Royal Academy and elsewhere from 1762 to 1815. Italy and Switzerland, which he visited in 1780, and the Lake District (1786), inspired his principal works, 'The Source of the Arveiron' (Victoria and Albert Museum) being a distinguished example.

Traini, Francesco (*b.* Pisa, active first half of the fourteenth century), Italian painter whose style is related to that of the early Sienese School. The famous fresco in the Campo Santo, Pisa, 'The Triumph of Death' (de-

stroyed in the Second World War), has been attributed to him and described by Bernard Berenson as, from an illustrative point of view, 'by far the greatest Italian achievement of the Middle Ages'.

'**Très Riches Heures du Duc de Berry, Les**', one of the most famous and beautiful of all illuminated manuscripts, the main part of which is ascribed to the three miniaturist brothers from Limbourg, Pol,

FRANCIS TOWNE—The Source of the Arveiron— Victoria and Albert Museum.

THE BROTHERS DE LIMBOURG—Les Très Riches Heures du Duc de Berry (The
Month of January—The Duke at Dinner)—Musée Condé, Chantilly.

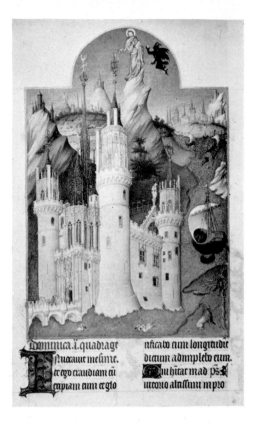

THE BROTHERS DE LIMBOURG—Les Très Riches Heures du Duc de Berry (The Temptation of Christ, showing the Château de Melun)—Musée Condé, Chantilly.

Hennequin and Herman (fourteenth to fifteenth centuries), who executed it for their wealthy patron, Jean de Berry. It was unfinished at the time of the latter's death in 1416. It is one of the great treasures of the Musée Condé, Chantilly. Though containing other miniature paintings, its main feature is the series of calendar illustrations depicting the occupations and background of nobles and peasantry in the months of the year. The various châteaux of the duke are minutely depicted, and figures and landscape beautifully combined in such masterpieces as the snow scene of February, the joyousness of spring, with its noble cavalcade, and the boar-hunt of autumn. (Colour, *see* list.)

Triptych, altar-piece of three hinged panels, the outer two folding over the central panel when required. Each side of the outer panels may be painted either to form a connected design when folded or as subsidiary compositions to the painting on the central panel when open.

Trompe l'Œil, painting which in the literal translation of the French phrase 'deceives the eye', persuading the spectator for example that a painted fly is a real one that has alighted on the canvas or that a piece of paper actually projects from it. As an exercise of ingenuity, it is to be distinguished from Naturalism and Realism (qq.v.), and is often of trivial interest, though a certain 'magical' quality has prompted its use as an element of design by some modern artists with striking effect.

Troy, Jean François de (*b.* Paris, 1679; *d.* Rome, 1752), French painter who came of an artist family, the pupil of his father, François de Troy. After six years in Rome he had a long and successful career in France as a painter of decorative compositions and portraits, also producing cartoons for Gobelins tapestries. He became director of the French Academy at Rome in 1738.

Troyon, Constant (b. Sèvres, 28 Aug. 1810; d. Paris, 20 Mar. 1865), French landscape painter, son of a painter at the Sèvres factory. He first won notice at the Salon with views of Sèvres and subsequently worked at Barbizon, being influenced by Rousseau and Dupré (qq.v.). After 1848 and a visit to Holland which introduced him to Cuyp (q.v.), he specialized in pictures of grazing cattle which were very successful, though not entirely in the spirit of the Barbizon School (q.v.), with which he is associated. He visited England in 1853, a sketch-book recording his impressions of pictures and scenes. The Louvre has many of his works and other examples are in the Wallace Collection and at Glasgow.

Trumbull, John (b. Lebanon, 6 June 1756; d. New York, 10 Nov. 1843), American painter of portraits and historical subjects whose first efforts were inspired by Copley. He had a year under West in London, 1785, and afterwards turned from individual portraiture to painting scenes from the American Revolution, including the likenesses of those still living who had taken part. In his spirited battle pictures he was no unworthy successor of Copley. In 1817 he was commissioned by Congress to paint four Revolutionary themes for the Rotunda of the Capitol at Washington.

Tura, Cosimo (b. Ferrara, c. 1430; d. April 1495), Italian painter,

C. TURA—Allegorical Figure—Layard Gallery, Venice.

[317]

the first outstanding representative of the School of Ferrara. He seems to have studied in the Squarcione workshop at Padua and to have been influenced by the sculpturesque style of the young Mantegna (q.v.), though not with the same antiquarian or classical tendency. He embellished his paintings of religious and allegorical figures with much fanciful ornament (dolphins and shells often figuring prominently), sometimes suggesting stone carving and sometimes sharply defined linear forms wrought in metal. He worked mainly for the Este court at Ferrara. Artists whose work is related to his are Francesco Cossa, Ercole de Roberti and the Bolognese Marco Zoppo (qq.v.).

Turner, Joseph Mallord William (*b.* London, 23 April 1775; *d.* there, 19 Dec. 1851), greatest of landscape painters, the son of a barber in Maiden Lane. He drew as a child; for a little time was with the architectural draughtsman Thomas Malton; and worked in the Royal Academy Schools, 1789–93, exhibiting a view of Lambeth Palace at the Academy when he was fifteen: though Ruskin was no doubt right in saying that Dr Monro was his real master. He learned much from copying the J. R. Cozens water-colours in Monro's collection and also from his fellow copyist Girtin, whose own original development in water-colour Turner set himself to rival. He began as a water-colourist in a meticulous topographical style, travelling for his material between 1798 and 1801, in Wales, Yorkshire and Scotland, also in Kent and the Isle of Wight, during this period already becoming loaded with commissions. He began to exhibit oils in 1796

J. M. W. TURNER—Ulysses deriding Polyphemus—National Gallery, London.

J. M. W. TURNER—A Frosty Morning: Sunrise—National Gallery, London.

and was made R.A. in 1802, the year of his first visit to the Continent (France and Switzerland). Thereafter until 1845 he travelled widely and continuously in Europe—in France, Switzerland, Italy, along the Rhine and in the Netherlands—as well as in various parts of Britain; always busy with his sketch-book and keenly observant of every effect in nature, dawn and dusk, sea and cloud, sun and storm. There resulted the prodigious quantity and variety of his work in which his genius constantly expanded until the end of his life.

From 1800 to 1820 he learned from and sought to vie with masters of the past, with van de Velde, Wilson, Claude: in the magnificent sea of 'Calais Pier', 1803 (National Gallery), he far surpasses his Dutch predecessor. He alternated between the masterly simplicity of the 'Frosty Morning', 1813, and elaborate subjects such as the 'Dido building Carthage', 1815, in which he imitated (but did not excel) Claude. The latter's *Liber Veritatis* suggested Turner's series of mezzotint engravings, the *Liber Studiorum*, 1807–19. His fondness for the legendary subject persisted, as in the 'Ulysses deriding Polyphemus' of 1829, though from 1819 (when he first visited Italy) he entered a phase in which light and colour gained a new significance of their own, culminating in the poetic visions of Venice, c. 1839. These and the 'Fighting Téméraire' were once thought to be a final splendour before his decline, but in the modern view the period between 1839 and 1850 is most remarkable of all in the power which converts air and solid matter into dynamic movement and force, 'Rain, Steam and Speed', 1844, and 'Snowstorm at Sea' being examples.

The art of Turner is a constant astonishment in its numerous

J. M. W. TURNER—Château of Blois (Gouache)—Ashmolean Museum, Oxford.

facets: Romantic in its infinite distances, Alpine heights, the turmoil of 'The Slave Ship' (Boston), the drama of 'The Burning of the Houses of Parliament' (Cleveland, Ohio); sometimes Impressionist in atmospheric colour; yet again Expressionist or abstract in such colour poems as the 'Interior at Petworth', while in the water-colours which parallel the development of his oils there are countless exquisite things, the masterly completeness of the Yorkshire views made at Farnley Hall, the *gouaches* of Blois and Tours (presented by Ruskin to the Ashmolean Museum), the glowing views of Constance or Lucerne, or even some small detailed study of birds or fish. The sketch-books in the British Museum are a rich mine for exploration. In figure painting also he can spring a surprise, as in the 'Jessica at the Window', with its jewels of paint (Petworth Collection). Turner died a rich man, partly through the great demand of his time for engraved illustrations of picturesque scenery for which he supplied originals; he left £140,000 to found a Charity for Decayed Artists. The obscurity often remarked on in his poetic effort *The Fallacies of Hope* extended, however, to the wording of his will, a cause of prolonged litigation, which fortunately did not prevent the enormous bequest to the nation of some 280 paintings and 19,000 drawings and water-colours divided between the National and Tate Galleries and the British Museum. Appraisal of his art was not perhaps made easier by Ruskin's defence and exposition in the first volume of *Modern Painters*, 1843, yet this justly emphasized a giant ability recognized today more fully than ever.

[320]

TURNER—Rain, Steam and Speed—National Gallery, London.

U

Ubertini, Francesco, *see* BACCHIACCA.

Uccello, Paolo (*b.* Florence, *c.* 1397; *d.* 10 Dec. 1475), Italian painter of the Florentine School, whose real name was Paolo di Dono, called 'Uccello' for no precisely known reason, perhaps because he loved birds or at some time painted them. He was trained as a goldsmith and *c.* 1407–12 was apprentice to Ghiberti when the latter was working on the doors of the Florentine baptistery. In 1415 he entered the Physicians' Guild at Florence as a painter. He worked mainly in Florence with an interlude, in 1425 and for a few years thereafter, at Venice, where he is said to have produced a mosaic for the façade of St Mark's. He bought a house in Florence in 1442 and evidently prospered for a time, though his old age was reputedly spent in poverty and isolation. He is famous for his study of perspective, though he used it imaginatively rather than with scientific accuracy or consistency. His works in fresco include his painting (in imitation of an equestrian statue) of the English *condottiere*, Sir John Hawkwood (known as Giovanni Acuto), 1436, in the cathedral at Florence, and a series in the Chiostro Verde of Santa Maria Novella, Florence, the principal composition being the 'Deluge' of *c.* 1445. He is, however, more celebrated for his panel pictures, notably the three pictures, 'Rout of San Romano' (q.v.), of the battle between the Florentines and the Sienese, 1432, painted for the Medici (Uffizi, Louvre and National Gallery). They were intended to be framed together, but each gives an effect of completeness and is wonderfully rich in design. Other remarkable works, showing his originality and vividness of imagination, are the 'Hunt' (Oxford, Ashmolean) and 'St George and the Dragon' (National Gallery). A series of portraits

P. UCCELLO—The Hunt—Ashmolean Museum, Oxford.

* L

by him (Louvre) suggests that he admired particularly Giotto, Donatello, Brunelleschi and the mathematician Antonio Manetti.

Uffizi Gallery, Florence, one of the world's greatest picture collections, created by Lorenzo the Magnificent and other members of the Medici family and taking its name from the Palazzo degli Uffizi or Palace of the Offices where the municipal government was carried on. It splendidly illustrates the whole development of the Florentine School from Cimabue and Giotto onwards, and the schools of Siena, Ferrara, Bologna and the Emilia, and also contains a number of works by Flemish, Dutch and German artists. 'The Holy Family' by Michelangelo, the unfinished 'Adoration of the Magi' by Leonardo, the 'Madonna of the Goldfinch' by Raphael, the masterpieces of Botticelli, 'Primavera', 'The Birth of Venus' and 'The Calumny of Apelles', and Bellini's 'Sacra Conversazione' are among its many treasures. A special section is devoted to portraits of painters which has grown from the nucleus formed by Cardinal Leopold de' Medici into a pantheon of art.

Ugolino di Nerio (active 1317–27), Italian painter of the Sienese School. A signed work by him was the high altar-piece of Santa Croce, Florence, a polyptych (his only authenticated painting). It was removed from its position in 1569 but remained intact, though evidently deteriorating, until the beginning of the nineteenth century when parts thought worth preserving were bought by an English collector. Fragments are in the National Gallery, London, at Berlin and in private collections. Ugolino's 'Greek manner', deplored by Vasari, can now be viewed as that of a close follower of Duccio's highly cultivated Byzantine style, though without Duccio's personal resource and elegance in design.

Ukiyo-e, translated as 'The Painting of the Transient Scene', the Popular School of Japanese art in painting and print making, which flourished in the eighteenth and nineteenth centuries, mainly in Yedo and Osaka. It had its origin in the *genre* painting which answered to the taste of a merchant class growing in wealth and influence but found its most typical and spirited expression in the colour print. Historical and legendary subjects, scenes of everyday life, theatrical portraits, landscape, animals, birds and flowers were depicted with fresh verve in terms of a democratic medium by a brilliant succession of print designers. Early masters were Moronobu (1625–94), who first saw the great possibilities of the woodcut, and Masanobu (1686–1764), who produced woodcuts hand-coloured or printed in two colours. A great advance was made by Harunobu (1725–70), who perfected the technique of colour printing, followed by the superb artists, Utamaro (1753–1806) (q.v.), Hiroshige (1759–1858) (q.v.) and above all Hokusai (1760–1849) (q.v.). Also of especial note are Sharaku (fl. late fifteenth century), celebrated for his prints of actors, Toyokuni (1769–1935), and Kunisada (1786–1864). Kuniyoshi (1797–1861), an artist of wide range and vigour, was the last outstanding representative of the colour-print. It declined with the

UKIYO-E SCHOOL—Colour Print by Utamaro—British Museum.

advent of European influence and also the importation and use of cheap and inferior colours *See also* JAPANESE PICTORIAL ART.

Umbria, with the Marches on one side and Tuscany on the other, may be regarded as a centre of art under the general heading of 'Central Italy', producing many great artists in the fifteenth century. In east Tuscany, Arezzo is famous for Piero della Francesca and his pupils Melozzo da Forli and Luca Signorelli. A great centre of Umbrian art was Perugia, where Perugino was outstanding, his followers and pupils including Fiorenzo di Lorenzo, Pintoricchio and Raphael. At Urbino, encouraged to practise painting by Melozzo da Forli and Piero della Francesca, was Giovanni Santi, the father of Raphael. Raphael's first master was Timoteo Viti at Urbino.

Underpainting, first stage of the traditional method of oil painting in which the composition is laid in in monochrome awaiting the application of glazes of colour.

U.S.S.R. Art Museums include the Hermitage, Leningrad, the collection of the Moscow Museum of Modern Western Art, the Pushkin Museum and the Tretiakov Gallery, museum of Russian art from the medieval icons to the paintings of recent times.

Utamaro (Toriyama Shimbi) (*b.* Yedo, 1753; *d.* 1806), Japanese artist of the Ukiyo-e or popular school, one of the great masters of the colour wood-block print. He is noted for the beautifully designed and

[323]

UMBRIAN SCHOOL—Resurrection of Christ (P. Della Francesca)—Galleria Communale, Sansepolcro.

UTRILLO—Place du Tertre—Tate Gallery.

coloured prints in which he depicts women of various social grades, and also produced landscape and bird and flower studies. He introduced many refinements of technique in colour printing. He was the first Japanese artist to become well known in Europe, many of his prints being sent to Europe during his lifetime by Dutch merchants resident at Nagasaki.

Utrillo, Maurice (*b.* Paris, 26 Dec. 1883; *d.* Dax, 5 Nov. 1955), French painter, the son of Suzanne Valadon (q.v.). He showed early signs of a neurosis which drove him to alcoholism and was encouraged by his mother to paint when eighteen as a therapeutic measure. He took instantly to art and from 1903 produced views of Montmagny, where he and his mother lived for a while, and cathedrals and villages taken from picture postcards. After an Impressionist phase he arrived at his characteristic 'white period', *c.* 1909–14, painting the streets and the peeling plaster of white walls in Montmartre, his native quarter, for which he had a deep affection, in pictures of great beauty. His style changed from about 1917, for a time deteriorating. Brighter colour and a more rudimentary kind of drawing characterized his later work, though in its final phases it showed some return to the style for which he is most esteemed. He produced delightful *gouaches* as well as oil-paintings.

V

Valadon, Suzanne (b. Bessines, nr Limoges, 23 Sept. 1867; d. Paris, April 1938), one of the most remarkable of French women painters and the mother of Maurice Utrillo (q.v.). In youth she lived a Bohemian life in Montmartre, was a circus acrobat and an artist's model posing for Puvis de Chavannes, Renoir and Toulouse-Lautrec, who discerned and encouraged her talent for drawing (as also did Degas). Married in 1909 to the painter André Utter, she took to painting in earnest, producing vigorous and original figure compositions, landscapes and still lifes. Like her son Maurice, who lived with and was devoted to her, she enjoyed success in the 1920's. The Musée d'Art Moderne, Paris, has some of the best examples of her work, including the portrait of Utrillo and his grandmother.

Valdés-Leal, Juan de (b. Seville, 4 May 1622; d. there, 15 Oct. 1690), Spanish painter and engraver of Portuguese descent. His youth was spent in Cordova but by 1656 he had settled in his native city, where he remained, painting religious and grimly emblematic subjects, such as 'The Triumph of Death' (Seville Hospital). He was one of the founders of the Seville Academy, 1660, becoming its president, 1663–6.

Valentin, Le (Valentin de Boulogne) (b. Coulommiers, Brie, ? 1591; d. Rome, 1634), French painter of religious subjects and scenes of popular life, who settled in Rome and there seems to have been a pupil of Vouet (q.v.). He worked in the manner of Caravaggio, derived perhaps through Manfredi (q.v.), and his 'Dice Players' (Dresden) was long mistaken for a painting by Caravaggio himself. The 'Martyrdom of Sts Processus and Martinian' (Vatican), copied in mosaic in St Peter's, is his only certainly authenticated work, but many others are accepted as his on reasonable grounds, including the 'Fortune-teller' (Louvre), a favourite picture with Louis XIV, 'Judith' (Toulouse) and 'Brawling Soldiers' (Munich).

Vallotton, Félix (b. Lausanne, 1860; d. Paris, 1925), Swiss painter who studied art and worked in Paris. He was a contributor to the *Revue Blanche*, the journal of the 'Nabi' movement with which he was associated, his style being related to that of such 'Nabis' as Maurice Denis (q.v.) and Paul Sérusier.

Values, see TONE.

Van de Velde, name of a Dutch painter family. **Esaias** (c. 1591–1630) was a painter of landscape, battle-pieces and *genre* who worked at Haarlem and as a court painter at The Hague, mainly noted for his small landscapes with figures. His brother, **Willem the Elder** (1610/11–1693), was a marine painter who took part in the naval

LE VALENTIN—Brawling Soldiers—Pinakothek, Munich.

warfare between Holland and England, but in 1672 was summoned to England together with his son to paint for Charles II. His son, **Willem the Younger** (*b*. Leyden, baptized 18 Dec. 1633; *d*. Greenwich, 6 April 1707), who had studied at Amsterdam under his father and Simon de Vlieger, collaborated with him and is the more eminent of the two. The brother of Willem the Younger, **Adriaen** (*b*. Amsterdam, 1636; *d*. there, 21 Jan. 1672), was an animal and landscape painter.

Van Gogh, *see* GOGH.

Van Loo, French artist family of Flemish extraction. Jean Baptiste Van Loo (*b*. Aix-en-Provence, 14 Jan. 1684; *d*. there, 19 Dec. 1745) was taught by his father and painted portraits, religious subjects for churches and decorative compositions. He went to England, 1737–42, being successful there in portraiture. His picture of Sir Robert Walpole is in the National Portrait Gallery. His eldest son, Charles Amédée (1719–95) also painted portraits and 'history' subjects and became painter to the King of Prussia. Carle (Charles André) (*b*. Nice, 15 February 1705, *d*. Paris, 15 July 1765) was the younger brother of Jean Baptiste and was taught by him, studying also in Rome. His subject paintings were admired in both Italy and France and he became court painter to Louis XV. His son and pupil, Jules César (1743–1821) was a landscape painter, noted for winter scenes.

Van Meegeren, Henricus Anthonius (Han) (*b*. Deventer, 1889; *d*. 1947), Dutch painter and notorious forger of pictures, the principal

[327]

instance of the disappointed artist who failing to win recognition by his individual work comes before the public in the guise of an old master. His remarkably skilful imitations of seventeenth-century painters included the supposed Vermeer, 'Christ at Emmaus' which long imposed on the world.

Vanni, Andrea (*b.* Siena, *c.* 1332; *d. c.* 1414), Italian painter of the Sienese School, a follower of Simone Martini in style. Employed (like Rubens later) on ambassadorial missions, he visited and worked at Rome, Naples and Avignon. He corresponded with St Catherine of Siena and painted her portrait. Paintings by him are at Siena and a fine triptych by him is in the Corcoran Gallery, Washington.

Vanucci, Pietro, *see* PERUGINO.

Vargas, Luis de (*b.* Seville, 1502; *d.* 1568), Spanish painter who was trained in Rome in the studio of Perino del Vaga (q.v.), and influenced in style by the followers of Raphael. Works by him at Seville include his altar-piece of the Genealogy of the Virgin.

Varley, John (*b.* London, 17 Aug. 1778; *d.* there, 17 Nov. 1842), English water-colour painter. He was in youth a protégé of Dr Monro and became well known as a teacher of art, David Cox and Samuel Palmer (qq.v.) being among the many he trained or encouraged. Views of North Wales are of note in his own work but his large output tended towards a mechanical facility. It was for him that Blake drew his famous 'visionary heads'. His brother Cornelius (1781–1873) painted architectural subjects in water-colour. His younger brother, William Fleetwood (1785–1856), his son, Albert Fleetwood, and two grandsons were also water-colourists.

Vasari, Giorgio (*b.* Arezzo, 30 July 1511; *d.* Florence, 27 June 1574), Italian painter, architect and art historian, famous mainly for his *Lives of the most eminent Painters, Sculptors and Architects*, first published in 1550 and partly rewritten and enlarged in 1568. He studied

E. VAN DE VELDE—The Ferry Boat—Rijksmuseum, Amsterdam.

W. VAN DE VELDE (the Elder)—Dutch Ships coming to Anchor (Grisaille)—National Maritime Museum, Greenwich.

art in Florence for a short while with Michelangelo, for whom he had an unbounded admiration, and also with Andrea del Sarto and Baccio Bandinelli. He studied the work of Raphael in Rome. He was successful as an architect and decorative painter and in 1547 built himself a house at Arezzo, now a museum, which he decorated lavishly. As a painter he has never been highly rated, though of interest as an instance of the Mannerist exaggeration which the devotion to Michelangelo produced. His *Lives*, however, is a classic, and, though corrected in a number of particulars by modern research, remains of the greatest value as a largely unbiased and delightfully written account of the progress of Italian art from the Middle Ages to the Renaissance.

Vatican, Rome. The works of art in the Vatican Palace include the paintings by Michelangelo and other masters in the Sistine Chapel, the paintings of the Stanze and Loggie by Raphael and his assistants, the paintings by Pintoricchio in the Appartamento Borgia, the Raphael Tapestry, and the picture gallery founded by Pius VII, mainly of pictures given back by the French in 1815 and including works by Raphael, artists of the Venetian School and of seventeenth-century Rome. The Chapel of Nicholas V has frescoes by Fra Angelico (1450–55).

Vecchietta (Lorenzo di Pietro) (*b.* Castiglione di Val d'Oreia, *c.* 1413; *d.* 1480), Italian painter and sculptor of the Sienese School, the pupil of Jacopo della Quercia and Donatello. In painting he follows Sassetta and had considerable influence on the development of Sienese art.

Vedder, Elihu (*b.* New York, 26 Feb. 1836; *d.* Rome, 29 Jan. 1923), American painter and illustrator. He studied under Picot in Paris, also in Italy, living for many years in Rome. His illustrations to the *Rubáiyát* in 1884 first made him widely known and later he produced a number of mural paintings, imaginative or mythological in theme, among them lunettes, and a mosaic for the Congressional Library, Washington.

Veen, Maerten van, *see* HEEMSKERK.

Veen (Venius), Otto van (*b.* Leyden, 1558; *d.* Brussels, 6 May 1629), Flemish painter of historical and religious subjects and portraits, who worked at Liège, Brussels and Antwerp and also in Italy in the studio of Federigo Zuccaro (q.v.), becoming Italianate in style. He settled at Antwerp in 1593 but left the city for Brussels in 1620.

Velazquez, Diego Rodriguez de Silva (*b.* Seville, 1599; *d.* Madrid, 1660), Spanish painter and one of the world's greatest artists. His first master was Francisco de Herrera (q.v.), from whom he went to the more cultivated guidance of Francisco Pacheco (q.v.), whose daughter, Juana, he married in 1618. His early works produced at Seville were 'bodegones', 'kitchen pictures', of the type then popular, with peasant figures and carefully detailed still-life detail, showing strongly the influence of Caravaggio's 'naturalism'. Examples are the 'Christ in the House of Martha and Mary' (National Gallery), the 'Cook' (National Gallery of Scotland) and the 'Water Carrier' (Apsley House). He went to Madrid on a short visit in 1622 and was recalled in the following year by Philip IV's minister, Olivares, when he gained immediate success and prompt appointment as painter to the king. A painting that established his reputation was 'The

**VELAZQUEZ—Philip IV—
National Gallery, London.**

[331]

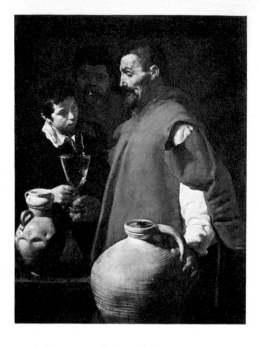

Topers' ('Los Bor-
rachos') of 1629. At
this time he met Rubens
in Madrid and was also
stimulated by his first
visit to Italy, 1629–31,
when he studied and
copied the great Vene-
tians in Venice and went
on to Rome and Naples
(where he met Ribera,
q.v.). His 'Forge of Vul-
can' (Prado) attempts
a reconciliation of the
mythological theme as
treated by Italians and
his native sense of
realism. From 1631 he
settled to an assiduous
court routine which
entailed various official
duties as well as painting, broken only by a second visit to Italy
(Genoa, Venice, Naples and Rome), 1649–51. Paintings of the royal
family, e.g. the full-length 'Philip IV' (National Gallery) and 'Prince
Baltasar Carlos dressed as a Hunter' (Prado) mainly occupied him,
though to this period belongs the greatest of historical compositions,
the 'Surrender of Breda' ('Las Lanzas') (Prado), painted before 1635
to commemorate the successful siege of Breda by Spinola. The second
visit to Italy (to buy pictures and to gain information useful for
the organization of a proposed Spanish Royal Academy) produced
Velazquez's portrait of Innocent X, his remarkable landscape sketch
of the Gardens of the Villa Medici (Prado) and the 'Rokeby Venus'
(National Gallery), in which he sought to emulate Titian. His later
years are marked not by prolific output but by a remarkable series of
masterpieces. His portraits of Philip IV's second wife, Mariana of
Austria, and of the Infanta Margarita combine exquisite colour with
breadth of design. In the famous group pictures—the 'Maids of
Honour' ('Las Meniñas') and the view inside the royal tapestry works
('Las Hilanderas'), both in the Prado—intricate themes are perfectly
resolved. The courtly side of Velazquez's life never obscured the sad
and intense contemplation of human reality, and the equivalent of
his peasant themes is given in his studies of buffoons and dwarfs and
the humble strength of his 'Aesop'. His pictures (which he signed
'Diego Velasquez' or 'Diego de Silva Velasquez') do not, it is estimated, number more than 170, and copies and versions were produced

Venice Vergós

by his assistants, among whom were Juan Paréja and Juan del Mazo
(qq.v.). His immediate influence in Spain, however, was small,
though Goya was to declare as the source of his inspiration 'Rembrandt, Velazquez and Nature', and many great artists since, such as
Manet, have been inspired by this most 'painterly' of great painters.

Venice was pre-eminent in pictorial art in the sixteenth century,
the fully developed Venetian School being then noted for its richness
of colour and sensuous beauty. The city, by virtue of its position,
maritime power and possessions on the mainland had previously
absorbed influences from west and east with fruitful result. Painting
first comes into prominence with the advent of Gentile da Fabriano
from Florence and Pisanello from Verona to decorate the Doge's
Palace in 1410. Other influences to be noted are those of the Paduan
School and of Antonello da Messina, who in 1475 brought to Venice
the oil technique of the van Eycks. The two leading families of early
Venetian painting, the Bellinis and the Vivarinis, both show these
influences. Jacopo Bellini was the pupil of Gentile and the father-in
law of Mantegna, whose work greatly affected that of Jacopo's sons
Gentile and Giovanni Bellini. Antonello's technique was adopted by
Giovanni Bellini and by Alvise Vivarini. The influence of Padua can
be seen in the work of Carlo Crivelli. The pupils of the Bellinis were
many. They included Francesco Bissolo, Vittore Carpaccio, Marco
Basaiti, Bartolommeo Montagna, Cima da Conegliano and Vincenzo
di Biagio (Catena), but the most important of Giovanni Bellini's
pupils were Giorgione and Titian, with whom Venetian painting passed
into a new and splendid phase. The sixteenth century saw a number of
distinguished artists working in the spirit of these great men: Palma
Vecchio, Cariani, Pordenone, Sebastiano del Piombo, Lorenzo Lotto,
Previtali, Schiavone, Bonifazio, Paris Bordone, the Bassano family.
The period culminated in the work of Tintoretto and Veronese. The
seventeenth century was something of an anticlimax, but the art of
Venice had a last notable phase in the eighteenth century when
Tiepolo revived the decorative splendour of Veronese. Other famous
Venetians of this period were the view-painters Carlevaris, Canaletto,
Bellotto and Guardi. The painters of *genre* Piazzetta and Longhi, the
decorative painters Marco and Sebastiano Ricci and the pastellist
Rosalba Carriera are also of some note.

Vereschchagin, Vasily Vasilyevich (*b.* Novgorod, 26 Oct. 1842; *d.*
Port Arthur, 13 Feb. 1904), Russian painter and war correspondent.
He studied in Paris under Gérôme and subsequently travelled widely
in India, Tibet, Palestine and Syria. He was with the Russian forces
in the Turkestan campaign, 1867, the Russo-Turkish war of 1877,
and was killed in the flagship *Petropavlovsk* during the Russo-
Japanese War. Many of his pictures were an exposure of the horrors
of war. His 'Kirghiz Hunter with Falcon' (Moscow, Tretyakov
Gallery) is a vigorous study of a robust local type.

Vergós, name of a family of Catalonian painters who worked in
Barcelona in the fifteenth century, having a workshop for the
production of retablos. They included Jaime Vergós, father and son

[333]

of the same name,
and the latter's sons,
Pablo and Rafael. They
were related in style to
Bermejo and Huguet.

Vermeer, Johannes
(**Jan**) (*b*. Delft, baptized
31 Oct. 1632; *d*. there,
buried 15 Dec. 1675),
Dutch painter, one of
the greatest European
artists, who spent his
life at Delft. He was probably the pupil of Carel
Fabritius (q.v.) and was
admitted to the Delft
Guild of Painters in
1653, being Master of
the Guild in 1662 and
again in 1670. He died
in poverty, the obliga-
tions of a large family
no doubt being a con-
tributory cause, while he was evidently not a prolific painter, less than
forty authentic works remaining. After his death he was forgotten
until in 1866 the French critic 'W. Bürger' (Théophile Thoré) rediscovered him, since when his greatness has been acclaimed. In
balance and simplicity of design, an exquisite sense of colour and of
colour in light, he attains a serene perfection. Italian influence may be
discerned in his early work, e.g. 'Diana and her Nymphs' (The Hague)
and 'The Courtesan' (Dresden), and the Chinese porcelain he would
see at Delft may have offered some suggestions of colour and simplification, but independent genius appears in his masterpieces: the
two great exterior views, the 'View of Delft' (The Hague) and 'The
Little Street' (Rijksmuseum); the interiors in which he transcended
the brilliance of de Hooch, Ter Borch and Metsu, such as the 'Lady
standing at the Virginals' (National Gallery) and 'The Painter's
Studio' (Vienna)—unsold at the time of his death; and such remarkable studies as the 'Maidservant pouring Milk' (Rijksmuseum), the
'Girl with a Turban' (The Hague) and the 'Girl with a Flute' (National
Gallery, Washington). Some plausible imitations of his earlier style
(notably 'Christ at Emmaus') by the Dutch forger van Meegeren
were exposed as forgeries in 1945.

[334]

J. VERMEER—The Painter's Studio–Kuntshistorisches Museum, Vienna.

J. VERMEER—Maidservant pouring Milk—Rijksmuseum, Amsterdam.

C. J. VERNET—Coast Scene—Prado.

Vernet, French painter family of which the principal member was **Claude Joseph** (*b.* Avignon, 14 Aug. 1714; *d.* Paris, 3 Dec. 1789). He studied under his father, Antoine, and at Aix, and worked in Italy, 1734–52. He was made a member of the Académie on his return in 1753, subsequently travelling in France until 1762 to paint the series of French seaports (Louvre) commissioned by Louis XV. He settled finally in Paris. His marines (storm, moonlight, rocky coasts) have a certain Romantic feeling. His son, **Antoine Charles Horace (Carle)** (*b.* Bordeaux, 14 Aug. 1758; *d.* Paris, 27 Nov. 1836), was a painter of horses and battle scenes, also of note for his caricatures of the *Incroyables* and *Merveilleuses*. The son of Carle, **Émile Jean Horace** (*b.* Paris, 30 June 1789; *d.* there, 17 Jan. 1863), friend of Géricault (q.v.), was a military and sporting painter.

Veronese (Paolo Caliari or **Cagliari)** (*b.* Verona, 1528; *d.* Venice, 19 April 1588). Italian painter of the Venetian School. He was the pupil of a minor painter, Antonio Badile, but learned much from the study of Titian and Tintoretto. Some part of his youth was also spent in the shop of his brother Antonio, who dealt in embroidery and rich stuffs such as were to play an important decorative part in his painting. From 1555 he lived in Venice, producing those huge decorative compositions with their representation of splendid architecture and crowds of luxuriously dressed figures for which he is famous. Many of his best paintings and frescoes are at Venice in the Doge's Palace, the church of San Sebastiano, the Accademia and the Villa Masiera, but masterpieces elsewhere are the great 'Marriage at Cana', 1562–3 (Louvre), the 'Family of Darius before Alexander', ? *c.* 1570 (National Gallery), and the 'Finding of Moses' (Washington, Mellon Collection). The 'Marriage at Cana' is typical in its pomp and luxury, containing more than 130 figures, including portraits of many celebrities of the time— Charles V, Francis I, Sultan Soliman II, Titian, Bassano, Tintoretto,

[336]

VERMEER—The Little Street—Rijksmuseum Amsterdam.

VERONESE—The Marriage at Cana—Louvre.

Aretino—together with an assortment of fools, dwarfs, Negro pages and dogs, in a grandiose architectural setting. This and a work similarly conceived, the 'Supper in the House of Levi' (Venice, Accademia), were considered irreverent in their treatment of a religious theme and caused Veronese to be questioned by the Inquisition in 1573. The Inquisitors pointed out that in Michelangelo's 'Last Judgment' there were no such 'drunkards nor dogs nor similar buffooneries' as Veronese had painted. He answered: 'Mine is no art of thought, therefore for this very reason it can do no harm; my art is joyous and praises God in light and colour . . . I am above all a painter and nought else but a painter.' In composition, in painting the figure and in tapestry-like schemes of colour, Veronese ranks with the greatest Venetians, and after an interval of time his work inspired the last brilliant efflorescence of mural painting in the eighteenth century as represented by Tiepolo. Veronese was assisted in his huge undertakings by his brother Benedetto and his sons Carlo and Gabriel, who carried on his studio after his death.

Verrocchio, Andrea del (b. Florence, c. 1435; d. Venice, 7 Oct. 1488), Italian goldsmith, sculptor and painter of the Florentine School, whose real name was Andrea di Cione. He studied as a goldsmith under Giuliano Verrocchi and was probably also a pupil of Donatello. He is famous principally as a sculptor, his bronze equestrian statue of Bartolommeo Colleoni in the piazza of SS. Giovanni e Paolo, Venice, being one of the great masterpieces of that art. As a painter he is less eminent; indeed only one picture, the 'Baptism of Christ' (Uffizi), is attributed to him with certainty; but his studio-workshop in which

VERROCCHIO—The Baptism of Christ—Uffizi, Florence.

VERROCCHIO—The Virgin and Child—Sheffield Art Gallery.

painting was one of many activities was an important Florentine training ground, and Verrocchio has a secondary fame as the master (and for some years employer) of Leonardo da Vinci, while Lorenzo di Credi (q.v.) was his principal assistant in painting. A well-grounded tradition has it that Leonardo painted the angel (at left) in the Uffizi 'Baptism'. His hand has also been traced in the background of the 'Virgin and Child' (Sheffield).

Verspronck, Jan Cornelisz (*b.* Haarlem, 1597; *d.* there, buried 30 June 1662), Dutch portrait painter, who worked throughout his life at Haarlem. He was the pupil of his father and Frans Hals and is especially notable for his portraits of children.

Victoria and Albert Museum, London, one of the world's greatest museums of fine and applied art, mainly of the post-classical periods. It developed from the Museum of Ornamental Art of 1852 and was renamed in 1899. It is arranged to show the development of periods of art with separate study collections of ceramics, metalwork, textiles, etc., and has large collections of oil-paintings, miniatures and water-colours, prints and drawings, as well as a great library open to students. It contains the seven cartoons by Raphael which are among the most important surviving examples of High Renaissance art.

Vien, Joseph Marie (*b.* Montpellier, 18 June 1716; *d.* Paris, 27 Mar. 1809), French painter, a pupil of Natoire and court painter to Louis XVI, who represents the antiquarian taste in art stimulated by the discoveries at Pompeii and Herculaneum and by the writings of Winckelmann. His classicism was a timid revolt against the rococo style which his pupil, David (q.v.), who accompanied him to Rome in 1775, was to infuse with vigour. Vien became a count of the Empire in 1808.

Vigée-Lebrun, Marie Anne Elisabeth (*b.* Paris, 16 April 1755; *d.* there, 30 Mar. 1842), French portraitist, daughter of a painter, by whom she was taught. She married the critic J. B. P. Lebrun in

1776. Her personal charm and ability to please with a style reminiscent of Greuze made her a society favourite in the Ancien Régime. Among her sitters was Marie Antoinette, of whom she painted more than twenty portraits between 1779 and 1789. When the Revolution began she escaped to Italy, repeating her early success in Rome, Naples, Vienna, Berlin, St Petersburg and London. She published her *Souvenirs*, 1835–7.

Viti, Timoteo (*b*. Ferrara, 1467, *d*. Urbino, 1523), Italian painter of the Umbrian School, he served apprenticeship as a goldsmith with Francesco Francia, who also taught him painting, and afterwards settled at Urbino, where he was Raphael's first master. Paintings by him are the 'St Mary Magdalene' (Bologna) and 'Annunciation' (Milan).

Vinci, Leonardo da, *see* LEONARDO.

Vivarini, family of Venetian painters of Murano, of importance in the development of Venetian art. **Antonio** (*b*. *c*. 1420; *d*. 1476+) collaborated with his brother-in-law, Giovanni d'Allemagna, in religious paintings of a Gothic character, supposedly influenced by Gentile da Fabriano and Pisanello (qq.v.). Some German admixture of style may have been due to Giovanni d'Allemagna, though the two painters are not distinguishable one from another. Antonio Vivarini's younger brother, **Bartolommeo,** at first collaborated with him but developed a style influenced by Mantegna (q.v.). The son of Antonio, **Alvise** (1447–1504), conducted a school at Murano rivalling that of the Bellini family and was noted for his portraits, being much influenced by Antonello da Messina (q.v.). He painted altar-pieces for a number of churches in Venice.

Vlaminck, Maurice de (*b*. Paris, 4 April 1876; *d*. there, 11 Oct. 1958), French painter of Belgian extraction. In youth he was a racing

ALVISE VIVARINI—Man
feeding a Hawk—Royal
Collection, Windsor Castle.

M. VLAMINCK—Snow
Scene—Photo: Tooth
Gallery.

cyclist, but he began to study painting when nineteen and, meeting André Derain (q.v.), worked in company with him. In 1901 he was greatly impressed by the van Gogh exhibition of that year, when he made the typically Fauve announcement that 'one should paint with pure vermilion, Veronese green and cobalt', and he was associated with Matisse, Derain and others in the Fauvist Salon of 1905. His mature work, however, did not pursue the implications of using pure colour. Following van Gogh only in emphasis, it was marked by heavy impasto and sudden transitions from dark to light, which gave dramatic effect to the stormy skies and snow-bound villages of his characteristic landscapes. These and still lifes in the same key were his main products. He was also something of a man of letters and wrote poetry, novels, film scenarios and criticisms of modern society.

Volterra, Daniele da (Daniele Ricciarelli) (*b*. Volterra, 1509; *d*. Rome, 4 April 1566), Italian painter, sculptor and architect, a follower of Michelangelo. His style was first formed by Sodoma and Perino del Vaga (qq.v.) and also by the study of Raphael, but Michelangelo, with whom he worked, became his main inspiration. He did not, however, disobey the order of Pope Paul IV to paint concealing garments over some of the nudities of Michelangelo's 'Last Judgment', Restless movement and exaggeration in his own work, as in his 'Descent from the Cross' (Rome, SS. Trinità dei Monti) and 'The Massacre of the Innocents' (Uffizi), show the trend of Mannerism towards baroque.

Vorticism, only British contribution to the 'isms' of modern art, inspired by Cubism and Futurism (qq.v.), though declaring itself 'anti-Futurist'. The Vorticist leader was Percy Wyndham Lewis

D. DA VOLTERRA—Descent from the Cross—Pinacoteca, Lucca.

W. ROBERTS—The Jockeys—Bradford Art Gallery.

(q.v.), who indeed has stated that 'Vorticism was what I personally did and said at a certain period', though his friend Ezra Pound seems to have invented the name. The aim was to build up 'a visual language as abstract as music' and also to make use of machine forms which constituted as real a world to the artist as the forms of nature. Its manifesto appeared in the publication *Blast*, June 1914, of which only one other issue came out, 1915. A number of distinguished artists had some association with the movement, including Henri Gaudier Brzeska, William Roberts, Edward Wadsworth, David Bomberg and others. The war halted the Vorticist activity but a number of Lewis's associates were later prominent in the London Group (q.v.).

Vos, Cornelis de (*b.* Hulst, Flanders, in the summer of 1585; *d.* Antwerp, 9 May 1651), Flemish painter of historical and religious subjects, family groups and portraits. He went to Antwerp as a boy and studied art there, settling in the city after travel, 1604–8, and frequenting the markets as dealer and antique collector. He is mainly known for portraiture, following Rubens and van Dyck (qq.v.) in style, his work having sometimes been confused with the latter's. His brother Paul (*b.* Hulst, *c.* 1596; *d.* Antwerp, 30 June 1678), also trained at Antwerp, was an animal painter and collaborator with Rubens and Snyders (q.v.) (who married the sister of the two brothers).

Vos, Marten de (*b.* Antwerp, 1531–2; *d.* there, 4 Sept. 1603), Flemish painter of religious and allegorical subjects and designer of tapestries, the son of the painter Peter de Vos and the pupil of Frans Floris (q.v.) and perhaps also of Pieter Aertzen (q.v.). He spent some years in Italy, at Rome, Florence and Venice (where he worked in the studio of Tintoretto), and on his return to Antwerp in 1588 was much employed in paintings for churches executed in the Venetian manner.

S. VOUET—Cupid and Psyche—Musée de Lyon.

E. VUILLARD—The Flowered Dress—Museum of São Paulo, Brazil.

Vouet, Simon (*b*. Paris, Jan. 1590; *d*. there, 30 June 1649), French painter of religious and decorative works, the pupil of his father, Laurent Vouet. Precocious in talent, he is said to have painted portraits in England when fourteen. He accompanied the French ambassador to Constantinople in 1611 and stayed in Italy, 1612–27, becoming president of the Academy of St Luke, 1624. An eclectic in style, he was influenced by Caravaggio and by the Mannerist and baroque art of Italy, but shaped and refined these elements successfully into a species of classicism which foreshadows that of Poussin (q.v.), e.g. in the 'Presentation in the Temple' (Louvre). He was Louis XIII's principal painter, carrying out works in the Luxembourg, Louvre and Château of St Germain, and the art of the Louis XIV period may be said to have originated in his studio, his pupils including Le Sueur, Le Brun and Mignard (qq.v.).

Vranckz, Sebastian (*b*. Antwerp, Jan. 1573; *d*. there, 19 May 1647), Flemish painter of battle scenes, popular life and interiors (q.v.), the pupil of Adam van Noort. He visited Italy probably about 1595 and was a captain in the civic guard at Antwerp, 1626–31. He provided figures for landscapes by Joos de Momper and 'Velvet' Brueghel (qq.v.).

Vuillard, Édouard (*b*. Cuiseaux, Saône-et-Loire, 11 Nov. 1868; *d*. La Baule, 21 June 1940), French painter, closely linked with Bonnard (q.v.), his friend from youth, and taking a parallel direction in art. He was a member of the 'Nabi' group (q.v.), though as he said there was 'nothing of the revolutionary' about him The term Intimist, applied both to him and to Bonnard, refers particularly aptly to the gentle and seclusive spirit in which Vuillard painted lamplit domestic interiors. He was less venturesome and more academic in tendency than Bonnard, though in colour lithography he developed, with the inspiration of Japanese prints, some brilliant and unconventional designs. He produced a number of decorations, for the Comédie des Champs Élysées, 1913, Palais de Chaillot, 1937, and the Palais des Nations, Geneva, 1938. His notebooks and diaries, left to the Bibliothèque Nationale, are not to be opened until 1980.

W

Walch, Jacob, *see* BARBARI.

Wallace Collection, art collection at Hertford House, London, originally formed by the fourth Marquess of Hertford and bequeathed to the nation in 1897. French art of the eighteenth century is its distinctive feature, including sculpture, furniture and small *objets d'art* as well as painting. There are also paintings of various schools including Velazquez's 'Lady with a Fan' and Hals's 'Laughing Cavalier'.

Wang Wei (Mo-ch'i) (699–759), Chinese painter, a native of T'ai-yüan, in Shanshi, renowned for his poetical landscape though his work survives only in copies. Poet, musician and official, he also ranks as a founder of the southern school of Chinese painting (q.v.). A main aim was to embody in a picture the emotion conveyed by a poem. He was also regarded as a founder of a type of brushwork in ink. He wrote a treatise on landscape painting, observing that 'in painting landscapes the idea should exist in the mind before the brush is taken up'.

Ward, James (*b*. London, 23 Oct. 1769; *d*. there, 17 Nov. 1859), English landscape and animal painter and mezzotint engraver. He studied engraving with John Raphael Smith and his elder brother

J. WARD—Bulls Fighting—Victoria and Albert Museum.

William, and later took to painting in imitation of his brother-in-law, George Morland (q.v.), producing many excellent animal studies. He was painter and engraver to the Prince of Wales, 1794, and made R.A., 1811. In his 'Bulls Fighting' he attempted the technique of Rubens's 'Château de Steen' and also tried to rival Paul Potter. Ambitious designs in his later years, e.g. an allegorical work commemorating Waterloo (1815–21), failed and involved him in distress, material and psychological. The Romantic aspect of his art is best seen in his huge and gloomy 'Gordale Scar', 1814 (Tate Gallery).

Water-colour, painting with pigments bound with gum and diluted with water. In principle it is to be found in many parts of the world at different times, fresco and tempera coming under the general description and oriental painting providing a particular form of water-colour on paper or silk. Transparent colour was used in some medieval manuscripts and the European old masters used it occasionally, Dürer giving landscape examples while Dutch and Flemish artists, e.g. Ostade, tinted some of their drawings. Its great development, however, was in eighteenth-century England, its rise accompanying the growth of interest in topography and landscape. Water-colour drawing in which a delicate tint was laid over a carefully executed monochrome was first widely practised, but the later trend of the art was towards water-colour painting with greater

P. DE WINT—Old Houses, Lincoln (Water-colour)—Victoria and Albert Museum.

A. MELVILLE—Bull Fight (Water-colour)—Victoria and Albert Museum.

completeness and force in brushwork. Paul Sandby was an early
master, but the outstanding masters of water-colour landscape were
J. R. Cozens, Thomas Girtin, John Sell Cotman and J. M. W. Turner,
to whom may be added David Cox, Peter de Wint and R. P. Bonington from among hundreds of practitioners. Great artists who used the
medium for other purposes than landscape were Thomas Rowlandson
and William Blake. The influence of early English water-colour on the
whole course of landscape was considerable, for the *art anglais* made
a decided impression in France at the beginning of the nineteenth
century, pointing to the advantages of a lighter scheme of colour than
was usual in oils and to the value of direct study of nature. In the
nineteenth century the water-colours of Samuel Palmer and D. G.
Rossetti are of note, and later those of J. S. Sargent, Whistler, Winslow
Homer and A. Melville. Though technically limited in comparison
with oil, it was used with beautiful effect by Cézanne, and the
American artist John Marin (q.v.) has shown its capacity for vigorous
and semi-abstract application. *See also* GOUACHE.

Watteau, Jean Antoine (*b.* Valenciennes, 10 October 1684; *d.*
Nogent-sur-Marne, 18 July 1721), French painter, the son of a tiler.
He had some lessons in his native place (a Walloon town anciently
French-speaking, it may be noted, though absorbed only six years
before his birth into the dominions of Louis XIV) and went to Paris in
1702. He studied under Claude Gillot, who painted the scenes and
characters of the Italian Commedia dell' Arte, and with Claude

[348]

A. WATTEAU—Gilles and his Family—Wallace Collection.

Audran (III), curator of the royal collections, who introduced him to the Luxembourg and its works by Rubens. He was taken up by the wealthy amateur, Crozat, whose open-air parties may well have given the first suggestion for the *fêtes galantes* which Watteau was to paint. These evocations of aristocratic diversion won him success and he was elected to the Académie in 1717, his diploma piece being the world-famous 'Embarkation for Cythera' (Louvre). His early days of privation were now over but tuberculosis had him in its grip. He went to London in 1719 to consult Dr Mead, Queen Anne's physician, but returned without hope. The crash of John Law's Mississippi companies in 1720 robbed him of his investments. He had one famous work still to execute, the shop-sign (now at Berlin) of Gersaint, the picture dealer with whom he lodged. Though he died when thirty-six the work of Watteau is extensive. It comprises, in painting, three types of subject: the scenes of military life, in its less formal aspect, painted in his youth; the pictures of characters of Italian comedy, as in the Louvre and Wallace Collection; and the *fêtes galantes*, at once gay and sad, theatrical and mysterious, real and unreal, in which his poetic and imaginative vision is fully displayed. The beauty of his landscape can be well appreciated in the 'Champs-Élysées' (Wallace Collection). Careless in his treatment of pigment, which has sometimes deteriorated, he was an exquisite colourist, deriving a silvery quality from Veronese and a warmth of flesh and sparkle of pigment from Rubens, but developing them into symphonies of his own. His many drawings in black and red chalks, sometimes heightened with white, made from life and forming a repertoire of figures for his paintings, are of incomparable beauty in their combined sensitiveness and precision. A masterpiece somewhat apart is the Gersaint sign, a return to realism. While an underlying personal melancholy is perceptible in Watteau, there was also a quality that can only be

[349]

called musical and a charm that transmitted itself to later eighteenth-century French art, re-appearing exquisitely in Fragonard (q.v.).

Watts, George Frederick (*b.* London, 23 Oct. 1817; *d.* Compton, 1 July 1904), English painter and sculptor. He frequented the studio of the sculptor Behnes as a boy and studied in the Royal Academy Schools, 1835. Winning in 1842 the prize of £300 in the competition for wall-painting designs for Westminster (a further premium fell to him in 1847), he went to Italy and met Lord and Lady Holland, with whom he stayed in Florence and who became his patrons. The curiously outdated Renaissance pattern of patron and household genius was later repeated in his thirty years' stay at Little Holland House in Kensington with Mr and Mrs Thoby Prinsep. Insulated from the world, he worked in high-minded seclusion on allegories, symbolic frescoes and portraits of those he admired. In his portraits of eminent Victorians, e.g. the 'Morris' and 'Tennyson' (National Portrait Gallery), idealism and reality were combined with distinguished result, while his portrayal of the young Ellen Terry (with whom his marriage was a fiasco) has much beauty. He is better known for such works of the 1880's as 'Hope' and 'Love and Death' (Tate Gallery), cloudily philosophic, and as in his 'Mammon' showing the desire of his age to teach and uplift. The influence of the Venetians and of the Elgin Marbles is traceable in his style, in which, however, failings in colour and form too often give painful prominence to his didacticism and ill-defined thought. His equestrian statue, however, 'Physical Energy', for the memorial to Cecil Rhodes at Cape Town (replica in Kensington Gardens), matches subject with style in a work of great originality. Watts was made R.A., 1867, and received the Order of Merit, 1902. His second wife had the gallery built at Compton, Surrey (near his house, 'Limnerslease'), where there is a permanent collection of his work.

Weenix, Jan Baptist (*b.* Amsterdam, 1621; *d.* Château Ter-Mey, nr

[350]

Utrecht, 1660), Dutch painter of landscape, still life and portraits, who studied under Bloemaert (q.v.) at Utrecht and spent four years in Italy, 1642–6, with marked results on his landscape style. He painted still life in the Flemish manner of Snyders. Jan Weenix (*b.* Amsterdam, *c.* 1640; *d.* there, 20 Sept. 1719), his son, who was his pupil, painted some Italian views in his father's manner but was mainly devoted to animal and bird painting (in which he may be linked with Hondecoeter, q.v.), specializing in dead stags and hares.

Wen Cheng-ming (*b.* Suchou, 1470; *d.* 1559), Chinese painter, poet, calligrapher and scholar. He is one of the most famous representatives of the courtly art of the Ming Dynasty and excelled in picturesque landscape.

Werff, Adriaen van der (*b.* nr Rotterdam, 1659, *d.* there, 1722), Dutch painter, engraver and architect. He studied with Eglon van der Neer and painted portraits and subject pictures much admired for their elegance and finish. He visited Germany and was retained by the Elector Palatine Johann Wilhelm to act as his court painter for six months in the year.

West, Benjamin (*b.* Springfield, Pennsylvania, 10 Oct. 1738; *d.* London, 11 Mar. 1820), American painter of religious and historical

pictures who worked in England. He studied in Philadelphia and worked there and in New York until, after a visit to Italy, 1760, he settled in England, 1763. He was patronized by George III, was a founder member of the Royal Academy, 1768, and succeeded Reynolds as its president, 1792. His 'Death of Wolfe', 1770, is famous as a new departure in the 'history picture' in representing a contemporary event with figures in contemporary dress, though Copley was to do the same thing better. If Byron's description of

A. VAN DER WERFF—
The Mousetrap—National
Gallery, London.

B. WEST—The Death of Wolfe—National Gallery of Canada.

West as 'Europe's worst dauber and poor Britain's best' was unfair, his merit as an artist was not great: yet his late picture, 'Death on a Pale Horse', showed feeling of a Romantic kind which left its impression on Turner, and he was a teacher of influence.

Weyden, Rogier van der (*b*. Tournai, *c*. 1399; *d*. Brussels, 16 June 1464), one of the greatest painters of the early Netherlandish School, born in what was then a French town, of Flemish parentage. He appears under various guises of nomenclature, as Roger of Bruges, Rogier de la Pasture and Rogelet de la Pasture, and is considered to have been a pupil of Robert Campin (q.v.). He became official painter to the city of Brussels in 1436, visited Italy (where he was regarded with admiration) in 1450 and had a busy workshop at Brussels until his death in 1464. Though he signed no paintings his work is as distinct as that of Jan van Eyck (q.v.), the products of his studio, now in many of the world's galleries, being a dominant influence in northern Europe during the second half of the fifteenth century. A lucid and graceful mode of composition, a feeling for relief (suggesting that he made use of effects observed in Gothic sculpture) and a warm humanity, observable in the play of human expression in which he had no contemporary rival, characterize his work and explain his eminent position. These qualities are displayed in the 'Descent from the Cross' (Escurial and other versions). The 'Pietà' (The Hague), the great polyptych of the 'Last Judgment'

[352]

R. VAN DER WEYDEN—The Descent from the Cross—Musée, Douai.

(Beaune), the 'Seven Sacraments' (Antwerp) and the 'Adoration of the Magi' (Berlin) are among his main religious works, while his portraits, such as the 'Portrait of a Lady' (Washington), have a comparable quality.

Wheatley, Francis (*b.* London, 1747; *d.* there, 28 June 1801), English painter of portraits and *genre*. He studied art in London and lived in Dublin, 1779–81, painting small portraits, then returned to London, exhibiting at the Royal Academy, 1784–1801, becoming R.A., 1791. He was popular for scenes of everyday life into which he infused some of the artificial charm of Greuze and is best known by the delightful 'Cries of London', engraved in 1795.

Whistler, James Abbot McNeill (*b.* Lowell, Massachusetts, 10 Aug. 1834; *d.* London, 17 July 1903), painter, etcher and lithographer, born in America, though taken when nine to St Petersburg, where his father was consultant engineer for the St Petersburg–Moscow railway. A cadet at West Point, 1851–4, he failed to qualify for the U.S. Army ('Had silicon been a gas I should have been a major-general,' he later remarked.) and went to Paris in 1855, after a brief period on the coast survey, Washington, to study art in the *atelier* of Gleyre. An important factor in this Paris period was his acquaintance with Courbet (q.v.), whose influence appeared in such early oil-paintings as 'Au Piano', exhibited at the Royal Academy, 1860, and 'The Blue Wave, Biarritz', 1862. He went to London in 1859, settling in Chelsea, a first remarkable achievement being the superb Thames series of etchings. During the 1860's he was friendly with Rossetti and the taste they shared for oriental china has its trace in 'La Princesse du Pays de la Porcelaine', 1864. He admired Albert Moore, in whose pictures (often without title) of 'classical' maidens he found a purely aesthetic element. In contrast he had the greatest contempt for the typically academic and anecdotal art of the time,

**J. McN. WHISTLER—
Nocturne, Blue and Gold,
Old Battersea Bridge—
Tate Gallery.**

witheringly expressed after the famous libel action against Ruskin, 1878, and in various subsequent conflicts with official art and criticism.

He attained his height as a painter after his (unexplained) visit to Valparaiso, 1865–6, and during the 1870's, Japanese colour prints influencing his exquisite care in arrangement and selection of colour both in his portraits and the night views of the Thames he called 'Nocturnes', no doubt with musical comparison in mind. Famous examples are the portrait of his mother, 1872 (Louvre), and the 'Nocturne—Blue and Gold, Old Battersea Bridge', 1877 (Tate Gallery). His Japonic decoration of the 'Peacock Room' (Washington, Freer Gallery), which caused a split with his patron, F. R. Leyland, was carried out in 1876. His sense of design extended to the placing of his famous signature device, the butterfly. A nominal victor in the case against Ruskin, whose criticism of the 'Nocturne—Black and Gold' (Detroit) was indeed outrageous, he became bankrupt and turned again to etching to bring in money. His later work was mainly (though not exclusively) graphic, including the Venice etchings, 1880 and 1886, an Amsterdam series and many delicate lithographs and pastels. His one-man war against critics, aesthetes and academic prejudice, conducted with brilliant and scathing wit, is chronicled in *The Gentle Art of Making Enemies* of 1890. Never an Impressionist in the French manner, out of his element in Victorian England (though he died in Chelsea) and an absentee from America, Whistler seems in many ways an isolated figure, yet his masterpieces proclaim him one of the great nineteenth-century artists.

White, John (active 1584–93), artist and Virginian pioneer, who sailed from England to America with Sir Richard Grenville and was one of the first settlers in Raleigh's colony in Virginia in 1585. He made studies in water-colour of great interest, depicting the life and customs of the Indians and the flora and fauna of the New World. A

[355]

J. McN. WHISTLER—Portrait of the Artist's Mother—Louvre.

set of sixty-five of these water-colours, 'counterfeited according to the truth', in his words, is preserved in the British Museum.

Whitney Museum of American Art, gallery of American painting and sculpture in New York, having special reference to twentieth-century art in the United States. (*See* Appendix—American Artists in the Whitney Museum.)

Wilkie, Sir David (*b.* Cults, Fife, 18 Nov. 1785; *d.* at sea, nr Malta, 1 June 1841), Scottish painter of *genre* and historical subjects, the son of a parish minister. He studied at the Trustees' Academy, Edinburgh, and the Royal Academy Schools, but engravings after Teniers and Ostade suggested the pictures of popular life in which he was to excel. 'The Village Politicians', 1805, won instant success and was followed by such other works as 'The Blind Fiddler' (Tate Gallery) and 'The Penny Wedding' (Royal Collection). He was elected R.A., 1811. After 1825, when he visited Italy and Spain, his style changed

SIR D. WILKIE—The Penny Wedding—Royal Collection, Buckingham Palace.

R. WILSON—Mount Snowdon—Nottingham Art Gallery.

under the influence of Velazquez and Murillo. He died on the way home from a visit to Constantinople and Palestine.

Wilson, Richard (*b.* Penegoes, Montgomeryshire, 1 Aug. 1714; *d.* Llanberis, 15 May 1782), landscape painter of Welsh birth. His father (who held the living at Penegoes) gave him a classical education and he studied art in London, 1729, under an obscure portrait painter, Thomas Wright, and until 1750 practised portraiture with some success, painting the Prince of Wales (George III) and his brother, the Duke of York (National Portrait Gallery), as well as Flora Macdonald (National Gallery of Scotland). He had, however, painted some landscapes before going to Italy in 1750, and during his stay there (until 1756) was encouraged to devote himself to landscape by the approval and commissions of Grand Tourists, and it may well be by the counsels of Zuccarelli at Venice and Claude-Jospeh Vernet at Rome. He painted at Rome and Naples, having several pupils, producing a type of 'classical landscape' deriving partly from Claude and Gaspard Poussin but also from Cuyp, whose golden light

Wilson greatly admired, while his convention for painting foliage seems to have been based on Ruisdael. His originality lay, however, in a structural simplicity of design, breadth of treatment and luminous atmosphere directly studied in nature. It is possible that the departure thus made from the artificialities then in vogue accounts for his lack of success when he returned to England. Though a founder member of the Royal Academy, he was unsuccessful in introducing mythology (as in his ' Niobe'); in remembered

THE WILTON DIPTYCH
(Right Panel)—Virgin and Child with Angels—National Gallery, London.

Italian scenes (uneven in quality and sometimes evidently 'pot-boilers'); or in his views of England and Wales. Yet he created masterpieces, among them 'The River Dee' (Barber Institute, Birmingham), 'Cader Idris' (National Gallery) and 'Snowdon' (Nottingham). He retired shortly before his death to live near Llanberis, and left an achievement fully appreciated by the following generation.

'Wilton Diptych', painting in tempera on two oak panels, *c.* 1395 (now in the National Gallery), showing Richard II presented to the Virgin and Child by his patron saints. On the left obverse panel the king kneels, while behind him are St John the Baptist, St Edward the Confessor and St Edmund, king and martyr. On the right is the Virgin and Child with a company of angels. The reverse panels show, left, a shield of arms and right a white hart, the badge of Richard II. It is assumed to have been painted some years before Richard's deposition in 1399. An example of the International Gothic style (q.v.), it has been variously ascribed to English, French and Italian hands but the balance of probability seems in favour of French authorship.

E. DE WITTE—The Fishmarket—Boymans Museum, Rotterdam.

Witte, Emmanuel de (*b*. Alkmaar, 1617; *d*. Amsterdam, 1692), Dutch painter, the pupil of van Aelst at Delft. He worked in various cities but mainly at Amsterdam, being the most distinguished of those who painted views of church interiors. Apart from this speciality he experimented in outdoor scenes of popular life, a splendid example of which is the 'Fish Market' (Boymans Museum, Rotterdam).

Witz, Conrad (*b*. Rottweil, Upper Rhine, *c*. 1400; *d*. Basel, 1447), Swiss painter, son of a painter who worked for the Duke of Burgundy. He went with his father to Burgundy and the Netherlands and from these sources derived some inspiration. He worked mainly at Basel, developing a strength and virility of design in which he departed from the 'soft' manner of German art at the time. His great powers can be seen in the 'Annunciation', *c*. 1445 (Nuremberg), but unquestionably his masterpiece is the 'Miraculous Draught of Fishes', 1444 (Geneva), with its beautifully rendered landscape background, the view of Lake Leman from Geneva, said to be the first identifiable landscape in European art.

C. WITZ—The Miraculous Draught of Fishes—Musée d'Art, Geneva.

Wolgemut, Michael (*b.* Nuremberg, 1434; *d.* there, 1508), German painter and engraver, head of a large workshop at Nuremberg which produced carved and painted altar-pieces and also woodcuts to his designs. Altar-pieces by him are those for Zwickau, 1479, and Schwabach, 1508, and he illustrated with woodcuts two celebrated books, the *Schatzkammer der wahren Reichthümer des Heils*, 1491, and the *Weltchronik* by Schedel, 1493–4, usually known as the *Nuremberg Chronicle*. He married the widow of Hans Pleydenwurff (q.v.), whose son, Wilhelm, was his assistant in woodcutting, and is perhaps best known as the master of Albrecht Dürer (q.v.).

Wollaston, John (*b.* England, active first half of the eighteenth century), portrait painter in colonial North America, who worked in a number of cities. His portraits were in the fashionable and artificial manner of Kneller.

Wood, Grant (*b.* Anamosa, Iowa, 13 Feb. 1892; *d.* Iowa City, 12 Feb. 1942), American painter, informally trained, best known for the illustrative skill with which he related human types and architectural background in his 'American Gothic', 1930 (Art Institute of Chicago).

Woodcuts and Wood Engraving, method of print-making in which the design is drawn on the surface of a wood block and the parts which are to print white are cut away leaving the black areas in relief. A knife is used for woodcuts, and a burin for wood engraving, as in line engraving (q.v.) though the line incised on wood appears as a white line in the print. Woodcut blocks were first used for printing on fabrics. The earliest examples on paper are ascribed to ninth-century China. In Europe they came into use at the beginning of the fifteenth century, (*a*) for the production of playing-cards and (*b*) for the 'block-books', in which both text and illustrations were cut on the block, these books

H. HOLBEIN—The Dance of Death, The Pedlar (Woodcut)

WILLIAM MORRIS and BURNE-JONES—Woodcut from the Kelmscott 'Chaucer' (detail).

preceding the use of movable type. Great designers of woodcuts in the sixteenth century were Dürer (q.v.) and Holbein (q.v.), the latter's famous 'Dance of Death' being cut by Hans Lützelburger. The process was popular with other German artists of their time, but was less practised than line engraving in the seventeenth and eighteenth centuries. In modern form it was revived by Thomas Bewick (q.v.) and beautifully used by William Blake (q.v.). In the nineteenth century it was a merely reproductive craft, but again revived by the producers of fine books, William Morris (q.v.), Charles Ricketts (Vale Press) and Lucien Pissarro (Eragny Press), and has since been used with effect by Eric Gill, Robert Gibbings and other twentieth-century artists.

Wootton, John (*b. c.* 1686; *d.* London, Jan. 1765), English painter of hunting and racing scenes, pupil of the Dutch-born artist Jan Wyck (painter of battle and hunting pictures). Wootton painted race-horses at Newmarket and was also an early English follower of Claude and Gaspard Poussin in landscape, his work being one of the minor sources from which Gainsborough's landscape style derived. His 'Members of the Beaufort Hunt', 1744 (Tate Gallery), marks a stage in the development of the English sporting picture.

Wouters, Frans (*b.* Antwerp, 1612; *d.* there, 1659), Flemish painter of religious and allegorical subjects and landscapes with figures. He

[362]

P. WOUWERMAN—The Halt of a Hunting Party—Dulwich College Picture Gallery.

J. WRIGHT OF DERBY—The Orrery—Derby Art Gallery.

worked at Antwerp, where he was a pupil of Rubens, and also in Austria and England, and was especially noted for his landscapes.

Wouwerman, Philips (*b*. Haarlem, baptized 24 May 1619; *d*. there, 19 May 1688), Dutch painter who worked at Haarlem. He studied under his father, Paul Wouwerman, Jan Wynants (q.v.) and Frans Hals (q.v.), but his landscapes, hunting scenes, horses and scenes of camp life, well composed and minutely finished, recall the style of Pieter van Laer (q.v.). His brothers, Jan (1629–66) and Pieter (1623–82), painted similar subjects.

Wright (of Derby), Joseph (*b*. Derby, 3 Sept. 1734; *d*. there, 29 Aug. 1797), English painter who mainly lived and worked in his native city. He studied portrait painting with Hudson (q.v.) but is best known for groups illuminated by artificial light. These distantly echo the effects attained by such earlier candlelight painters as Honthorst but stem more directly from the Romantic and industrial trends of his time, as in his 'Experiment with the Air Pump' (Tate Gallery) and 'The Orrery' (Derby). A visit to Italy, 1773–5, led him to add Vesuvius in eruption to his effects of illumination, though he was stimulated as much by the lighted windows of a factory seen by moonlight and, it has been said, was the first painter to 'express the spirit of the Industrial Revolution'.

Wtewael, Joachim Anthonisz (*b*. Utrecht, *c*. 1566; *d*. there, 1638), Dutch painter of religious subjects, the son of a glass painter. He studied in Italy and France before settling in Utrecht and his work shows the Mannerist character so gained, 'The Adoration of the Shepherds' (Ashmolean Museum, Oxford) being a typical example.

Wu Tao-tzu (eighth century), Chinese painter, a native of Yang-ti, Honan. He is considered the greatest master of the T'ang Dynasty and one of the greatest of all Chinese artists, though his work can only be estimated by copies. He executed many mural paintings for Buddhist temples.

Wyant, Alexander Helwig (*b*. Port Washington, Ohio, 11 Jan. 1836; *d*. New York, 29 Nov. 1892), American landscape painter. He studied in Germany and was influenced by the work of Turner and Constable on visiting England. In a realist approach to landscape he diverged from the Hudson River School tradition. He was attached to a government exploring expedition in the west of America in 1873, the hardships of which caused his health to give way; though paralysed on one side he learned to paint with his left hand and later painted much in the Adirondacks.

Wyeth, Andrew Newell (*b*. Chadds Ford, Pennsylvania, 12 July 1917), American painter, the son of the illustrator N. C. Wyeth, by whom he was trained. His highly detailed paintings of aspects of contemporary life have an imaginative intensity which goes beyond illustration.

Wynants, Jan (*b*. Haarlem, *c*. 1625; *d*. Amsterdam, 1682), Dutch landscape painter who worked at Amsterdam. His paintings of sandy lanes and undulating country were influenced by Ruisdael's early work and usually had the addition of figures contributed by Wouwerman or other artists.

Y

Yeats, Jack Butler (*b*. London, 29 Aug. 1871; *d*. Dublin, 27 Mar. 1957), Irish painter and graphic artist, son of the painter John Butler Yeats, and brother of the poet William Butler Yeats. His youth was spent in Sligo and his early work consisted mainly of pen and water-colour drawings, lively impressions of country and sporting life and character in Ireland. From 1930 onwards he devoted himself to oil paintings with an emotional violence of colour that might be called Expressionist, and in his later years was considered the most eminent representative of Ireland in art.

Yugoslav Painting. The countries of Eastern Europe now forming Yugoslavia, being a great cross-roads of west and east, have benefited by the international influences of art and in the Middle Ages from the thirteenth to fifteenth centuries were one of the main channels in the spread of Byzantine influence. (*See also* BYZANTINE PAINTING.) Artists, both Greeks trained in Constantinople and native Slavs, produced remarkable frescoes, mainly in the monastic churches of the south-west, celebrated examples being those of Mileševo from *c.* 1235 and Sopočani, *c.* 1260. The Turkish conquests of the fifteenth century put an end to this phase of art and many works were whitewashed over and have only been restored to view in recent times. Dalmatia, long a Venetian province, has linked Yugoslav art with that of Venice. Thus one finds Schiavone—the Slavonian (Andrea Meldolla of Sebenico, 1522–82)—among the painters of the Venetian School, a disciple of Titian, though otherwise Turkish rule for centuries repressed activity. The national existence created after the war of 1914–18, its unity strengthened by the trials of the Second World War, has in recent years fostered new activity in both painting and sculpture, non-figurative painting having been enthusiastically taken up by the younger generation.

Z

Zenale, Bernardino (*b*. Treviglio, 1436, *d*. 1526), Italian painter, a friend of Leonardo da Vinci, whose influence appears in some of his work. He is mainly noted for the polyptch in the church of San Martino, Treviglio, in which he collaborated with Bernardino Butinone.

Zeuxis (fl. 425–400 B.C.; *b*. Heraclea), Greek painter belonging to the Ionic School, apparently influenced by Apollodoros (q.v.). He was the contemporary and rival of Parrhasios (q.v.). His reputed masterpiece was a picture of Helen which he painted for Crotona, combining in the figure the beauties of five maidens of that city. That realistic imitation was valued in his time may be suggested by the well-known story of the birds pecking his painted grapes. No work by him exists but an 'Infant Hercules strangling the Serpents' found at Pompeii may give some idea of one of his most anciently renowned paintings. Aristotle considered him inferior to Polygnotos (q.v.).

Zingaro, Lo, *see* SOLARIO, ANTONIO DE.

Zoffany, Johann (John) (*b*. Frankfurt, Mar. 1733; *d*. Kew, 11 Nov.

J. ZOFFANY—The Life School at the Royal Academy—Royal Collection, Windsor.

F. ZUCCARELLI—Landscape with Figures—Royal Collection, Buckingham Palace.

1810), German painter who came to England about 1758 and won popularity by small theatrical scenes, featuring Garrick and other actors, and conversation pieces. He was a foundation member of the Royal Academy in 1768. From 1783 to 1790 he was in India painting notabilities of ' John Company'. Two paintings of detailed documentary interest are his two groups, 'The Life School at the Royal Academy', 1772, and 'The Tribuna' of the Uffizi (showing British *cognoscenti*). Both were painted for George III and are in the Royal Collection.

Zoppo, Marco (*b.* Cento, *c.* 1432; *d.* Venice, *c.* 1478), Italian painter, trained in the studio of Squarcione (q.v.) at Padua, *c.* 1453, who worked mainly at Venice. His style shows the influence of Cosimo Tura (q.v.).

Zuccarelli, Francesco (*b.* Pitigliano, 1704; *d.* Florence, 30 Dec. 1788), Italian painter of pastoral and fanciful landscapes. His style was formed in Venice and under the influence of Marco Ricci (q.v.), and he seems to have encouraged Richard Wilson (q.v.), whom he met in Italy, to devote himself to landscape. He visited England, staying there 1751–62 and again 1768–*c.* 1772, his light, decorative style winning much success. He was a foundation member of the Royal Academy in 1768 and exhibited there, 1769–73. The consul, Joseph Smith, was one of his patrons and from him several works came into the Royal Collection.

Zuccaro (**Zucchero**), name of two Italian painter brothers. **Federigo** (*b.* Sant' Angelo, 1542; *d.* Ancona, 20 Aug. 1609), the younger of the two, was his brother's pupil and a leading exponent of the Mannerist style. They worked together on the decoration of the Sala Regia at the Vatican and in the Villa Farnese at Caprarola. Federigo also finished frescoes in the cathedral at Florence begun by Vasari (q.v.). He travelled in Italy, France and the Netherlands and visited England in 1574. A number of English portraits are freely attributed to him by Walpole, though the only certain productions of his short stay are the portrait drawings of Queen Elizabeth and the Earl of Leicester in the British Museum. He also worked for a time in Madrid for Philip II. He was a founder of the Academy of St Luke at Rome and also wrote on the theory of art. His brother, **Taddeo** (*b.* ? 1529; *d.* ? Rome, 1569), was the pupil of his father, Ottavio, and was the principal partner in the decorative works in which he collaborated with his brother.

Zuloaga, Ignacio (*b.* Eibar, 26 July 1870; *d.* Madrid, 3 Oct. 1945), Spanish painter of Basque origin. He first studied architecture in Rome but turned to painting later in Paris, though he was mainly influenced by Velazquez and Goya. He settled at Segovia and in landscape, *genre* and portraits applied himself vigorously to bringing out national and picturesque characteristics.

Zurbarán (**Salazar**), **Francisco de** (*b.* Fuente de Cantos, 1598; *d.* Madrid, Aug. 1664), Spanish painter of peasant extraction apprenticed as a boy to a painter in Seville, Juan de las Roelas (q.v.). He settled in Seville in 1628, painting many religious works for churches and monasteries. He was the friend of the young Velazquez and was influenced in style by him and by the dark manner of painting then cultivated in southern Spain and derived from Ribera (q.v.) and the Neapolitan School and other sources. He lived in

ZURBARÁN—St. Francis in Meditation—National Gallery, London.

[368]

Madrid in later life and in 1650 was appointed one of the painters to
Philip IV, but his austere and simple art suffered in competition with
the vaporous and sensational productions of Murillo (q.v.). He is now
recognized as one of the greatest Spanish painters. Characteristic of
his work are paintings of monks at prayer or in the solitary meditation
enjoined by Jesuit precept. He also painted a number of portraits of women, in seventeenth-century dress but described, according to a poetic custom of the time, as female saints; the charming ' St
Margaret' of the National Gallery being an example. A third remarkable aspect of his art is to be found in his still life, in which there is
the same concentrated simplicity as in his figures. A masterpiece of
this kind is the ' Oranges, Lemons and a Rose' (Uffizi).

APPENDIX A

Supplementary List of British Artists represented in the Tate Gallery and other public galleries in Britain

ARMSTRONG, JOHN (*b.* 1893). Painter in oil and tempera of imaginative subjects.

AUSTIN, ROBERT SARGENT, R.A. (*b.* 1895). Etcher, designer of currency notes.

BAWDEN, EDWARD (*b.* 1903). Water-colourist, engraver and illustrator

BEECHEY, SIR WILLIAM, R.A. (1735–1839). Portrait painter.

BEERBOHM, SIR MAX (1872–1956). Author and caricaturist.

BELL, ROBERT ANNING, R.A. (1863–1933). Decorative artist in the Pre-Raphaelite tradition.

BELL, VANESSA (1880–1961). Painter of landscape, portraits, still life and murals.

BEVAN, ROBERT POLHILL (1865–1925). British Post-Impressionist painter.

BOMBERG, DAVID (1890–1957). Member of the Vorticist group, landscape painter.

BOUGHTON, GEORGE HENRY, R.A. (1833–1905). Landscape painter.

BRABAZON, HERCULES BRABAZON (1821–1906). Water-colourist and free copyist of old masters.

BRATBY, JOHN (*b.* 1928). Painter of domestic subjects in a bold realistic style.

BROWN, FREDERICK (1851–1941). Landscape and figure painter, Slade Professor of Fine Art, London.

BURRA, EDWARD (*b.* 1905). Water-colour painter of imaginative subjects and still life.

BURTON, WILLIAM SHAKESPEARE (1824–1916). Painter influenced by Pre-Raphaelitism.

BUTLER, SAMUEL (1835–1902). Author of *Erewhon*, painter of 'Mr Heatherley's Holiday'.

CALDERON, PHILIP HERMOGENES, R.A. (1833–98). Subject painter.

CALLCOTT, SIR AUGUSTUS, R.A. (1779–1844). Landscape painter.

CALLOW, WILLIAM (1812–1908). Topographical water-colourist.

CAMERON, SIR DAVID YOUNG (1865–1945). Scottish landscape painter and etcher.

CATTERMOLE, GEORGE (1800–68). Water-colourist and illustrator.

CHAMBERS, GEORGE (1803–40). Marine painter.

CHINNERY, GEORGE (1774–1852). Painter of portraits and landscapes in India and China.

CLAUSEN, SIR GEORGE (1852–1944). Painter of rural scenes and open-air effects.

COLDSTREAM, SIR WILLIAM (*b.* 1908). Figure painter and art teacher.

COLLIER, THOMAS (1840–91). Water-colour landscape painter.

COLLINS, CHARLES ALLSTON (1828–73). Painter until 1858, a follower of Pre-Raphaelitism.

COLLINS, WILLIAM (1788–1847). Painter of landscape and *genre*.

COLLINSON, JAMES (1825–81). Painter, early member of Pre-Raphaelite circle.

COLQUHOUN, ROBERT (*b.* 1914). Painter, graphic artist and stage designer.

CONNARD, PHILIP (1875–1958). Painter of conversation pieces, landscapes and decorative works.

COOPER, THOMAS SIDNEY, R.A. (1803–1902). Animal painter.

CRANE, WALTER (1845–1915). Illustrator and designer.

CRAXTON, JOHN (*b.* 1922). Figure painter.

DADD, Richard (1817–87). Painter and water-colourist of psychological peculiarity.

DANIELL, THOMAS, R.A. (1749–1840). Landscape painter and engraver of eastern subjects.

DAVIE, ALAN (*b.* 1920). Abstract painter.

DEVERELL, WALTER HOWELL (1827–54). Painter, early member of Pre-Raphaelite circle.

DICKSEE, SIR FRANK, P.R.A. (1853–1928). Painter of romantic and sentimental subjects.

DOWNMAN, JOHN, A.R.A. (1750–1824). Portrait painter.

EAST, SIR ALFRED, R.A. (1849–1913). Landscape painter.

EGG, AUGUSTUS LEOPOLD (1816–63). Painter of social subjects.

ELMORE, ALFRED (1815–81). Painter of Victorian subject pictures.

FERGUSSON, JOHN DUNCAN (1874–1960). Scottish painter of landscapes, portraits and still life.

FERNELEY, JOHN (1782–1860). Painter of horses and sporting subjects.

FILDES, SIR LUKE, R.A. (1844–1927). Painter of social themes.

FISHER, MARK, R.A. (1841–1923). Painter of landscape on Impressionist lines.

FLINT, SIR WILLIAM RUSSELL, R.A. (*b.* 1880). Water-colour painter of landscape and figure, etcher.

FOSTER, MILES BIRKET (1825–99). Water-colourist and illustrator specializing in rustic scenes.

FURSE, CHARLES WELLINGTON, A.R.A. (1868–1904). Painter of portraits and open-air subjects.

GEAR, WILLIAM (*b.* 1915). Abstract painter.

GERE, CHARLES MARCH (1869–1957). Painter, book illustrator and decorative artist.

GERTLER, MARK (1892–1939). Painter of portraits and still life.

GILMAN, HAROLD (1876–1919). British Post-Impressionist painter of portraits, landscape and still life.

GINNER, CHARLES (1878–1952). Painter of intimate landscapes and urban subjects.

GOODALL, FREDERICK (1822–1904). Painter of Egyptian and biblical subjects.

GOODWIN, ALBERT (1845–1932). Water-colour landscape painter.

GORE, SPENCER FREDERICK (1878–1914). British Post-Impressionist landscape painter.

GOWING, LAWRENCE (*b.* 1918). Painter of landscape, portraits and still life, of the Euston Road School.

HADEN, SIR FRANCIS SEYMOUR (1818–1910). Graphic artist, etcher, founder of the Society of Painter-etchers, 1880.

HARDING, JAMES DUFFIELD (1798–1863). Water-colourist and lithographer.

HEMY, CHARLES NAPIER, R.A. (1841–1917). Marine painter.

HERKOMER, SIR HUBERT VON, R.A. (1849–1914). Painter of social subjects.

BRITISH ARTISTS

HERRING, JOHN FREDERICK (1795–1865). Painter of animals and sporting subjects.

HILLIER, TRISTRAM (b. 1905). Painter of landscape and surrealist subjects.

HITCHENS, IVON (b. 1893). Landscape and still-life painter, abstract in tendency.

HODGKINS, FRANCES (1869–1947). Painter of landscape and still life.

HOLL, FRANK (1845–88). Painter of social subjects and portraits.

HOLLAND, JAMES (1800–70). Painter of town views.

HOLMES, SIR CHARLES JOHN (1868–1936). Director of National Gallery, 1916–23, painter of industrial landscape.

HOLROYD, SIR CHARLES (1861–1917). Director of National Gallery, 1906–1916, painter-etcher.

HOOK, JAMES CLARKE, R.A. (1819–1907). Marine painter.

HORSLEY, JOHN CALLCOTT, R.A. (1817–1903). Subject and mural painter.

HOUGHTON, ARTHUR BOYD (1836–75). Painter and book illustrator.

HUNT, WILLIAM HENRY (1790–1864). Water-colour painter of rustic subjects and still life.

IBBETSON, JULIUS CAESAR (1759–1817). Landscape painter.

INCHBOLD, JOHN WILLIAM (1830–88). Landscape painter and etcher.

JOHN, GWEN (1876–1939). Sister of Augustus John, painter of portraits and single figures.

JONES, DAVID (b. 1895). Water-colourist and engraver.

KELLY, SIR GERALD FESTUS, P.R.A. (b. 1879). Portrait painter.

KENNINGTON, ERIC HENRI, R.A. (1888–1960). Painter and pastellist of war subjects and portraits, sculptor.

KNIGHT, DAME LAURA, R.A. Painter of landscape, portraits and circus life.

LAMB, HENRY, R.A. (1885–1960). Painter of portraits and figure subjects, portrait draughtsman.

LAMBERT, GEORGE (1710–65). Landscape painter.

LEADER, BENJAMIN WILLIAMS, R.A. (1831–1923). Landscape painter.

LEAR, EDWARD (1812–88). Author of *Book of Nonsense*, landscape painter and humorous draughtsman.

LOWRY, LAURENCE STEPHEN, A.R.A. (b. 1887). Painter of industrial townscape and character.

McTAGGART, WILLIAM, R.S.A. (1835–1910). Scottish Impressionist, landscape painter.

MAY, PHIL (1864–1903). Pen draughtsman.

MELVILLE, ARTHUR (1855–1904). Water colour painter.

MENINSKY, BERNARD (1891–1950). Portrait and figure painter.

MOYNIHAN, RODRIGO (b. 1910). Figure painter, abstract in later work.

MÜLLER, WILLIAM JAMES (1812–45). Painter of oriental life and scenery.

MULREADY, WILLIAM (1786–1863). Painter of *genre*.

MUNNINGS, SIR ALFRED, P.R.A. (1878–1959). Painter of hunting, racing and other sporting subjects.

PEPLOE, SAMUEL JOHN (1871–1935). Painter of still life and Scottish landscape.

PINWELL, GEORGE JOHN (1842–75). Water-colourist and illustrator.

PIPER, JOHN (b. 1903). Painter of architecture and landscape, designer in stained glass and mosaic.

PROUT, SAMUEL (1783–1852). Topographical water-colourist.

RAVILIOUS, ERIC (1903–42). Water-colour painter, engraver and designer.

REDGRAVE, RICHARD, R.A. (1804–88). Painter and author of *A Century of Artists*.

REYNOLDS, ALAN (*b.* 1926). Landscape and abstract painter.

RICH, ALFRED WILLIAM (1856–1921). Landscape painter in water-colour.

RICHARDS, CERI (*b.* 1903). Abstract painter.

RICHMOND, GEORGE, R.A. (1809–96). Follower of William Blake, later portrait painter.

RICHMOND, SIR WILLIAM BLAKE (1842–1921). Painter of classical subjects and portraits, designer of mosaics in St Paul's.

RICKETTS, CHARLES, R.A. (1866–1931). Painter, engraver and connoisseur.

ROBERTS, DAVID, R.A. (1796–1864). Painter of city views in Spain and elsewhere.

ROBERTS, WILLIAM, A.R.A. (*b.* 1895). Painter associated with the Vorticist group, specializing in modern *genre*.

ROGERS, CLAUDE (*b.* 1907). Landscape painter of Euston Road School.

ROTHENSTEIN, SIR WILLIAM (1872–1945). Portrait and landscape painter, lithographer and etcher.

RUSHBURY, HENRY, R.A. (*b.* 1889). Water-colour painter.

RUSSELL, JOHN (1745–1806). Crayon portraitist.

SANDYS, FREDERICK (1832–1904). Portrait draughtsman and illustrator.

SCOTT, DAVID, R.S.A. (1806–49). Painter of imaginative subjects.

SCOTT, WILLIAM (*b.* 1913). Still-life and abstract painter.

SCOTT, WILLIAM BELL (1811–90). Painter of historical subjects.

SERRES, DOMINIC, R.A. (1722–93). Marine painter.

SHANNON, CHARLES HAZLEWOOD, R.A. (1863–1937). Painter of imaginative subjects, wood engraver and lithographer.

SHANNON, SIR JAMES JEBUSA, R.A. (1862–93). Portrait painter.

SHEE, SIR MARTIN ARCHER, P.R.A. (1769–1850). Portrait painter.

SHORT, SIR FRANK, R.A. (1857–1945). Graphic artist in etching, aquatint and mezzotint.

SMIRKE, ROBERT, R.A. (1752–1845). Painter of *genre* and illustrator.

SOLOMON, SIMEON (1840–1905). Draughtsman and illustrator.

SPEAR, RUSKIN (*b.* 1911). Portrait and *genre* painter.

STARK, JAMES (1794–1859). Landscape painter of the Norwich School.

SWAN, JOHN MACALLAN, R.A. (1847–1910). Animal painter and sculptor.

SWYNNERTON, ANNIE LOUISA, *née* Robinson, A.R.A. (1844–1933). Painter of allegorical subjects and portraits.

TENNIEL, SIR JOHN (1820–1914). Cartoonist and illustrator.

THIRTLE, JOHN (1777–1839). Landscape painter of the Norwich School.

TONKS, HENRY (1862–1937). Painter and Slade Professor of Fine Art, London.

TUKE, HENRY SCOTT, R.A. (1858–1929). Painter of outdoor figure subjects, mainly on the Cornish coast.

TURNER, WILLIAM ('Turner of Oxford') (1789–1851). Painter of landscapes near Oxford, also in Wales and Scotland.

WADSWORTH, EDWARD, A.R.A. (1889–1949). Painter in tempera of landscape and formalized still life.

WALKER, FREDERICK, A.R.A. (1840–75). Painter and illustrator.

WALLIS, HENRY (1830–1916). Painter influenced by Pre-Raphaelitism.

WEBSTER, THOMAS (1800–86). Painter of village and domestic *genre*.

WINDUS, WILLIAM LINDSAY (1823–1907). Painter influenced by Pre-Raphaelitism.

WOOD, CHRISTOPHER (1901–30). Painter of Cornish and Breton subjects and still life.

WYLLIE, WILLIAM LIONEL, R.A. (1851–1931). Painter of ships and the sea.

APPENDIX B

Supplementary list of American Artists represented in the Whitney Museum of American Art, the Museum of Modern Art and other public galleries in the United States

ADAMS, WAYMAN (*b.* 1883). Painter of street scenes and portraits.

ALBERS, JOSEF (*b.* 1888). Painter of geometric abstractions.

ALBRIGHT, IVAN LE LORRAINE (*b.* 1897). Painter of minutely detailed still life and symbolic subjects.

ALEXANDER, JOHN WHITE (1856–1915). Portrait and mural painter.

BAZIOTES, WILLIAM (*b.* 1912). Abstract-Expressionist painter.

BEAL, GIFFORD REYNOLDS (*b.* 1879). Painter of the contemporary scene.

BIDDLE, GEORGE (*b.* 1885). Portrait, *genre* and mural painter.

BLAKELOCK, RALPH ALBERT (1847–1919). Painter of romantic landscape.

BOHROD, AARON (*b.* 1907). Painter of the contemporary scene.

BOIS, GUY PÈNE DU (*b.* 1884). Painter of American *genre*.

BOUCHÉ, LOUIS (*b.* 1896). Painter of the contemporary scene.

BROOK, ALEXANDER (*b.* 1898). Figure and still-life painter.

BROOKS, JAMES (*b.* 1906). Abstract-Expressionist painter.

CADMUS, PAUL (*b.* 1904). Tempera painter of symbolic and figure subjects.

CALCAGNO, LAURENCE (*b.* 1916). Painter of contemporary subjects.

CARROLL, JOHN (*b.* 1892). Figure painter.

CASTELLANOS, JULIO (1905–47). Mexican painter, muralist and graphic artist.

CATLIN, GEORGE (1796–1872). Painter of Indian life.

COLEMAN, GLENN O. (1887–1932). Painter of the contemporary scene.

DAVIS, STUART (*b.* 1894). Painter of formal abstractions.

DEHN, ADOLF ARTHUR (*b.* 1895). Water-colour painter and lithographer.

DEMUTH, CHARLES (1883–1935). Figure and landscape painter and illustrator, a pioneer of modern art in the United States.

DICKINSON, Preston (1891–1930). Painter influenced by Cézanne and Cubism.

DURAND, ASHER (1796–1886). Landscape painter of the Hudson River School.

DUVENECK, FRANK (1848–1919). Portrait painter and art teacher.

EILSHEMIUS, LOUIS (1864–1942). Painter of imaginative landscapes and figure compositions.

EVERGOOD, PHILIP (*b.* 1901). Painter of social subjects.

FIENE, ERNEST (*b.* 1894). Landscape painter and graphic artist.

FRANCIS, SAM (*b.* 1923). Abstract (tachist) painter.

GORKY, ARSHILE (1905–48). Abstract-Expressionist painter.

GOTTLIEB, ADOLF (*b.* 1903). Abstract-Expressionist painter.

GROPPER, WILLIAM (*b.* 1897). Painter of satirical comment.

GUSTON, PHILIP (*b.* 1913). Abstract and mural painter.

HART, 'POP' (GEORGE OVERBURY) (1868–1933). Water-colour landscape painter, etcher and lithographer.

HARTIGAN, GRACE (*b.* 1922). Expressionist painter.

HENRI, ROBERT (1865–1929). Portrait and landscape painter, art teacher.

HIRSCH, JOSEPH (*b.* 1910). Painter of social subjects.

[375]

AMERICAN ARTISTS

JARVIS, JOHN WESLEY (1780–1839). Portrait painter.
JENKINS, PAUL (b. 1923). Abstract painter.
JEWETT, WILLIAM (1795–1874). Portrait painter.
KANE, JOHN (1860–1934). Modern primitive painter.
KARFIOL, BERNARD (b. 1886). Figure painter.
KELLY, ELLSWORTH (b. 1923). Painter of formal abstractions.
KLINE, FRANZ (b. 1910). Abstract painter.
KUHN, WALT (b. 1880). Painter of portraits and still life.
KUNIYOSHI, YASUI (b. 1893). Painter of the contemporary scene.
KOONING, WILLEM DE (b. 1904). Expressionist painter.
LAM, WILFREDO (b. 1902). Cuban Surrealist painter.
LIBERMAN, ALEXANDER (b. 1912). Painter of formal abstractions.
LUKS, GEORGE (1867–1933). Painter of the contemporary scene.
MARTIN, AGNES (b. 1916). Painter of formal abstractions.
MAURER, ALFRED HENRY (1868–1932). Pioneer of Fauve and Cubist
    influences.
MILLER, KENNETH HAYES (1876–1932). Painter of city *genre* and art
    teacher.
NEWMAN, BARNETT (b. 1905). Painter of informal abstractions.
PERLIN, BERNARD (b. 1918). Painter of the 'Symbolic realism' School.
PICKENS, ALTON (b. 1917). Painter of the 'Symbolic realism' School.
PICKETT, JOSEPH (1848–1918). Modern primitive painter.
PIPPIN, HORACE (1888–1946). Modern primitive negro painter.
POOR, HENRY VARNUM (b. 1888). Decorative painter and designer.
RAY, MAN (b. 1890). Painter and photographer, pioneer of abstract design
    in the United States.
REINHARDT, AD. (b. 1913). Painter of formal abstractions.
ROBERTSON, ANNA MARY (Mrs 'Grandma' Moses) (1860–1961). Modern
    primitive painter.
ROTHKO, MARK (b. 1903). Painter of highly simplified abstractions.
RUSSELL, MORGAN (1886–1953). Abstract painter.
SCHREIBER, GEORGE (b. 1904). Painter of scenes of working life.
SHEETS, MILLARD (b. 1907). Landscape painter.
SHINN, EVERETT (1876–1953). Portrait painter, muralist and decorative
    artist.
SMITH, LEON (b. 1906). Painter of formal abstractions.
SPEICHER, EUGENE (b. 1883). Portrait painter.
SPENCER, MILES (1893–1952). Painter of industrial landscape.
STELLA, JOSEPH (1880–1946). Painter in the Futurist manner.
STEUMPFIG, WALTER (b. 1914). Painter in the Surrealist manner.
STILL, CLYFFORD (b. 1904). Painter of the Abstract-Expressionist school.
TAMAYO, RUFFINO (b. 1899). Mexican painter and muralist.
TCHELITCHEV, PAVEL (1896–1957). Surrealist painter and designer for
    ballet and theatre.
TOMLIN, BRADLEY WALKER (b. 1899). Painter of calligraphic abstractions.
TWACHTMAN, JOHN HENRY (1853–1902). Landscape painter in the Im-
    pressionist manner.
TWORKOV, JACK (b. 1900). Painter of the Abstract-Expressionist school.
WALDO, SAMUEL LOVETT (1783–1861). Portrait painter.
WEBER, MAX (1881–1961). Painter of Cubist and Abstract trend, a pioneer
    of modern art in the United States.
WOLFSON, SIDNEY (b. 1914). Abstract painter.
WRIGHT, JOSEPH (1756–93). Portrait painter.

INDEX OF ILLUSTRATIONS

COLOUR PLATES

VOLUME ONE

VOLUME TWO

BLACK AND WHITE ILLUSTRATIONS

VOLUME ONE

INDEX OF ILLUSTRATIONS

INDEX OF ILLUSTRATIONS

[1] Now transferred to Tate Gallery.

INDEX OF ILLUSTRATIONS

INDEX OF ILLUSTRATIONS

[381]

INDEX OF ILLUSTRATIONS

INDEX OF ILLUSTRATIONS

[383]

INDEX OF ILLUSTRATIONS

INDEX OF ILLUSTRATIONS

INDEX OF ILLUSTRATIONS

INDEX OF ILLUSTRATIONS

INDEX OF ILLUSTRATIONS

INDEX OF ILLUSTRATIONS

INDEX OF ILLUSTRATIONS

INDEX OF ILLUSTRATIONS